Tom Fletcher CM   Principal at Hertford College, Oxford. He is a British diplomat, a writer, and a campaigner. He was foreign policy advisor in No.10 Downing Street to Tony Blair, Gordon Brown and David Cameron, and from 2011 to 2015 was the British Ambassador to Lebanon. He is a Visiting Professor at New York University and author of two works of non-fiction.

Also by Tom Fletcher

The Diplomat Thrillers

The Ambassador
The Assassin

TOM FLETCHER

THE
ASSASSIN

1☉CANELO

First published in the United Kingdom in 2024 by Canelo

This edition published in the United Kingdom in 2024 by

Canelo
Unit 9, 5th Floor
Cargo Works, 1–2 Hatfields
London SE1 9PG
United Kingdom

A CIP catalogue record for this book is available from the British Library.

Ebook ISBN 978 1 80436 650 9
Hardback ISBN 978 1 80032 899 0
Paperback ISBN 978 1 80032 898 3

Cover design by Nick Venables

Cover images © Arcangel

Look for more great books at www.canelo.co

Printed and bound in Great Britain by Clays Ltd, Elcograf S.p.A.

1

To the peacemakers and activists protecting my descendants.

'It's a hoax. In my opinion, you have a thing called weather, and you go up, and you go down. The climate's always been changing.'

President Donald J. Trump

'How can we lose when we're so sincere?'

Charlie Brown, Peanuts

'We practise selective annihilation of mayors and government officials, to create a vacuum. Then we fill that vacuum. As popular war advances, peace is closer.'

Peruvian Shining Path guerrilla general

Part One

Three Stories

1

Game Theory

The sunset was blood red behind Mount Kenya. The heat of the day receded as the dead man drove towards the trophy hunter.

There was snow on the jagged, triangular peak of the mountain. Elias Abu Khalil kicked the orange dust from his khaki desert boots and stretched his legs out as he sank into the green canvas chair. The soil smelt of rain. He hated the din of the crickets, but it gave him an excuse for another shot of Black Label. It was cold and sharp in his dry throat.

It had been another good day. Abu Khalil had expanded his collection of elephant tusks. Only the Moldovan had a fuller set. They had tracked the mother for two hours in the Land Rover, before crouching downwind, still in the shade beyond the water hole, watching as she and her two calves drank. Their trunks had blown and sucked in the water, a cacophony of air and sound, the mother always watching over her children. Uncomplicated lives, unaware of the danger. After several minutes, as their bodies cooled, they had stopped drinking and started to play. One calf boisterously ran between his mother's legs, while the younger calf wallowed in the muddy water.

He had steadied himself, knees in the mud, while his Kenyan guide made the final checks of the weapon. He had licked the salty sweat from his upper lip. The late afternoon sun was hazy, intense. He felt his breath slowing, visualising the finger on the trigger. The last breath before her death.

The enjoyment was in the challenge. Man against beast: surely the ultimate test of courage.

In his house, in the mountains above Beirut, was a vast room built to exhibit his kills over the decades. Stuffed tigers, lions, elephant heads. Animal skins on the floor: he enjoyed watching his visitors wondering whether it was polite to walk around them. The product of years of hunting, not all of it his. Millions of pounds of fees for guides and bribes. He loved to offer his male guests their cigars below the largest beasts. Skill and patience were not enough: this was a hobby that demanded hard cash and sacrifice. It sorted the men from the boys, the strong from the weak. His sons understood that.

The younger of the calves had nestled against its mother's side. At first, she seemed to ignore her offspring, and then brought her trunk laboriously towards it and sprayed water along its back. The second, now jealous of the attention, had shoved against its mother's flank, nestling its head into her gnarled, leathery thighs. Elephants were more affectionate than any humans Abu Khalil had encountered. A sign of weakness.

Once, an idealistic young diplomat had questioned Abu Khalil on his expensive hobby. Abu Khalil had listened patiently, curious as to why others didn't see the world as he did. How little some people understood about nature, and man's domination of it.

4

As he saw it, this mastery over the natural world was humanity's story, or certainly the story of man. The money spent on this trip alone would sustain all the struggling families around the Lewa Downs reserve for a year. And wasn't the hunter just one more predator in a world packed with them? Better to kill animals than other men. Abu Khalil had seen plenty of both, and knew which he preferred. He was a predator. And if he didn't do it, someone else would. Survival of the fittest.

A fly had disturbed the enjoyment of the moment before the kill, buzzing around his left ear. He had tried to swat it away, hoping for a few more minutes to relish the feeling of power and strength. A life hanging by a thread. The executioner waiting, the victim unaware that these were her final moments. But he was becoming irritated. The anticipation was no longer enough. He knew that the sun would soon start to fall behind Mount Kenya and night would shift the odds away from him and back towards the wild. A glance at the guide – a lean, quiet Samburu – who nodded. The family of elephants were finishing and would soon move on. They might track towards the denser bushes and the treacly orange mud where even the Land Rover would struggle to follow.

Abu Khalil caressed the trigger, feeling it warm against the skin of his finger. He aimed it at the side of the elephant, well away from the head. The flanks were worthless but there was skill in the sighting, minimising the damage to the carcass. A long slow breath. Three short pops, the ricochet hard against his shoulder to minimise the recoil. The animal looked startled, at the noise before the pain. She stood shocked for a moment, only her eyes moving, alert to the danger to her calves.

Her two children panicked, restless in the water, as she stood, unsteady. And then her front knee bent. She paused like that for a few seconds, her head now cocked in pain. He wondered whether to take an extra shot, fearing she might stand and bolt. But why risk soiling the head? For a last moment she was strong. Then time slowed and she fell, undignified, into the mud. The sounds and smells of Africa seemed to recede. Her body twitched a little as it sank. The guide fired several further shots in the air, but her children refused to leave her side. In the end they drove the Land Rover into the water hole, revving its engine, to drive them away.

The calves had stood watching at a distance, distressed and unsteady as Abu Khalil and the guide hacked at the elephant's neck with a panga, the crude but effective knife that many of the locals carried. The guide was swift, efficient, finding the angles through the bone and leathery skin. The blood was hot as it surrounded the carcass in the muddy water. There was skill in the butchery. Abu Khalil rested a foot on her flank as he watched, relishing the mastery.

A good day, then. But tonight would be better. Some argued that hunting was only about conservation, or protection of a way of life. Not Abu Khalil: for him it was about power. He had made a sizable bet with friends that he would kill a white rhino. There were only a handful still in the wild in Kenya, the product of a decades-long conservation project. Most were carefully guarded, with rangers nearby twenty-four hours every day. Abu Khalil's fixers had needed to pay off several senior Kenya Wildlife Service directors. And he had secured the services of a company of ex-Russian soldiers, now mercenaries, to provide security in case they ran into a trigger-happy anti-poaching unit.

Everyone here was a mercenary – you just had to pay more than the other guy.

The elephant's head now stood to the side of the camp. The guide had cleaned it up, tenderly scrubbing away the mud and the gristle of the neck. Abu Khalil cocked his own head as he looked at the trunk and tusks. She looked humbled. Her eyes would need to be pinned back open for the display case, maybe replaced with replicas. Once he had the rhino head, both would be carefully preserved, driven to Mombasa on the coast, and then shipped via Lamu to Cyprus, and then from there to Beirut. More expense, but every bit of it worthwhile for the dinners he would host beneath their heads, cigar smoke and the cool aniseed of the *arak* hitting the back of the throat as he told once again the story of the raw intensity of the struggle between man and beast. These were victories to be savoured again and again.

He listened as the Land Rover approached. His *askaris* – all muscular bustle and tattoos – were alert. They did not know the new British guide, and they distrusted strangers. Many had seen colleagues killed or injured by anti-poaching teams, often trained and armed by the Brits. But Abu Khalil was relaxed. His friends in Syrian intelligence had carried out all the checks on this mercenary. A former sergeant major, said to be mentally damaged by years of conflict in Iraq but skills intact. Now one more gun for hire in a region full of them. They would simply have to keep him off the whisky until the job was done. It would be good for the Russians to see a Brit in action. Keep them on their toes.

7

The Land Rover pulled up. A green, short wheel-base, with wheels caked in orange mud. The mercenary switched off the ignition and stepped down. He moved smoothly towards Abu Khalil, showing no signs of stiffness from the journey. He was tanned, lines around the alert eyes, two days of stubble, no sunglasses, and a dark brown cork hat. He wore khaki shorts and a light brown cotton polo shirt, open at the neck. A wiry, muscular physique but not tall, or bulging with the macho bravado of the Russians. Abu Khalil reckoned he had a couple of inches on the man.

'Elias-*bayk*.'

Abu Khalil smiled at the honorific. He had been a deputy prime minister in a short-lived Lebanese government. At that time, he had been on the other side, and the Syrians had tried to assassinate him in a car bomb. But he was tougher than the others. Guests were often told the story of him turning up afterwards to a cabinet meeting with his saline drip and cigar, as though it was the most normal thing in the world. He was a predator, he would tell them, never the prey.

'And your real name, Sergeant Jones?'

The soldier took his hat off and grinned. Aby Khalil felt there was something surprisingly innocent, childlike, to him. A man who travelled light.

'You know that if I told you that I'd have to kill you.'

Abu Khalil guffawed and slapped him on the back. The right answer.

'And we go tonight?' he asked.

'If you're ready.' The soldier stared back at him. Abu Khalil liked the nonchalant confidence. A simplifier not a complicator. He wanted to know more about him. Get his money's worth. Make him part of the story he would tell.

'We go. But first we eat.'

They did not speak much as they ate their simple meal of rice. No fire for now, so as not to draw attention to the camp. That was part of the drama. There would be plenty of time later for meat. And Abu Khalil preferred to hunt on an empty stomach. Jones ate efficiently and without relish, chewing slowly and carefully scraping the sides of the bowl with a hunk of bread.

'You eat like a hungry man, Jones.'

The man was impassive. 'When you've missed as many meals as I have, you don't waste them.'

Abu Khalil grunted his approval. It had been a while since he had missed a meal, as his doctor kept reminding him. Something stopped him from showing Jones the head of the dead elephant. Later he would wonder if it was the only decision about Jones that he had got right.

They checked the weapons methodically and climbed into Jones's Land Rover. Abu Khalil's security guards had looked over the vehicle, checking for any threats, and now stood scowling to one side. They had barely acknowledged the British soldier's quiet bonhomie. Abu Khalil waved them away, pleased to see that he had impressed the soldier. He was probably used to escorting Japanese or Saudi glory hunters, not real men who had also known real violence. They were both predators. The only difference was that Abu Khalil was paying.

And then they were out into the African night. The crickets were quieter now, the pulsating noises of the afternoon replaced by the tension of the bush: hunger, survival, death. The soldier drove carefully but confidently, the lights of the vehicle off. It was clear he knew the tracks and the car. Abu Khalil relaxed, holding his gun on his knees, relishing the feeling of adrenalin and the confidence of the whisky. They did not speak.

After half an hour the soldier stopped the vehicle, and held a finger to his mouth. They sat in silence for a few minutes, before the soldier nodded for them to get out. Abu Khalil recognised the water hole where he had killed the elephant earlier. He tried to make out the hulking remains of the carcass in the dark. There was no sign of the calves. Would they last the night without their mother to defend them?

When he had first begun to hunt, he would sit for hours near the kill, watching as Africa disposed of its dead. The lions, never far away, would arrive first to tear at the flesh, and sink their faces into the entrails, leaving their faces soaked in the light red blood. At first there were moments of terror for the prey, and yet often the shock would kick in, and only the eyes would show the pain. When the lions were too full – groggy on their feed – to care to fight them off, the hyenas were normally next: ugly, deformed creatures that dragged the bones in different directions to take off any remaining flesh and suck noisily on the cartilage. Cackling and screeching, the jackals would spar with them for the remains. Then the vultures, waiting impatiently, would rip apart whatever was left, gnawing deep into bone to suck out the marrow. And then finally, the unseen insects would dispose of the fragments. Every last piece of nutrition was drained from the creature.

Abu Khalil liked the sense of hierarchy to it; a natural order. The problem with humans was that they had lost that sense of order.

He enjoyed the way his voice became deeper after whisky. He wanted to prolong the moment. 'There's always a more powerful beast, Sergeant Jones. And tonight, that's me.'

The man glanced at Abu Khalil's ostentatious watch. 'Not just tonight, I hear, Elias-*bayk*. All those arms sales to the factions in Syria? How can you keep up with who is on which side?'

Abu Khalil shrugged. 'There will always be war. If I don't sell the weapons, someone else will. You're a man of violence: you know that. And you know who I am, where I'm from. You can't wait for death.'

The man nodded. Abu Khalil's father had been killed by a militia in front of him, late in the civil war. They had spared no one in the house but him, a child of four. He sometimes claimed to remember watching them as they debated whether to kill him too, standing over his bed. He had later made them regret sparing him from the slaughter, seeking them out one by one. He had tied the man who killed his father between the bumpers of two of his cars, and had him pulled slowly apart. Even his toughest bodyguards had looked away as the screams intensified. But Abu Khalil had stood close enough to hear the joints popping and the flesh continue to tear long after the whimpering had stopped.

Abu Khalil shrugged away the memory. 'Like every orphan, I learnt that you have to use your power if you want to keep it. Survival of the fittest.'

The soldier noticed the way the hunter looked up at him. Somehow seeking approval. A boy of four again. For a brief moment he hesitated.

But the moment passed. The soldier handed Abu Khalil the night vision glasses and gestured to a break in the trees. They moved slowly towards the spot and the soldier placed a canvas on the ground, checking carefully for snakes. Abu Khalil lay on his front, scanning the open space ahead of them. The joy of big-game hunting was in the tracking of the prey. It was easier tonight: the white rhinos were tagged, part of the conservation process. A significant element of the cost of the evening was the bribe to one of the monitors of their movements and the kit to hack the system. They waited, the soldier following the path of the rhino on a laptop. It was moving slowly towards the water hole. Twenty minutes, no more.

'You have kids, Jones?'

The soldier was silent. Abu Khalil sniffed, partly in irritation, partly in complicity. You gave every advantage to your kids, and they were never grateful. The men waited.

Through the sights they eventually saw the white rhino lumber into view. It was magnificent. One of the last males. Ponderous, heavy, but powerful. The animal's calves were creased by the heavy, slate grey wrinkles of the hide. Abu Khalil grunted with pleasure and took out the weapon. The soldier nodded at him and edged back, leaving him to his moment.

'Worth it, Mr Abu Khalil?'

Abu Khalil didn't notice the man's voice lose some of its deference.

'Not yet.' Abu Khalil grimaced. Why the need to be so talkative now?

But Jones persisted. 'And what next, after the white? Is there anything you haven't yet killed?'

Abu Khalil felt his anger rising. The soldier was only a cameo in this story. He sniffed. 'People? I've seen plenty killed. There's no pleasure in that.'

The soldier nodded, grim-faced. 'Agreed.'

Abu Khalil grunted as he found a more comfortable position. 'But I respect animals more than humans. Less complicated.'

'I'm with you on that too.'

Abu Khalil watched the animal for a while, relishing once again the feeling of power and mastery. But he knew that the window for the kill would close. The white would not stay near the water for long. And the anti-poaching units were everywhere. After the shot they would need to move fast to hack and saw the head from those powerful shoulders, get back to the camp, and clear out.

He breathed out as he squeezed the trigger.

But nothing. He glanced at the weapon with frustration.

Again. Nothing. Abu Khalil cursed silently. It might take months to get the chance again. Getting the kit right was what he paid other people for. He was impatient now. 'Jones, give me your fucking weapon.' But there was silence behind him.

Amateurs. 'Jones, fucking get on with it. We don't have long.'

Abu Khalil rose to his knees, feeling the stiffness in the joints, and turned. The soldier was standing behind him, his face hard to see in the dark. For the first time Abu Khalil felt uncomfortable. His eyes narrowed. The soldier was impassive.

'What's happening, Jones?'

The voice was quiet, lower, more authoritative. 'We're evening it all up a bit.'

Abu Khalil was careful to avoid any catch in his throat. He stood. A first pang of regret that he hadn't brought some of the Russians along.

'Evening it up?'

The soldier nodded. His face was still impassive. Without relish he drew a revolver and shot Abu Khalil once in each knee. Abu Khalil gasped as he jerked first left and then right, and lurched forward onto the tarpaulin, sharp pain leaving him retching for air. He tried to reach for his weapon, but the soldier kicked it away.

The soldier's voice remained efficient, calm. 'It's no use to you now.'

Abu Khalil was dizzy with the pain. There was blood spreading around him on the green canvas. He felt for his right knee, his hand sliding into a bloody mess of cloth, bone and flesh. He screamed with the pain.

Where there had been silence, the sounds of Africa in his ears now felt deafening.

He choked back a groan, trying to show no weakness. 'But why?'

The soldier had placed the weapon back in the holster. 'It doesn't matter. Perhaps you just met a more powerful beast. I'm leaving now. Take this as an opportunity to show your famous courage.'

Abu Khalil looked at him with fury. 'You bastard. I won't last an hour out here.'

'Not if you raise your voice like that. If you stay quiet I'd give you until just dawn, probably. That's when the marsh pride normally arrive. You should hope they find you first. It will be far quicker with them than with the jackals and hyenas. Save your energy.'

Abu Khalil felt despair flood through him. 'I'll pay you whatever you want. Anything. I can make your wildest dreams come true.'

The soldier cocked his head. 'Believe me, you just have.'

He turned, walked slowly away, and started the vehicle, the sounds of Abu Khalil's curses in his ears.

Abu Khalil tried one last time to stand but fell forward again on the tarpaulin. He rolled onto his side to try to reach the weapon but the pain in his legs was overwhelming. He strained his eyes in the darkness, looking for the first signs of movement. The night felt suddenly cold.

'Do me one last favour. Tell me your real name.'

The soldier stayed long enough to watch the white rhino lumber off.

'You can call me Nemesis.'

2

Make America Hate Again

Orla Fitzgerald had expected to find her more charming. President Elizabeth Hoon's public persona was tough, steely, sharp. She liked it when people called her uncompromising, because she had learnt the hard way that compromise was weakness. The magazine profiles had been carefully choreographed to craft a sense of a private person, devoted to her job. Of course, there were plenty of pieces out there telling the other side: the political coups, the driving ambition, the ruthlessness with opponents and allies.

Orla had been writing about people like this for decades. She didn't want to tell either of those versions. Saccharine hagiographies were boring and unpersuasive. Hatchet jobs were predictable and rarely lasted beyond a media cycle: the public knew there must be more going on. Anyone could write a one-dimensional character. Orla was not going to be that writer.

Orla had got where she had as a journalist by combining intense scrutiny with clinical detachment. The best profiles told a story, leaving the reader to draw their own conclusions. That meant that she had to find a way to stay detached and non-judgemental. But she also had to gain President Hoon's trust, maybe even her friendship. Certainly her complicity.

But to do that, you had to get close. Which meant breaking down resistance from President Hoon and her aides. And now that she was closer, it was hard to be detached. No one had got this far in before. But what she had found was still, somehow, one-dimensional. It was beyond frustrating. Orla wondered if she was losing her powers of observation, her ability to see behind the curtain.

However, this was a great gig. The ultimate. Not to be wasted. Orla had spent years getting them to agree to her profiling the president. Perhaps Hoon had only agreed because she had wanted someone to find another dimension, to see some shades of grey. She had always scoffed at second-term presidents who sought a legacy, a place in history. She was not in politics to be loved, for gratitude. And yet, was it too much to ask to be understood?

Orla had started with three questions. Who is Hoon, really? What does she actually stand for? And how had the presidency changed her?

Orla's method was meticulous. She interviewed everyone she could, recording the conversations on her iPhone and filing them carefully. She read every word she could find on Hoon's background, upbringing, family, home, community. And she observed, seeking out quiet corners into which she could disappear.

It was from one of those corners that she had seen the real president. Hoon debating with aides about how to defend a signature policy on immigration control against opposition attacks that it was victimising minorities. The language had been worse than Orla could have imagined. In one meeting, Hoon had spat out the words 'vermin, human scum, rats'. Aides had looked awkwardly at each other, clearly immune to the tirade. They had heard it all before, but seemed embarrassed that someone else was there to witness it.

But Orla hadn't heard it before. And she felt she was finally behind the veil, seeing Hoon without her guard up. Hoon had asked for more detail on migrant crime. 'Give me stories, human stories. Good, honest, hardworking people in our communities whose lives have been ruined by these people.' When the accounts had been presented, she had pushed the folder of papers aside. 'I need *better* stories.'

When these had failed to materialise, she had pushed for more. 'Then create the reality. Move more of these scum into peaceful areas. Make the confrontations happen. Wait until they do, and then make sure everyone sees what these invaders are really like. Let the *libtards* defend them if they still want to.'

In the weeks that followed, young male migrants from East Africa were denied food and then dropped off by vans in family restaurants in white, upper middle-class areas. The most violent migrant gangs were released from prisons, and straight back onto the streets. Migrant beggars were delivered each day to shopping malls. Hoon wanted them seen for who she knew they were. The American people needed – wanted – a threat. They're not like us. We need to protect ourselves. Hoon's television network kept the issue at the top of the news agenda, fed off the backlash from liberals.

Orla wrote and deleted, wrote and deleted. She wanted more texture, more nuance. But the challenge was that Hoon gave her none to work with. 'Hoon is a president setting out to prove her critics right. A celebrity billionaire who has cast herself as the voice of the ordinary American. A nation built on the promise of migrants is led by a president who hates them. Her presidency is the resignation of America as the beacon for liberty.'

And in the background, Hoon's media maintained the steady drumbeat of messaging. *These people are different to us, they threaten our way of life, they are overwhelming our communities, changing our values. It is out of control. We have been too soft for too long. We can take you back to a time when the world was fairer, when you had more dignity. Everyone agrees with you really. Don't let yourself be silenced. Life is unfair. We can give you a feeling of power again. Look at them, close up: they are not like us.*

Sooner or later, every political leader needs someone to blame for the fact that they cannot change the world. Elizabeth Hoon had not taken long to decide who she blamed. After another on-stage tirade in which she had likened Mexican immigrants to snakes, Orla had asked her if she really believed it. She had hoped to detect the slightest of pauses, something she could write up as hesitation or even self-reflection. But Hoon had grinned past her, waving a fist at the adoring crowd, high on camaraderie and hate. The convoy had swept on, oblivious to the broken lives it would leave in its wake.

Orla had not yet managed to forget everything she had been taught by the nuns at her convent school. It seemed to her that President Hoon had inverted the prayer of Assisi. 'Where there is love, let me sow hatred; where there is pardon, injury; where there is union, discord; where there is faith, doubt; where there is hope, despair; where there is light, darkness; and where there is joy, sadness.' She had not come to politics to unite, but to divide.

And in her wake, others – in America and beyond – had concluded that this was the new politics. Autocrats in South America, Asia, Europe were taking pages from her playbook, growing in bullishness. America still set the tone, but the tone was one of sinewy rancour. The city on the hill was no longer shining. The message went out: to protect the people we must control them, through fear and misinformation.

Orla had hoped to extract some sense of apology or regret from Hoon, as the violence increased and the polarisation intensified. Migrant centres were burned, schools were barricaded, places of worship were vandalised. But Hoon offered nothing: she had nothing to regret. American carnage was where she drew her strength.

Sometimes Orla envied Ed Barnes his belligerent idealism. Sometimes she missed it more than she could admit to herself. Perhaps she even missed him a bit. She hadn't laughed enough in Washington. It was all so earnest.

After three months trailing Hoon around the White House and the country, Orla had realised that she couldn't publish the profile. She couldn't find the extra dimensions she needed to Elizabeth Hoon. She couldn't tell a nuanced, challenging story.

Orla had found the answers to her three questions. Elizabeth Hoon was a monster. She stood for nothing. And the presidency was making her even more dangerous.

3

A Good Man in Africa

Her Majesty's high commissioner to Kenya hated reading before breakfast about who might kill him after it. Instead, he placed the red folder of intelligence to one side and returned to his scrambled eggs. He looked out over the lush Nairobi garden; his respite from the relentless platitudes and smug small talk of the diplomatic circuit.

Ed Barnes had been in Nairobi for a year. His permanent secretary, Sir Angus Green, had taken advantage of the departure of the unlamented foreign secretary, Lynn Redwood, to quietly rehabilitate him after what the Foreign Office were now calling, with typical understatement, 'his Paris *adventures*.' Angus hadn't meant the description as a compliment. And, if he was honest, Barnes didn't care.

Barnes had been walking on the South Downs when the call came. Angus, as ever, clipped, precise, infuriating. 'Afternoon, Ed. Still saving the world?'

Barnes tried to suppress any excitement in his voice. Was this the lifeline? Angus needed no encouragement in imagining how much Barnes needed the call.

'Mainly just trying to save myself these days.' Too much bonhomie? 'What do you need, Angus?'

The deflection. 'Stephanie doing okay?'

For someone who had helped a woman commit suicide to save her father from the truth about his wife's affair? His daughter was 'okay'?

'She's fine, Angus.'

A diplomatic pause. Neither wanted to pursue the conversation, yet they both knew it had to be given space before they could move on. 'I gather she is still quite a... handful?'

The Saudi ambassador had stormed out of a recent reception that Barnes and Stephanie had attended, seething at Stephanie's questions over mistreatment of migrant workers in his country. When the Saudi had said that women had equal rights, Stephanie had asked when that meant a woman would be head of state. The inevitable complaint had come in from the embassy in London, straight to Angus.

'I wouldn't want it any other way,' Barnes grunted. He might once have made excuses. 'And your lot?'

Barnes could imagine the shrug at the other end of the line. So many of his diplomatic relationships seemed to come down to a shrug. The problem with understanding the theatre of diplomacy was that you recognised that everyone else was also acting.

But at least they were both ready now to get to the substance.

Yet Angus paused again, this time a genuine hesitation. His wife had died in the first wave of the pandemic. 'They miss her. We... I... but we're fine.'

He was silent for a moment and Barnes let it rest, wondering as ever how many intelligence agencies were listening to the call. What was there still to say, anyway? Would his grandchildren dig up a Russian file cataloguing the moments that would have been better forgotten?

A lifetime of changing the subject. 'Congrats on the Oxford job.' Angus was soon to be installed as a master of a college. Ideal combination: decent endowment, dons said to be not too restless, incompetent predecessor. 'You'll be glad to be free of all the intrigue.'

'I'll be happy there will be so much more of it. They asked me at the interview whether I had any experience of negotiation.' A chuckle. 'I said that apart from the IRA, Hamas and the Shining Path, I'd not had much use for it. One don muttered something about how an Oxford governing body would be much harder than all that.'

Barnes smiled, despite himself. 'I've always wondered what those jobs actually involve.'

'Me too. Hosting dinners; the rites of passage; a bit of ceremony; some glad-handing; impromptu speeches. Setting the *tone*. So should be well within the comfort zone.'

Barnes was happier for his old friend than he could let on to him. Angus had let him down, but his *adventures* in Paris had taught him that there were only so many grudges you could hold. Seeing death up close was the ultimate reminder that life was short. Too short.

'So what do you really need, Angus? I'm assuming you're not calling to tell me I'm your successor?'

Angus had the kindness not to laugh out loud. 'Indeed. But we do need you, actually. We all feel bad that you had such a, erm, rough landing. I'll be finished soon, and a new generation will forget us both. But Lynn Redwood's gone, thank God. It's time for you to come back. You look a bit, erm, aimless, *listless*.'

'Back?' Barnes looked out across the hillside, towards the English Channel.

'The mothership, Ed. You and I aren't really built for anything else. I don't see you on the government relations circuit. And I suspect you don't have the patient acquiescence for an Oxbridge college. Your tolerance for bullshit seems to have become less honed than mine.'

Barnes waited. If it was a big job Angus would have got to it by now. There would be more of a sense of relish, less of an air of faint embarrassment. He felt the resentment of the power imbalance surge again. He kicked the chalky ground.

Let's get it over with. 'But… Angus. There's bound to be a "but"?'

Angus hesitated. 'You're still pretty toxic. You know that. Not many ambassadors go rogue, charging around Lebanon, France and Denmark, leaving a trail of destruction. We do prefer you to remain on-piste. The Americans will be livid when they find out we're rehabilitating you.'

Rehabilitate. Barnes didn't want to play another power game. 'If it's got this far, you've asked them already. And they've worked out if they care enough to make something of it.'

Angus chuckled. 'Touché.'

Barnes felt his old friend enjoying the moment of power. He prepared himself to be disappointed or magnanimous. And to ensure Angus didn't know the difference. Perhaps Angus was tiring too. The next meeting would be waiting: another colleague to humiliate, or visiting ambassador to patronise. 'It's Nairobi, Ed. You always told me you wanted to go back one day. It's the least I can do.'

'Indeed. The very least.' But Barnes felt more positive than he let on. Far from London. Sunsets and sunrises. His own ship again. Gin. A bit more edge in former colonies, even if you took the blame for it all.

Angus let his exasperation show. 'Come on, Ed. There's lots going on: the terrorist threat from al-Shabab means the Home Office will read your reports. Trying to keep our DFID colleagues on the same reservation. Trying to keep the spooks within – or at least close to – the lines. Tricky – um – historical baggage, corruption, a shaky mission, bit of business, decent weekends to escape on safari. And you've always said you liked going back to the places you served in. Plays to that sentimental nostalgic in you.'

Barnes thought of his old and violent friend Max Crawford, buried in the ruins of a warehouse in Copenhagen, giving his life to protect him. Max would approve of Kenya. Get off grid. *Proceed until apprehended.*

'Let me think about it, Angus. I genuinely appreciate you giving me another run. I know you will have spent some genuine capital.'

Angus allowed a small amount of calculated irritation to come through. 'Can you think about it fast? I don't have much margin, and I need to let the frontrunner down. She won't be happy.'

Barnes had continued his walk. The hills had been a refuge. But also a prison. He had left Angus hanging two days longer than Angus had asked, and then agreed to go. But on one condition: that he became a UK climate change envoy. Nairobi housed the ineffectual UN climate HQ, UNEP. He would be accredited to that. He might learn something. It would keep him sharper. And provide an alibi when he needed to say no to receptions.

But mainly it might be the only way to get Stephanie to come with him. And that was the only way to make it all stack up.

And here she was now, arriving at the same moment as more tea, toast and scrambled eggs. All served on white crockery with a British crest. White cotton dress. Hair swept back. There was a light breeze and the air was still cool.

'Enjoying the intel, Pops? Is today the day they're going to splat you?' She made the bomb gesture with her hands.

He rolled his eyes theatrically, but he was pleased to see her. And pleased she cared. 'Late one, Steph?' he asked.

She shrugged. 'Think so. We found a great club, basement, decent live Zanzibari music. No expats or Kenya cowboys. *Real* people.'

'Decent Tusker, too?'

'They were serving *dawa*, "medicine". Vodka with lots of honey, fresh limes, ice. You should come next time. You might like it more than you realise. Maybe even meet someone? Or invite Orla along?' She winked.

They tucked into the eggs with gusto.

'How's the day looking?'

Better already. He always felt so much better when she was there.

'Heavy. I'm sending a management officer home for misconduct. Need to kick the visa section: they seem to see their job as saying no to as many Kenyans as possible in as unpleasant a manner as possible. Doesn't help that their minister agrees. And I need to get on top of the programme for the Princess Jane visit. President Obwocha is miffed over something about human rights the junior minister said in parliament. So, no drama really. The usual.'

'All sounds in your comfort zone, Pops. I read something cool on Twitter. Write down a list of those who energise you. Work more with them. Write down a list of people who leave you feeling drained and unexcited. Work less with them. Talking of which, did you read that the Lebanese arsehole disappeared?'

Barnes had known Elias Abu Khalil — 'the Lebanese arsehole' — during his time in Lebanon, when he had been invited to dinner at the man's macabre house, surrounded by dead animals. He had felt duty-bound to invite Abu Khalil back when he had heard he was visiting Kenya.

The man had sat at the residence table like he owned it, barking orders at Barnes's staff, holding court with legs spread wide. A status watch. Stephanie had inevitably fallen out with him fast.

Barnes had just seen the article in the *Daily Nation*. 'I'm curious. Maybe the anti-poaching lot. Decent scalp for them, if so. I'm sure the spooks will tell me. Unlamented, I agree.'

'Too right. One less *bwana mkubwa*, treating Africa like he treats women.'

They ate in silence for a moment, Barnes refilling her tea before the cup was finished, trying to hide his slight disapproval at his daughter's enthusiasm for the hunter's death. If the story hit the UK press, it would knock the tourist numbers. Not a problem for Barnes: fewer Brits, fewer headaches. But a kick for the travel guides, the bird spotters, the Kenyans working in the lodges. The small people always took the real hit.

'You okay, Pops? Your shoulders are sagging. Surely Jim and David can handle all of that?'

The High Commission had a gay couple as deputy high commissioner, job sharing. Each would work two to three days a week in the mission, where they hosted popular dinners. Some of the Kenyan ministers sniggered, but Barnes was delighted. Partly because they were so good at it all. Partly because they were fun to work with. And partly out of mischief, enjoying how much it unsettled some of those same sniggering ministers.

He sighed. 'I just worry it's all a bit futile. We're just reacting to events, reporting events, never behind the events. Everyone used to think we were running this country, even when we weren't. Now they don't think we're competent enough to be that cunning. Global Britain is a joke. Moving the chairs on the Titanic has become Britain's national sport. What's it really all for?'

Stephanie slammed down the cup and turned hard towards him. Her eyes were piercing, bright. 'Then stop moving the chairs around, Dad. Snap out of it. Start doing stuff. The only issue that really matters here is climate. The only issue that matters anywhere is climate. You know that. You're only a few weeks away from the biggest climate conference in years. You need to get up to UNEP and shake the place by its throat, before it is too late. Why are they there? Where's the urgency? Maybe it will take a few more dead bad guys?'

This was not the first time she had flared up on this. He hadn't yet found a way to respond. He glanced towards the house, wondering if he could manufacture a reason to escape. 'I know, I know. I care as much as you do. Really, I do. But I'm just trying to work out which levers to pull, what they connect to. The Jordan conference is off-track. Make or break, as our leaders say about every climate conference. The last summit that can make the change, before it is out of our hands. A minute to midnight. And all we're doing is haggling over communiqué language. As usual. I spent three days last week trying to get small island states to agree to a trade-off over finance for adaptation: yet half of them won't exist in twenty years.'

She placed a hand on his arm, preventing him from rising from the table. 'So why not tell the world that?'

Barnes raised his hands in mock defeat. 'Diplomats are the ripples in the pond, not the stone that creates them. What's idealism without a bit of purpose? It's just virtue signalling, Steph.'

'But purpose without idealism is just activity, Dad. Do you want attention for what you're doing, or who you are?'

'Can I not have both?' Why was he always losing the argument with her?

Stephanie glared back at him. 'The trouble with you is that you're too stubborn to acknowledge how stubborn you can be.'

Barnes felt his anger rising. 'Me? You're the stubborn one in this family.' And then he caught her eye, the sense of mischief back. They both grinned.

She cocked her head. At least he was exasperated. She wanted more of that.

'Well, you better get on with it. We've not got long.'

Barnes nodded, relieved they were back on a level. 'We'll get another few years here.'

Stephanie rose from the table and gave her father a supportive squeeze on the shoulders. She felt him relax.

He saw the intensity return. 'Seriously, Pops? Not you and me in Kenya, swanning around the diplomatic circuit with the Excellencies. The whole fucking lot of us.'

4

The Dealer

Michael Cameron ran his hands through his hair, then checked his teeth and nostrils in the changing room mirror. He hated nasal hair. It reminded him of his father.

It had been another great show. The transgender activist had got angry under the presenter's persistent questioning of their motives. Michael had felt the moment where the audience shifted in the anchor's favour, and had gently backed off, leaving space for the guest to over-reach and get angry. By the end of the interview, they had been blustering, allowing his star presenter to quietly turn to the camera, pause, and get the catchphrase in: 'You're still *just about* free to think. Make your own minds up.'

This was free speech in glorious, unrestrained action. The combat of the arena. He didn't personally have a problem with the woke brigade – nagging and feeble as they were – though they could be tiresome in their exhausting sincerity. Neither did his network really have an axe to grind: it was just good TV. Sometimes it was great TV. But they knew their audience at home were incensed at being treated like bigots, at being asked to hold their tongues. When had their views been deemed unacceptable? And who decided? They wanted the inconsistencies in the arguments exposed, or at least confirmed in their own eyes. They were sick of feeling guilty, of being corrected by their kids, of having their prejudices called out. Their free speech mattered, and they had woken up to find they no longer knew what they were allowed to say any more.

The section with the environmental activists had also been strong. As ever, Cameron had watched from midway back in the audience, feeling every twist and turn through their reactions. Sensing the mob twist and turn, hearing their buttons being pressed. The producers had done well in finding two such unsympathetic characters. The middle-class, entitled, grunge wannabe, chaining himself – or whatever his pronouns were today – to petrol pumps until Dad's trust fund money ran out. Curling his lip at decent, hardworking Americans as they tried to fill their tanks and get on with their lives. A great nemesis.

And the Mexican immigrant. Spending her days protesting against the country that had taken her in with generosity and without hesitation or complaint. If she hated America so much, why not go to somewhere where climate destruction was really happening? Brazil, for example. Why weren't they chaining themselves to the rainforest rather than American cars? The room was kept warm to increase the audience's sense of discomfort and anger.

It was the hypocrisy of it all that he loathed. And that was what he loved to expose. The gently chiding questions. The innocent misunderstandings. Beating them with their own arguments. Exposing the inconsistencies. The audience numbers for *Wake Up America* were growing. And if defending freedom of speech was so lucrative, surely that was a win/win. Next week was abortion, always a polariser. Then gun control, guaranteed to create waves. There were two sides to every story and the public deserved to hear both of them, at volume, even – especially – if that hurt the feelings of the woke brigade and their snowflake social media allies.

There was always a feeling of triumph after a great show. The noise of the audience. The lights. The adrenalin. The defeated adversary. The pumped-up presenter. The backslaps of the producer. Sometimes, on the best days, a rare text from his dad to say *well done*. The dopamine hit of seeing the video clips start to go viral. YouTubers would watch along and share their videos, whooping with delight as the interviewees took the hits.

The TV show built on the idea that there were two sides to every story. The social media follow-through was built on sharing just one of them, pumping it into the starch and sugar belt of those left behind by America. For his presenters, and for the network, this was the sweet spot. The deplorables had a right to deplore something too. Anger sold. It was a way to make the powerless feel more powerful, by giving them someone or something to hate.

The melancholy usually came later, as the thrill wore off. But tonight, he was determined to stall that moment. He had arranged for a fresh delivery of cocaine. Pure, reassuringly expensive. He was waiting for his man in the room that he insisted was always sixty-four degrees Fahrenheit. He tried to control the impatience, one knee rocking as he scrolled through his phone.

The Dealer arrived at precisely the moment he had been promised: ten p.m. Two short but firm knocks on the door. Security had been asked to let him through: looking after the Cameron family often involved looking the other way. The bodyguard opened the door swiftly, ushering the man inside and nodding at his boss.

The Dealer was taller than Cameron, but most people were. That was one of the reasons why he preferred being off-camera. The Dealer was also older than he had expected, despite being told by the middleman that he was not the usual type. White, rugged, slightly tanned. Smile wrinkles around the eyes and the sides of the mouth. He wore a dark blue shirt, closely fitted, and dark blue cotton trousers. He was clearly fit but didn't feel the need to show it.

As with everyone he met, Cameron looked immediately for weakness. Broken family? Insecure about ageing? Race? Class? Poverty? Running from a distant crime? This guy might tick all the boxes.

'Thanks for coming. I hear great things about your product.'

'You made it worthwhile.' The Dealer's voice was gruff, curt. That was normal. They were not here to make friends.

But Cameron was still pumped up. 'Watch the show tonight?'

A brief shake of the head. 'TV is overrated.'

Not blessed with charm, this one. The English accent was less polished, less entitled, than those Cameron knew from the parties he and his father threw for the UK politicians on their books. Obviously not a decent school. And yet a sense of confidence in it. A man used to being listened to. Ex-military? He was intrigued. But he knew the drill: you never asked their name.

'Is it true you bring this up yourself from Peru?' The Cameron family had growing interests in Peru. Fossil fuels.

A big untapped market, especially with many companies feeling the pressure from the wokerati to disinvest.

The Dealer shrugged. 'Yes. My clients prefer me to supervise it all myself. That works for me too. I'm in no hurry to be somewhere else.'

'It's a pretty violent trade, isn't it? Getting worse, I hear?' Cameron was still probing for the mask to slip, the point of leverage to become obvious. Or at least for a decent story to recount later.

The Dealer's face was impassive as he placed his bag carefully on the table. 'I've seen worse.'

'You like killing?'

The Dealer held his gaze for the first time since they had shaken hands. Cameron thought he saw sadness behind the stubborn resolve. Maybe a flash of anger suppressed. Then impassive again. 'Not usually.'

The Dealer unzipped his bag and placed the two packets of white powder on the table between them. He opened the face of his palms to signal that Cameron should try it. Powerful hands.

Cameron shook his head, dismissively. The checks had all come through fine. Personal recommendations combined with some intel on the Dealer. Enough of a backstory. And the man would know that Cameron could drive him out of town if he let him down. Suitably anonymous, discreet. There was no need to prolong this. He wanted to be alone with the product. This guy was clearly not going to be as interesting as what he had delivered. People tended to be a disappointment.

'I'll make the transfer tonight.'

The Dealer seemed to sigh, like a man unreconciled to himself. 'Try it first. I want to make sure you're happy.'

Cameron shrugged. He didn't need to be asked twice. He leant forward over the table, licked a finger. The anticipation was always the best part. He inhaled the cool of the room. He deserved this moment.

Minutes later the security team looked away as the Dealer headed quietly back down the corridor and out into the New York night.

–

They found Cameron's body an hour later, face down in the cocaine. His neck had been expertly broken. When they checked his account, the money had been transferred to a small charity in the UK for the families of military veterans.

His father, more heartbroken than either he or Cameron would ever have imagined, decided not to contest it or to publicise the case. Better to erase the boy from the family story. A key adviser at the firm had called it 'sunk costs'.

But the costs were not completely sunk. The media empire that had seemed so unassailable was now heirless and grieving. It started to break apart, the air knocked out of it. The Peru deal fell through, and a new government in Lima banned other international companies from fossil fuel exploitation. The planet gained some time. The Dealer disappeared.

5

Off the Record

Orla watched Brad Curtis carefully. The White House chief of staff had put on even more weight in recent weeks. He had always looked anxious, but the nails were now bitten further, the eyes more deeply sunk. He looked like a man defeated rather than a victorious *consigliere* with the world at his feet. A walking heart attack.

She had been pushing for some time for the interview. At last, she had a chance to build some fresh material into the Elizabeth Hoon story, perhaps to finally find the glimmer of humanity in her subject. Failing that, maybe some kind of new evidence against Hoon could justify this increasingly hopeless mission that Orla realised she had undertaken.

Curtis didn't look like he wanted to be there. Or anywhere. The usual dance over attribution, eventually settling on his wishes: 'Deep background, not for quoting. So why are you really writing this, Orla?'

He took a long swig of his red wine, not pausing to savour it. Orla had pressed him to do the interview over dinner, away from the White House. There had been many false starts. Even now his eyes darted to his phone, face-up on the table so that she could see the messages come in. How long did she have?

Orla didn't really have a plan. She was going on instinct. Find a connection. Join the dots. 'You've read the files, Brad, you know what I do. I find the personality behind the public figure. Bring that out for the reader. The real question isn't why I'm here, but why you let me in.'

Curtis glanced again at his watch. A small grin of acknowledgement. He knew that Orla knew that he had strongly opposed the invitation to her. In the end it had been Hoon's narcissism that made it happen. What harm could the Irishwoman do? If she wrote a hatchet job, ignore it, or tell the base that it was another liberal effort to stop their person delivering for them. And Hoon never had any doubt that proximity to her would win anyone over. Failing all that, well – as she had made clear – then it was her chief of staff's job to make it go away. Or she would find a chief of staff who could.

Curtis added more ketchup to his well-done steak, stealing a glance at the way Orla's blouse was taut across her breasts. At least she was a looker, amid the silicon and botox of the Hoon entourage. Was he relaxing a little? 'And are you getting anywhere with our dear leader?'

Curtis had of course seen Orla's notes, at least the ones she kept on her laptop. He had felt the frustration in the feedback from her increasingly curt interviews with staffers.

'You know I'm not, Brad. So what am I missing? How can I make this fresher?'

She leant across the table, taking off her glasses. A small smile at the side of her mouth as she tried to hold his eye. Curtis shifted uneasily in his seat. He glanced again towards his phone. A shrug. Orla sighed: this wasn't the way to him.

'Is this where you threaten my access, Brad? Make it even harder for me? Or are you just here to make sure that you come out of it well?'

Orla was searching his face for clues. He looked uncomfortable, but then he always did. Why did anyone want that job? She wondered how much longer he would live at this intensity. Hoon had burnt through four chiefs of staff. She scented blood. Just a speck of it, but there was something there. Another change of tack.

'So what's your plan, Brad, once all this is done?'

A pained smile, but he put down his cutlery. 'I've always wanted to visit Ireland. Explore my ancestors a bit. Get in touch with my roots.'

Orla was used to this conversation. It seemed everyone in Washington was part-Irish. She had long stopped rolling her eyes when they took it in this direction. If flirtation and menace were not the way through, perhaps nostalgia was.

'Where would the family be from then?' She heard herself dial up the accent.

Curtis was more engaged now. 'Kinsale, we think. I've done a bit of research, in moments in airport lounges or when the president is sleeping. We seem to have run a small guesthouse on the cliffs. Overlooking the sea.'

Orla heard his voice soften, and leant back in her chair, letting him enjoy the fantasy. She despised him.

'It's a beautiful part of Ireland, Brad. You'd love it. So much sky and sea and air. The fish is to die for. Good people.'

They sat in silence for a moment. Without checking, Orla ordered them two more glasses of red wine. Curtis had started hacking at his steak again. Orla took a bite of salad, more out of politeness than hunger. She leant forward so that he could see more of her neck.

'So how is she *really*, Brad?'

Curtis smiled, one eyebrow raised. 'Off the record still? To be honest, by this stage of the presidency, the challenge is not rationing the time that other leaders get in the White House but rationing the amount of time our dear president spends alone.'

Orla cocked her head slightly. 'But you pretty much fill her diary, Brad.'

His tongue flicked across his mouth, but missed the piece of spinach between his front teeth. 'The alternative is more dangerous. But I reckon I've developed the art of predicting her unpredictability. President Hoon watches two television channels, one of which she owns. She doesn't read and never listens to her briefings. So while you can't necessarily control what she hears, you at least know what she is hearing.'

Let him show off a bit. 'So that's why you always get the friendly commentators – the Loony Hoonies – on when you know she is unscheduled, when she must be watching.'

Curtis hesitated for a moment, but he was now starting to thaw. 'I guess so. Our media strategy is no longer about influencing the public – the White House has long given up on that. It is now purely about keeping the most powerful woman on the planet from chucking her toys out of the pram and her weapons out of the Pentagon.'

This was better than expected, but still not really any kind of revealing insight. 'So that's how you see my role? Writing truth to power, but not too much truth? And meanwhile she continues to prove her critics right. The administration mires itself even more in policy paralysis and inertia. Key jobs are left unfilled. Washington girds its loins for another long attritional battle against you all in the White House. And all that suits Hoon. But does it really suit you, Brad? Personally?'

Curtis now leant back in his chair. He was appraising her carefully. The ruthless political operator was back. He scratched his chin. A weaponised silence. She could see him choosing his words again. Another change of tack.

'Who does she actually *like*, Brad?'

He smirked. 'Not me, for sure. And not her voters.' Hoon was notorious for avoiding any physical contact with her base, or anyone else.

'And yet she trusts them?'

Brad Curtis half choked, half coughed. 'Certainly not them. She joked the other day that her voters were too dumb to be allowed guns.'

Orla stored this fact away. Quite a handy quote from a White House source even if he would not put his name to it.

She narrowed her eyes. 'I'm just trying to figure out how she ended up like this. That suit of armour. Okay Brad, scratch that. Tell me about today. You get more time with her than anyone. What does that involve? You know how this works: I need some colour, some detail.'

Curtis chewed his lip. She could sense him deciding whether to advance or retreat. A large fan whirred into action above them. 'The polls were terrible this morning. I'm not sure our drive-by shtick is working. It has served us well: pick a new target and focus all the attention on the fight with them. Whip up emotions. Then move on before everyone turns up with facts and reason. The problem is that, after a while, you've used up all the targets. I need to find her more adversaries, ideally domestic ones.'

Orla sensed that at last he was ready to show the part of his hand that he had come to show. 'And if not, Brad?'

'Then she'll start to choose the *wrong* targets. We are now in uncharted waters. Today I had hoped to get to her before she switched on cable news or – more dangerous – her Twitter account. I neutered the coverage on the panels she watches first thing, threatening lawsuits against the channels, barking at our donor pals who own the networks.'

Orla thought about interjecting, but decided to let him carry on.

'But social media is another ball game, as you can imagine. Usually I meet the president in the Oval for the intelligence briefing. Our officials have been instructed to share no sensitive intelligence that might be retweeted or repeated during the day. So there was little of any real substance. But I use the session to give myself the authority within the system to make the calls I know America wants. The arrangement works well for all of us. The president doesn't need to be in on the detail of where US troops are kicking ass, which leaders to blow off or blow up, or how to manage the fucking UN Security Council. I can handle all that for her.'

Orla picked up her notepad to make a note. Curtis paused, more for theatre than because he was worried about which parts were on or off the record. They were beyond that.

'Don't worry, Brad, you know I won't use anything you don't want me to.'

Curtis guffawed. 'Orla Fitzgerald, I wouldn't be saying anything I didn't want you to use. A bit of whimsical Irish coastline, intriguing tits and a decent steak doesn't change that. The only question is how and when you use this. On that, we negotiate.'

She refused the bait, and nodded at him to carry on.

Curtis waved a waiter away. 'Today, I opted not to wait in the Oval. Instead, I told staffers – who were already nervous about what might happen today – that I would brief the president in her private apartment. If she'd been online, I would need to act as a shock absorber. I can't risk more staff being bullied towards resignations, tell-all books – probably with you – and primetime interviews. Arriving in her living room, it was damn clear that she'd been online. Tables arse over tit. A TV ripped out of its bracket. A vase smashed, flowers scattered and water running down the wallpaper. I tracked the carnage into the next room. It looked like a tsunami had crashed through. Or the president had pressed the nuclear button. She was sat deep in an armchair, arms draped over the edges. A prize-fighter who had taken one bout too many.'

Orla raised an eyebrow. Good colour. Not useable anytime soon, but would add to the narrative. But why was he telling her all this now, even on background?

Curtis picked up a toothpick, started to manoeuvre gristle from his teeth, and continued. 'Looking to buy time, I briefed her on the China situation. More military exercises around Taiwan. I wanted enough clearance to take to the NSA for us to push back harder. We look too weak. But I overdid it. The president made clear to me, in her way, that she regarded China's actions as off-limits. She went into conspiracy mode. *They've always hated me.* Some pretty racist stuff, even by our standards. I tried to reason but she became more fired-up. Against my counsel, she demanded to see the chiefs.'

That hadn't appeared anywhere on the calendar shared with the press corps. She tried to ignore the toothpick in his mouth. 'This was today, Brad?'

No hesitation. 'Yes. Clearly a bad idea. But I'm just her chief of staff, as she loves reminding me. And meeting the chiefs *always* puts her in a worse mood. She thought that they were patronising her. Right, of course. The meeting went real bad. She demanded information, targets. The chief admiral argued that she was playing into our enemy's hands. But you know the president. Her mind was elsewhere. She was impatient for the fight. I think she's getting dangerously fixated on the wrong threat.'

'China? I get why we shouldn't dial it up. But why the wrong target?'

Curtis winced. 'That's why I need you to write. That's why I've come round to your project.'

Orla flushed. 'I'll write what I want. That's always been the deal.'

Curtis leant across the table, one fist clenched, fully present now. 'Write it *how* you want, Orla, but you've got to get the message across to the president that this *is* the wrong target. Stick to migrants, Mexicans, Arabs. Queers. Minorities. Single moms. Targets that can't fight back.'

'And what if I choose not to write that?'

Curtis snarled. 'Then I'll give the biggest story in Washington to someone else.'

Orla was not put off. She still needed the quote. A senior source. Maybe a senior White House source. Something that she could use with complete authority. She paused to let the bait settle. But not so long that Curtis could move on.

Her voice was calm, slower now. 'And what's the biggest story in Washington, Brad? What is the thing you're dying to say?'

He chuckled, admiring her patience but relishing the moment. He stood to leave, but paused and moved to her side of the table. Stood over her, too close. She ignored the strain of the stomach against the shirt buttons, the theatrical adjustment of his groin, and held his gaze. She wondered whether he would be angry later about the spinach between his teeth.

Curtis thrust his hands into his pockets. She felt the intensity in him rise and then subside, saw the insecurity, saw for the first time the deep fear. She resisted the urge to prompt him again. *Let him get there.*

His voice was thinner. 'That the greatest threat to US national security is our own president.'

6

Red List

There is a heightened threat of terrorism, including terrorist kidnappings, across Kenya.

Attacks, including terrorist kidnappings, could target Westerners, including British nationals. Attacks could occur at any time, including around religious or other public holidays or celebrations.

Attacks could be indiscriminate in places frequented by foreigners, including hotels, bars, restaurants, sports bars and nightclubs, sporting events, supermarkets, shopping centres, commercial buildings, coastal areas including beaches, government buildings including embassies, airports, buses, trains and other transport hubs. Places of worship including churches and mosques have also been targeted. British nationals are advised to be extremely vigilant in these areas. You should avoid regular patterns of movement and aim to travel during daylight hours.

UK travel advice, July 2023

Ed Barnes arrived at the High Commission feeling more energised than he had expected. The road down from Muthaiga to the centre of Nairobi had been less congested than usual, mercifully, and Henry had made better time, swinging in and out of the traffic with bravado. They used the Jag very rarely, normally for state occasions or business events where he needed a bit of extra dash. For day-to-day movements he, and his security team, preferred armoured Range Rovers; much easier to manoeuvre between tight spots, and higher off the ground. Both the driver and the principal bodyguard, sat in the front, were armed. Barnes had long since stopped noticing the weapons. The system only worked if you trusted it completely.

Today Raoul was the main BG. He would be with Barnes everywhere he went outside the High Commission, and was dressed as closely as possible to him. However bad you are with names, Barnes had told a younger colleague heading out to a high threat post, you never forget a BG's name. He had watched the training exercise where they took the bullet for him. He had imagined how he would try to explain that to a widow.

A second black Range Rover followed, occasionally swapping places with the car carrying Barnes. It had long stopped being disorientating to swing in and out of traffic and take sudden detours.

Keep moving forward; don't be predictable. Max Crawford would have approved.

Barnes thought often of Max. Had it really just been loyalty, maybe even friendship, that had motivated him to save his life in Copenhagen? Barnes didn't feel that same sense of loyalty to any individuals any more, except Stephanie. For Emma, the wife who had left him, he felt instead a residual pool of affection, the product of shared experience, of accumulated time. And he knew how important she still was to Stephanie, despite his daughter's continued fury at her betrayal. Whatever had come between them, they had created something extraordinary.

Max Crawford had protected Stephanie, too, like his own daughter. Protected her in ways that Ed could not have done.

Barnes had been at Crawford's funeral. Invited as an ambassador rather than a friend, which is what Crawford might have expected. After the formalities at the Hereford base, the last post and flag at half-mast, they had moved to a quiet church in Hay. Barnes had listened closely as the sons told their stories, quietly and without drama. There had been none of the derring-do and adventure that Barnes had anticipated. No former commanding officers reading the citations for valour. Instead, simple recollections of family and friends. Crawford watching sport, mending a fence, camping in the garden with the boys, listening to music, doing the washing up. An ordinary life in between the unspoken – of extraordinary moments. One of his former command had spoken about him as a mentor, calm under pressure, never striking fear into his men in the same way he did to his enemies. Quietly kind. Genuinely loved, genuinely respected.

It had all been swift and unfussy, as Crawford would have probably insisted it would be. His favourite quote, from General Gordon. 'England was never made by her statesmen; England was made by her adventurers.' A quiet dignity to the family, a 1950s funeral in an Instagram world. As his last ambassador, Barnes had read 'If', his favourite poem. His voice had only faltered in the first line, on keeping one's head while everyone else was losing theirs.

Barnes thought of Crawford often. Sometimes he felt he heard his voice.

No casket, with the body still somewhere under the wreckage of the US air strike in that Copenhagen warehouse. Crawford had always claimed not to want an 'oak suit'. No press coverage beyond a small piece in the regiment's gazette, giving the official story of a training accident. Barnes had sat briefly with the family afterwards. There had been little emotion: they were managing the day, managing the guests. Steely, resolute, chips off the old block. Talk of logistics, plans, the news, moving forward. No sense of regret. Stoic sacrifice. It was always hardest watching the family.

He had not wept that day until he got to the car. He had pulled over twice on the way home as the grief took him and shook him.

Barnes sniffed and cleared his head as the Range Rover pulled up to the gate of the High Commission. This was always the point of maximum threat: the one predictable move between leaving the residence and getting to the relative safety of the main compound. The bodyguard in the front seat shifted in his seat, eyes darting up and down the road. The guards on the gate swiftly ran the mirrors under the vehicle for car bombs, signalled for the bollards to come down, and they were through. He no longer noticed the slight unclenching in his stomach.

Sometimes in the early days Barnes had looked at stationary cars as they passed, wondering if they would be the one that would kill him. Would they waste a decent car for the bomb? Or were the clapped-out rust buckets really the ones to worry about? One unwanted Lebanese export to Kenya had been expertise on wiring up a parked vehicle. He had seen the smouldering wreckage of the armoured car of one Lebanese prime minister: the armour only went so far. Henry opened the heavy door and Barnes jumped out, a spring in his step.

He nodded at Raoul, the hint of a wink. The alternative to survival never discussed between them. 'Thanks, see you for the Chinese do. Let's see what joys my colleagues have waiting for me today.' As ever the BG half-smiled back, professional complicity but no more. He didn't know or care what happened in the high commissioner's meetings. He was looking forward to his coffee.

Barnes always took the stairs up to the office. Partly to send a message to the staff about saving energy, leading by example. But mainly because he – quietly backed up by Stephanie – was determined that Kenya shouldn't be the three stone posting it had been for his unlamented predecessor.

Penny Rainsford was waiting for him outside the office. She had followed him from the embassy in Paris once his return to the diplomatic service had come through. She had worked professionally enough with his successor there, an ambitious and slightly wearing ex-No 10 private secretary. But the narcissism had been exhausting, even for someone so used to the foibles and neediness of male diplomats, and she had been relieved to get back to the labrador earnestness of Ed Barnes, even in less glamorous environs.

She was enjoying it all more than she let on. Barnes needed more scaffolding since the events in Paris. But she knew he enjoyed it more than he let on too. She liked it when he had his bounce back.

'Morning, Ed. You look up for it.'

Barnes raised his eyebrows. 'Papers full of the usual political pantomime?'

'And that's just the UK?'

'Very funny, Penny. Here *and* at home. Just less corruption here. Who's on today? Jim or David?'

Penny walked ahead of him, enjoying his wince as she held a door open for him. They stood for a moment, Barnes awkwardly gesturing for her to enter. She shook her head in fake frustration and went through first.

'Jim,' she said. 'He wants to see you urgently about the travel advice.'

Barnes suppressed a groan. 'Again? Okay, let's get him in.'

Jim's office was on the same corridor. He grinned as he entered the office. They had worked each other out early after Barnes's arrival at post, when Barnes had backed his deputy's choice not to send home a young diplomat who had ended up in the residence swimming pool after a couple too many drinks at the annual king's birthday party. Jim knew that his boss had taken more flak for it than he let on. Barnes was making them both a coffee, fiddling with the Nespresso machine. The pods were stuck again.

'Espresso okay?'

'Dave's the espresso, Ed, remember? Something more lungo for me, please.'

'Oh God, sorry, it's not deliberate.'

Jim laughed. Of all the confusions – genuine or confected – over his joint posting with his husband, the high commissioner's were easy to take. And the apologies were always genuine. As his boss strode towards him with the coffees and gestured to the table rather than the armchairs, he decided to hold back for a moment on the travel advice. Ed Barnes was in earnest mode. It was always better to let him discuss something on his mind before giving him the bad news.

Barnes furrowed his brow. 'We've got to get back to climate, Jim. I'm sick of these pointless UNEP meetings. There's no sense of reality. I need to get out there, highlight areas where climate change is happening right now, show what that means, get it up the agenda. Maybe we could even *do* something about it?'

Jim nodded along. He had heard this before, mainly from Stephanie. 'The Kenyans know what climate change means. They are living it. At least the ones outside Nairobi.'

'Not just for them, Jim. For the people at home. For the Chinese, Indians. Anyone holding up this deal. Where's the sense of jeopardy? The meetings feel like we're debating credit default swaps, not the end of the world.'

Jim sighed. 'Then you've got to convince the Americans, too. No deal gets off the table without them. You know that.'

Ed paused. Fair point. 'Yes, maybe I should take *Her Excellency*.' Jim knew that he never used an honorific as a compliment. 'Either way, we have to get a bit of urgency back into the room.'

Having experienced the worst of US ambassadors in Paris, Barnes was slightly in awe of his new US counterpart. Early fifties, a political appointee, formidable, charming, Kenyan grandparents. She had worked in the White House in better times. The best Australian ambassadors brought camaraderie. The best Scandinavians brought a sense of purpose, and a lack of pomposity. The best US counterparts brought camaraderie and decent intel.

They were all, of course, still raw competition.

Jim nodded. 'We'll get you north again, Ed, I promise. Help make the case more convincingly. Connect it to people's lives. But, on the subject of people's lives, we also have something more pressing here…'

Barnes deflected again. 'And get the political team to pull together something on the elections. President Obwocha's prospects. No one in London will read it, obviously, but sometimes we need to remind them we're still here. Try to get me in to see Obwocha next week. I want to make him feel that the world will do something in response if he tries to stir violence up again in the north. He needs to know there are consequences. The last thing we need are another round of clashes up around the areas where we're trying to train up the anti-terrorist units.'

Jim wrote a note in his book. He'd include that argument in the draft of the telegram for London. Barnes liked colour: the choice Obwocha's militia had given local kids at the last elections of losing their arm at the wrist or elbow. And Barnes liked to close them with a comment linking the discussion to the most eye-catching issue for ministers. He paused to ensure that his high commissioner had seen him take the note, and then seized his moment. 'Actually, boss, it's the anti-terrorist units I wanted to talk about.'

Barnes drained his coffee, looked in frustration at the smear on the cup. He wanted to get on with his day. But Jim saw that he now had his full attention. Barnes nodded at him grimly.

Jim leant forward. 'London are back on the charge. They want the travel advice changed. The elections, the violence, now the media coverage of this missing Lebanese businessman. Your mate, the big-game hunter. It's all creating a sense that we need to be more cautious. Much more cautious. They want to warn against *all* travel to Kenya, just until we're through the next month. We've got another video conference at eleven. It's increasingly hard to hold the line on no change.'

Barnes was standing by the window now. Impatient. The view extended from the scented five-star hotels and manicured lawns of central Nairobi towards the fetid slums of Kibera. The energy was out there. He preferred Kibera.

He crossed his arms. 'Once again, no.'

Barnes noticed Jim cross his arms in response. Always the body language that was hardest not to replicate. 'Ed, you need to think this through again. Everyone there knows that you're the only one holding out on this. Ministers are covering their backs. If there is an attack against tourists, from al-Shabab or whoever, and you know how likely that is, there will be plenty of people saying, "I told you so."'

Not for the first time, Barnes said to himself. Or the last. The problem with desk officers in London was that they took the title as an instruction to stay behind their desks. And they were terrified of this generation of ministers. Too many senior people had been bullied out.

'Enemies of the people.'

Barnes heard the gulp, felt the change in register from his deputy. 'Your stock isn't exactly high in King Charles Street, Ed.'

Barnes smiled ruefully. It bothered him more than he wanted to let on. But he suppressed the flash of anger and frustration.

'The problem is that we've all become too risk-averse. It's always easy to take the path of least resistance. London used to be far enough away that the guy on the ground could make these calls. It would be months before the capital could judge whether he – yes, always *he* then – had got them right. And anyone coming to Kenya owned the risks rather than expected us to hold their hand. But if I allow this change, it has real consequences. To real people. All those lodges without visitors. All those local shops and hotels unvisited, quietly laying off staff. Think of all those Kenyan guides who have trained up as experts on their environment. A flick of the switch in London is the flap of a butterfly's wings. Tourists go elsewhere, jobs are lost, people fall further into poverty. More poaching, more conflict, more degradation. And then – perhaps this lot of ministers will notice this, at least – more migration, more terror. We have to factor all that in, too. You can minute in black and white that you tried again to convince me but I overruled you. Say that at eleven. I'm happy to own the risk.'

Jim hoped that his boss couldn't see the barb hit home. He tried one last time. 'Boss, you've got to watch your back. There's no point fighting every battle. You need to build some capital in London. And…' A deep breath. 'People are starting to say that this talk doesn't sound like High Commission policy, but Stephanie's. We all love her to bits. But she's at one end of the scale on climate change. And it's a long way from where our ministers are. We also have a responsibility to our own citizens.'

Barnes hesitated. Let it go. Take the point. A small smile, and he held his hands up in mock defeat. 'We also have a responsibility to Kenyans, Jim. And to our *future* citizens. Hold the line on that call. Buy me some more time to build the case against change in London. I'm not completely out of the game.'

Jim sighed. It was hard to dislike Ed Barnes, however stubborn he was. But increasingly he seemed motivated by a desire to stick it to the system. People said that he could have got the top job if he hadn't screwed up in Paris.

'Okay, okay. I'll hold London off. But at some point we'll have to listen to our – your – bosses.'

Barnes thought of Amina, the human rights activist murdered in his Paris embassy. Of the doors closing to him when he sought the truth. Of the insipid cowardice of the politicians they were asked to serve. Of Stephanie trying to shield him from the truth of the end of his marriage. Of Max Crawford, sacrificing everything to protect him. Of the futility of it all in the face of inertia, laziness and fear.

He grinned at his deputy. 'Nice try, Jim. You're a great DHM. And I'll be persuaded on everything else...' Barnes gestured him towards the door. '...but I think we all know I'm well past the point of worrying about my career.'

7

Killing Time

Nigel Banks never flew in his own planes. It continued to amaze him that anyone ever did.

In the early days, when he was building the airline, he had monitored everything personally, right down to the choice of soap and the font on the sick bag. But for the last few years, he had found himself unable to go to the airports his company used. The smell of the queue disgusted him. Overweight tourists with their heads in their mobile phones. Crisps and chocolate bars. Long queues for the toilets. Pints at nine in the morning: how did being at an airport make that okay? His marketing manager had come up with the idea of making the line for the check-in pass through the shop, so that they could sell more snacks, sweets and celebrity magazines. Small plastic bottles of expensive water. Gossip and grease, all marketed to the mob at a decent mark-up. And his people had stitched up the transit from the airport to the capital cities they were meant to serve, normally a distant ninety minutes away.

Banks liked to describe himself as a bull in a china shop. He elbowed his way into other people's cars, lifts, meetings, portfolios, business deals, offices, marriages – anything to further his agenda. He rarely paid for the lunch, cab, apartment, failed relationship or failed business.

It was partly disgust at what he had used to call the clients, partly his utter derision for a system that kept letting him get away with it. British politicians didn't need bribing. Of course not. They just needed a board seat, or a few days of strategic advisory work. One had asked him what he would be required to actually offer his strategic advice on. Geopolitics? The state of global supply lines? Banks had laughed out loud, leaving the feeble ex-MP bewildered. Strategic advice was the last thing he needed them for. They were cattle, just like the passengers he still pretended to call customers.

Banks had once seen a documentary about US cattle farming. Animals packed together, tired and hopeless. Every inch of space maximised. Every margin considered. What was the minimal amount of food required to keep a calf alive? What was the best time for the market to kill it? The soporific gloom of the animals as they were fattened up with chemicals. The rest of the family had been appalled. His daughter had gone off to work for some green charity, another bunch of muesli-weaving sandal-wearers. A gap year in tofu and wokery for those whose parents could afford it and were dumb enough to indulge it. Nigel Banks didn't believe that cow farts were killing the planet, any more than his business was. The world had always changed temperature. She'd be back soon, once he cut the allowance.

But Banks had been inspired by the film.

He was now working on his next venture. Banks liked people to think he was a lucky chancer. But he read more books than anyone he knew. And they told him that millions of people would be on the move in the next decade, leaving the parts of the world hit hardest by climate change. It was the great secret of the powerful that they had no answers to this, except to build bigger fences. The politicians on his payroll were appalled by the prospect of people on the move, but unable to think beyond the next election. But Banks was on the side of those wanting to move. He would make it much easier for them.

Not, of course, the asylum seekers, who could take their chances among the storms and vigilantes on the Med: there was not enough money in dinghies, and too many thugs, police and bedraggled corpses. He'd leave that market to the Albanian people traffickers and the right-wing politicians and media who lapped it all up. That was just a distraction.

Nigel Banks planned instead to focus on the next tier up: those who could afford to fly, even just once. Low-cost, low-question, single-ticket journeys with every inch of baggage space filled and charged. He would feed on desperation, on the survival instinct. A new range of airports in North Africa and Asia. His people had mapped the areas that would become uninhabitable, bringing in experts on deforestation and the expansion of the Sahara. He was building basic airports near the regions that would heat fastest to help people escape the sun. Meanwhile he would continue to fly everyone else in the other direction to get their sunburnt all-you-can-drink two-week holidays. Those beef farmers knew what they were doing.

The basic business model was that there were two markets for low-cost flights: those fleeing the heat and those seeking it. Those looking for a new life, and those looking for a suntan. Those who needed to migrate, and those who voted against immigration. He would cater to both. Someone had to. The fun would be that neither would know who had sat sweating in their cramped seat just a few hours earlier.

Banks had bought the country house from another family of fallen aristocrats. Cheaper cocaine and more expensive private schools were making it harder to hold family wealth beyond three generations, which was why Banks planned to enjoy his own money while he could. There was always someone on the way down for every person going the other way. He had torn out the ballroom and replaced it with an indoor swimming pool and hot tub, replaced the dining table with a full-sized pool table, and then replaced his third wife with his fourth. Much cheaper than the Botox-and-breasts bill.

He stood at his favourite window, looking down across the estate towards the lake and the fields beyond. It was a crisp, clear morning. The bleak sound of crows in the distance. The mist was lifting. It was now a proper pad. He had also had to put a decent security fence around it. Too many people knew how much his airline was making. Or at least the public figures. And the friends in high places who came to his pool parties wanted complete certainty that they had complete privacy. No camera phones or wives after ten p.m.

So he was surprised to see the figure striding slowly but purposefully up the centre of the main lawn. Like he owned it. A gardener here early? Unlikely. The lazy bastards were still on their second coffee at this time. And they were more – what would be the word? – cowed. They moved like he owned them. This man was not cowed.

Banks pressed the buzzer for the security on the front gate. No response. Muppets.

Banks was a short man, but he was proud of his strong upper body. He had told his personal trainer to focus on the pecs. The Instagram filters, head-hair restoring creams and body-hair removal creams would do the rest. He pushed his shoulders back and walked out onto the terrace at the top of the garden. It was colder than he had expected. He'd see if he could get those crows shot.

'What the fuck are you doing?'

No reply as the figure moved closer, seeming not to have heard. He was coming straight towards the house. He didn't look to be carrying any tools or equipment. How the hell had he got in?

Banks shouted again, hearing the urgency in his voice. 'Hey, who the fuck are you? This is private property.'

The man continued towards him until he was three metres away, stopped and looked him up and down. Banks squinted. He didn't recognise him. Ex-forces probably. Taut, wiry. But no match for his security. A chancer? Blackmailer? Maybe a disgruntled ex-pilot from the last round of layoffs? Banks had often had to use his fists in the early days, before he could pay other people to do it.

Banks squared up. 'You've got one last chance to tell me who you are, and then you can fuck right off back down the hole you came from, whoever you are.'

The man had a quiet assurance to him. He cocked his head slightly to one side, looking at Banks with a bemused curiosity.

'What are you doing here?'

The man paused. 'I'm still deciding. Do you like what you do, Mr Banks?'

Not much of an accent. Hard to place. Banks had no intention of humouring him. Must be a journalist.

Security would be here at any moment. He shivered slightly in the cold.

'None of your business. Not really. But I do what I have to. Last chance: why are you here?'

The man sighed. 'Customer feedback.'

Banks grinned. A nutter. A few every year. No doubt with a sob story of a lost bag or a night on the airport floor. What did they expect for sixty-nine quid: the Orient Express? He buzzed for security again. No response. Why did this man make him feel apprehensive? He needed to kill time.

Banks sneered. 'And you? Do you like what you do, Mr...?'

The assassin straightened up, the curious twinkle gone, and looked him in the eye.

'Not really, Banks. Not at all. But I do what I have to do.'

'Just like me, then.'

Banks saw the brief flash of anger in the man's eyes. 'No. Not like you, Banks.'

The sound of the crows seemed shriller to Banks, the air colder, as a mist rolled over the valley. A faint smell of silage from the bastards in the farm down the hill. There was enough money in the smaller safe to buy this guy off, if security didn't get to him first. He'd encourage them not to be too gentle. His eyes glanced up towards the house.

Banks didn't have time to be frightened, let alone to move. The man had both of his arms pinned behind his back before he was able to react. Forced him to the ground. He gasped, the wind gone from his lungs. The last thing he felt was the sharpness of the gravel against his knees. He struggled for a moment, cursing his security, cursing his assassin, cursing the world.

The security team found him an hour later, face down on the pool table. There was no evidence of anyone having breached the security fence. Nothing on any of the cameras. The police found no evidence of value. There were no signs of a search of the house. Nothing had been taken. Except a life.

It was as though he had broken his own neck, quietly and efficiently.

Banks had left no succession plan in place for his business: he had never wanted to encourage the sense among his senior colleagues that he might ever be in any way disposable. He had never really imagined life after he left it. His kids didn't want to take the business on. The airline's assets – car parks, airports, planes and people – were quietly sold off by the lawyers and the company's core business was quickly torn apart by hungry rival airlines.

But his death prompted such increased media interest in the salacious accounts of his laddish parties, corrupt networks and inhumane business practices that no real successor emerged to fill the gap in the market that he left. Nigel Banks might have been comforted by that: the last of the Mohicans.

More importantly, people started to notice that there were a series of low-level sabotage attacks against airports and planes, delaying fuel deliveries, disrupting flight patterns, making the margins harder to find. Perhaps, the industry murmurs suggested, the murder of the unlamented last of the low-cost plane tycoons was connected to a wider campaign.

His daughter went on to run a climate NGO, channelling her share of the inheritance into activism against fossil fuels and an asylum welcome centre.

She chose not to speak at his funeral.

8

Follow the Story

Orla Fitzgerald was an advocate of the shoebox theory of writing books. Rather than do it chronologically, she would wake up each morning, make a large coffee, and write the passage that most excited her in that moment. At the end of each session, she would print the piece and place it in a box with a label on the outside. At some point the boxes had become virtual files on her laptop rather than physical ones. Over time, some boxes would grow, becoming chapters, or sometimes whole sections of the book. Others would not. The book took shape based on where the writing took her.

This approach, however, wasn't working for her book on Elizabeth Hoon. As ever, the alarm had gone off at six a.m. When she was writing well, she would be at her desk by 6:15 a.m., coffee hot in her hand, eager to start. But with this book she found it too easy to seek distractions. Not least from the endless social media theatre that was generated about Hoon each morning. It was hard to hear any signal through the noise. Maybe that was Hoon's political strategy: all noise, no signal.

She curled her legs under her as she looked at the cursor blinking on the page. She was wearing a long Jimi

Hendrix T-shirt, her hair held back from her face with a band.

Orla chewed her lip. The coffee was starting to take effect. She was beginning to understand what she would be able to write. But she was finding herself unable to explain to herself *why* she was writing. A US bestseller would do her no harm. But for it to sell well it either had to take on Hoon and appeal to one faction, or build her up, and appeal to the other. To do the first felt boring, too easy. To do the second felt a betrayal of her values, of what she would never knowingly call her craft. To do either required her to say something *new*. And she wasn't confident in her content.

She looked at the shoeboxes. There was plenty on Hoon's early life: she had hoped to open up her personality. Perhaps it was all about the parents, or a class bully. But in the end it was all about Hoon. And she *was* the class bully. She had just found a bigger class. The writing was heavy, weighed down, lifeless.

The same went for the rise to power. There was no moment when Hoon found her vocation. Just a relentless narcissism. All that advantage, and never quite getting the prize. And even when the successes started to come, that sense that she wasn't really appreciated. Orla had enjoyed writing these kinds of stories about politicians, finding what drove them. But the writing wasn't leading her here.

The file on interviews with staffers was huge. Washington-speak and platitudes. Occasional nuggets. But most of Hoon's political colleagues were cautious and boring. And those who had left had already told their stories. The White House was a court. But not a court of a young monarch, full of energy and intrigue. The court of an ageing monarch, full of bitterness and fear. The stench of decay.

The digital shoebox marked *ideas* was empty. Hoon's administrations were most notable for what they had chosen not to do, or what they had stopped doing. Regulation of business. Climate change policy. International engagement and coalition building. Tackling climate finance. Media regulation. Always a belligerent 'no'. There was a gaping vacuum at the heart of the Hoon project.

With a sigh, Orla looked down the rest of the file list. Key allies. Donors. State of US politics. Media. Policy.

The belligerent 'no' served the allies and donors. And it was fuelled by the media, and the state of US politics. Orla felt her heart quicken. The writing had more life here. The questions seemed more interesting. What if she could join the dots? Between the people who backed Hoon, and the benefits for them. Not a classic trade-off on donations for ambassadorial positions, one of those issues that really wound up Ed Barnes.

She looked again at her notes on the dinner with Brad Curtis. There was a headline there, of course. And a killer quote. The throwaway line on Hoon's voters not deserving guns was worth coming back to: it could be hugely damaging to her re-election chances. But by the time she published, would the story not have moved on? With Hoon's disorientating approach to communicating policy, she might say something worse – or do something worse – at any moment. And who knew how long Curtis would last in the role anyway. Of course, it was alarming that the president's chief of staff thought that the president was a grave threat to national security. And of course, the risk of escalation with China was a growing story. But it was a long-read article at best, not the *why* for a whole book. And if she wrote it, she would lose all access to the White House.

So why not write the book that could bring down the president? The problem was that everyone else was already writing that. Hoon had built a career on being shocking, on doing the wrong thing. The people who hated her would not be surprised by any insight that Orla could add. And the people who worshipped her would dismiss it as just another bout of liberal snowflakery. If they heard about it at all. The one truly new story she had got was the fact of Hoon's abortion. The irony of the woman who had done more than anyone to deny women the right to choose having exercised that right herself. But it was beneath Orla's journalistic integrity to use that. She would not stoop that low.

Orla got up from the desk, frustrated. She paced to the apartment window, and looked out at the view down towards the Lincoln Memorial. What would he have made of this moment of populism and autocracy? Did liberal democracy inevitably fracture when it was forced to choose between liberalism and democracy?

Orla thought of the journalist who had taught her the shoebox theory. She had last seen him in Paris, weeks before he died. A career dodging bullets in the Middle East. Heavy drinking in the bars of Beirut, Damascus and Cairo. Those were the days when a journalist wore a white suit, knew every warlord, and was known to every barman. He had leant across the table, wine glass in hand, eyes bright in a weathered face. She could taste the confit de canard. 'Write what you know. Write what excites you. The only great work comes from when you let the story lead you.'

The last piece that had really excited her was the one that had won the prizes. It had almost killed her to write it, which was why she hadn't shown up to receive them. The story that had led her back to Ed Barnes, back to Paris, back to the mountains of Lebanon, and on the trail of the Heretics. The links between big data mining, public health and academia. But it had also led her through danger and trauma. Maybe writing it had been the easy part.

She had not seen Barnes since. She had received emails with half-invitations to Kenya, always with that sense that Ed couldn't quite find the right register. Stephanie shared photos and mischievous updates about life at the High Commission. Orla had enjoyed seeing that world, and Ed Barnes, through Stephanie's nonchalant but affectionate scepticism. Stephanie had recently sent her a book: *The Ministry for the Future* by Kim Stanley Robinson. Alongside exploration of different technical fixes for climate change, it imagined a group taking direct, violent action to prevent climate change. Extinction Rebellion with guns.

But Orla had held back from reconnecting properly with Ed and Stephanie. To get too close to them both might have led her closer to a truth she could not write. A writer's instinct for a story wrestled with a writer's sense of what they needed to do to preserve themselves. She had seen a similar tension in Ed Barnes: to be or to do.

Orla chewed a knuckle. The caffeine was now doing its job.

Back in Paris Ed had taken the plunge, in his own way. He'd pursued the Heretics, risking everything. Sooner or later every writer had to ask themselves: is it our job to hold up a mirror to the world or try to change it?

Let the story lead you. Brad Curtis wanted to be seen as a restraint on the president. Didn't they all? But she couldn't do it without them. Hoon didn't operate in a vacuum: she was allowed to operate. *Enabled* to operate.

She padded across to the coffee machine again, not feeling the cold of the tiles on her bare feet.

She looked at the shoebox on Hoon's donors. Airline owners. Financial speculators. Hard-right politicians. Media owners. Oligarchs. All linked to each other in subtle ways. Networks of corruption and influence. And all linked to President Hoon. All getting more powerful while the pantomimes in Washington distracted the citizens from the checks and balances meant to restrain them. And – why did Ed Barnes's voice always come back to her when she was trying to be creative – from the international alliances meant to protect citizens and the planet itself. All shovelling a percentage of that power back towards Elizabeth Hoon.

A vicious cycle. But not a victimless crime. *Enablers.*

Orla felt a small victory over the cursor, still flashing accusingly at the top of the empty page. The writing was taking her where she needed to go. Brad Curtis was wrong that the greatest threat to US national security was the president.

It was the enablers.

9

Blood on Their Hands

The six-seater plane landed smoothly on the narrow landing track at Eldoret airport in northern Kenya. There was a single shed by the airstrip, onto which someone had daubed the words *departures* and *arrivals*. A lone guard lounged in a chair, legs spread wide, shirt off, his gun by his side and a cigarette in his mouth. The heat was intense as Ed Barnes and Lucy Featherstone descended the steps. They could taste the dust.

Lucy had been at the High Commission for three years. Earnest, with a Masters in Development Economics which she had quickly concluded was irrelevant to the actual work as development counsellor. Mid-thirties, bright, adventurous. She oversaw the UK's projects in East Africa, with a team spread across the region. Unlike most of her colleagues, she was not seething at the merger of the development department into the Foreign Office: she saw aid and diplomacy as intimately connected. Part of the same toolkit. Fortunately for her, Barnes didn't really understand development, and left her to it. She was happy to use his clout where it helped. Today he had been keen to visit communities hit by tribal conflicts, always a feature of the run-up to Kenyan elections. She suppressed

70

a smile that he was wearing his usual ageing Brit travel TV presenter uniform: mustard chinos and a light blue shirt.

As ever, Barnes had relished the flight, savouring every moment. The slums around Nairobi had given way to the verdant green of Laikipia, with snow-capped Mount Kenya to the east. The logo from the Paramount films, craggy with ice on the upper peaks. He had climbed it as a young diplomat, head pumping from the altitude. Tougher than Kilimanjaro. The Kikuyu tribe had once believed that it was the home of God. He had taste.

As they climbed north the terrain had become dryer, oranges fading to browns. Vast stretches of browns, with the abundance of the central plains giving way to arid dust. He and Lucy looked down in silence. Barnes sighed. He could hear Stephanie's urgency. The flush in her cheeks as she worked herself up at dinner with well-meaning but dull diplomats. Her ability to charm the excellencies even as she berated them. He pushed his hands through his hair, motioning to Lucy. 'Every climate change denier should come here and see the retreat of nature.'

They were met by the airstrip by his driver, Henry. The local roads were pretty good, the product of the last president's tenure. A Kalenjin, he had known that it would be decades before the more numerous Kikuyu let another of his tribe back into the State House. He had moved fast to deliver for his community. Tarmac mainly: the currency of the African *bwana m'kubwa*, big man.

Barnes opened the car door for Lucy before climbing in himself. She suppressed a giggle: no one else still did that any more. She was not sure whether she was meant to think it inappropriate or charming. It didn't really matter out here.

As they drove north, and beyond the former president's region, the roads became bumpier, and the pace slowed. Parts were almost impassable, with deep craters gashed into the road, and Henry had to manoeuvre the vehicle off the main track and between the holes. Barnes and Lucy gripped the handles by their heads as they rocked back and forth, bodies swaying to the movement of the vehicle. The dust started to get into their eyes and mouths.

Barnes looked freer to Lucy than he did in Nairobi. There was an air of boyish excitement. She always found him lighter, happier on the road. 'What's first, then?'

She had thrust the briefing notes into the seat pocket, to avoid them being scattered by the lurching vehicle. But she didn't need to look at them and wanted him to know that.

'District commissioner. From the coast. Been here a year. Sounds decent. Then out with the local church group to see two communities hit by the clashes. There's a school we're rebuilding, and a health centre I think we should try to help.'

Barnes nodded as the front right tyre thudded into another hole in the road. 'And Pejeta? When does he show up?'

Ole Pejeta was the local MP. Ambitious, shrewd, articulate. He had long implored Barnes to visit his area, hoping that it would bring some UK funding. Barnes had long stopped trying to explain how little influence he had over where Lucy and her team spent the actual money. So Pejeta would be delighted that she had come too.

Pejeta was also still in the dock for instigating clashes before the last election. Barnes had been chided by one visiting junior minister that he should not have contact with politicians with blood on their hands. That would rule out just about everyone up here. You couldn't remain an MP in the north otherwise, as communities jostled for territory and diminishing resource. Barnes had thought about explaining this to his minister, with a homily about the realities of diplomacy, but he couldn't be bothered: there had been five Africa ministers in three years. There would be a new one soon enough. Pejeta would still be there long after the minister had become a lobbyist for fossil fuels or a sewage company.

At the district commissioner's office, Barnes was ushered into a room with a large fan and a huge visitor's book. He flicked through the previous pages. Kenyan ministers always signed flamboyantly across an entire page, an expression of power and disdain. He confined his name to a line. The DC looked disappointed.

'Quieter now, Mr District Commissioner?'

The DC sighed as he sipped his heavily sugared mint tea. His gold watch hung baggily off his wrist like a bracelet. 'Temporarily. There are too many constituencies up here with mixed populations. The Pokot have always herded cattle across the borders between them. They are not confined to neat lines on a map. We know that, even if your predecessors didn't.'

Barnes let it go. He was used to the early jab. And the DC had a point. Further west, there was a sizeable kink in the border between Kenya and Tanzania because Queen Victoria had gifted Kilimanjaro to her German nephew.

'And we're in the raiding season?'

Another sugar lump in the tea. 'It's always the raiding season, High Commissioner. Always has been. In Mombasa we only fight when there is a good reason, normally to protect ourselves from pirates or invaders. For this lot up here, it's a way of life. Part of the ritual, a rite of passage.'

District commissioners were always posted far from their home communities, to reduce the risk of political pressure and corruption. It only worked partially. He was youngish, early thirties, quite earnest but slightly crest-fallen. A precise voice. Probably wouldn't last long.

The heat in the office was stifling. Barnes wondered whether to ask for the instant coffee. No capsules to worry about up here, but it was still Nestlé.

'So what can you do to protect the civilians?'

'Not much. Cattle raids were fine when the Pokot only had bows and arrows. It was all part of the normal back and forth. An arrow can cause some serious damage, of course, especially if the tip's poisoned, but tends to target those actually doing the fighting. It's different now. They're raiding further and further south each year because of the droughts. And they're much harder to stop when they are armed to the teeth. These automatic weapons do not discriminate between warriors and children. And I don't have many soldiers to help.'

'So why not do more to stop the weapons getting in? Make it harder for the gun runners?'

The DC rolled his eyes theatrically. 'Above my paygrade, Mr High Commissioner. *Well* above it. Maybe above yours? As you know very well.'

They both drained their tea. Lucy asked a series of questions about the local population size, water supplies, school enrolment numbers. The DC answered efficiently but without enthusiasm. Barnes could see that Lucy was impressed, earnestly noting the statistics in her black leather notebook. Barnes let his mind wander.

When she had ticked through her list, Barnes leant forward across the desk. He was grateful for a gust of cooler air from the fan pumping behind his host.

'And *Manishmewa* Pejeta? Your MP. Is he part of the solution, or part of the problem?'

The DC hesitated, glancing at the door. 'It depends on your perspective. Perhaps it is important to him that the Kalenjin here don't vote, or vote somewhere else. It is not for me to speculate on the world of politics. You are the ones who insist on all these elections, all this democracy. I'm just trying to get things done. *Despite* all the elections and democracy.'

Another awkward silence. The whole structure of provincial and district commissioners had been a colonial inheritance. Even the visitor books. Barnes wondered if he was the only person in the room that felt it hadn't all been bad.

The DC cleared his throat. 'May I accompany you to the school?'

Barnes glanced at Lucy. He hated too much entourage; white men turning up in big cars with large crowds of officials to look at projects they probably would not fund. But she nodded gently: the new policy was to try to work with local leaders, and this one was a decent guy. She had learnt not to use the word 'empower' with Ed Barnes.

Barnes spread his arms in a gesture of welcome. 'Of course, of course, Mr District Commissioner. It is your country, your district. I'm just a guest. You have been generous with your time.'

After twenty minutes, they turned off the main road on what looked like a small track that led to a single house, Barnes trying not to resent the convoy as it kicked up the dust. But they ground along it for another hour, the cars manoeuvring ponderously between the holes. Barnes and Henry had to stop twice to let the DC catch up. Occasionally they would pass a group of children, or a woman carrying provisions. People seemed to know where they were going. But they had less of a carefree nonchalance than Barnes had often observed this far away from the cities.

They could smell the smoke before arriving at the settlement. Not the woodsmoke of a cooking fire, but the smoke of destruction. The huts and school buildings were smouldering. Groups of villagers sat around in the debris. Children gathered around the vehicles as they pulled in, staring glacially at the outsiders.

Barnes stepped down from the car. The DC was quickly out too, barking orders at the villagers, who stared back impassively.

A young clergyman stepped forward, black shirt pristine even in the heat, as was his bright white dog collar. 'Thank you for coming, High Commissioner, and you, of course, dear Lucy. It is good of you to bear witness.'

A warm smile. Lucy reciprocated, but Barnes could see the anxiety in her face. Aid policy wasn't theoretical out here. 'You're in the midst of it, as ever, Peter.'

The priest gestured them to the remnants of the first hut. An old man sat outside it, gazing into the middle distance. His arm was bandaged at the elbow, where the forearm had been.

A recent bandage, but already filthy with dried blood and dust.

'*Habari yako, mzee.*' Barnes used the honorific for age.

The man was silent.

The clergyman stepped forward. 'He doesn't speak much Swahili. Doesn't speak much of anything at all anymore.' He spoke to him in Kalenjin. The old man shrugged disconsolately, and then let loose a flow of anger. The priest translated. 'Thirty raiders, they burnt everything, killed three younger men, including his son, cut the old men, burnt the voting cards, took away some male teenagers to fight and the girls to...' He tailed off while he tried to find the polite translation.

Barnes bent to sit by the old man. They said nothing. He felt an empty despair, the old man's exhaustion moulding with his own sense of hopelessness. What was there to say? He could only bear witness. But did that make it any better?

After a few minutes, Peter gestured to Lucy. Should they move on? VIP guests always did at this point, anxious to get somewhere easier.

She glanced at Barnes and then back at the priest and shook her head. She had seen him like this before. When there were no words to be said, he chose to sit. In the midst of the horror, it was at least a gesture of solidarity. A way of demonstrating respect for the dignity of the survivors.

Eventually, Barnes rose and shook the gnarled remaining hand of the old man. He held the hand for some time. There was nothing left in the old man's eyes.

Barnes's voice was quiet but angry. 'Let's see the school.'

The DC and priest led them to the remains of the building. It was hard to picture it as a school. A female teacher stood to one side, a small group of children around her. 'We were in the middle of an English lesson when we heard them. We were learning about Paddington Bear. I was trying to tell the children what marmalade tastes like. The kids hid in one room. They shot in the air above us to make us leave, and then burnt it. They were high on

77

something. We didn't know what they might do to us, to our girls.'

Barnes looked around the group of children. 'Good morning.'

They recited back, 'Good morning... how... are... you?'

Even amid the despair, one giggled to hear it. He smiled at the girl. 'What's your name?'

'My... name... is... Mary.' She looked at her teacher for approval, who smiled with encouragement. They were all grinning again now.

Lucy was quizzing the teacher. 'Is there anywhere else they can study?'

She shook her head. 'The nearest school is over three hours' walk. These kids have to be close to their grand-parents. The parents are in the cities, or long gone. I will do my best here.'

Barnes grimaced. The DC was again by his side. 'They need help from you, from Britain. You can rebuild the school. Give them hope.'

Barnes turned to him, eyes blazing. 'But it's false hope. Isn't it? The Pokot will be back. They'll burn the place again. Or worse. They want to make it impossible to stay here. For the land, for the elections, for whatever they are told is the reason to hate. These kids are up against impossible odds, *whatever* we try to do.'

He felt Lucy's look, even from behind him. *Breathe.*

There was the roar of a four-wheel drive, and two Pajeros came through the bush towards them, skidding to a stop. Ole Pejeta jumped out of the first vehicle. Six armed men followed him, glowering at the villagers, who avoided their eyes. The DC moved fast to greet him, a small bow, dismissed with a flick of the hand by the MP.

A huge grin at Barnes, and he strode forward, arms out for an embrace. 'Mr High Commissioner, my friend, welcome to my constituency. *Karibu sana.* But you should have waited for me. I wanted to show you around.'

Barnes held a hand out to avert the hug. Pejeta smelt of roast meat, Tusker beer, sweat and power. There was a menace to him that Barnes did not feel when they met in the leafy hotels of Nairobi, where a British high commissioner still held the advantage.

This was Pejeta's turf now.

Barnes stood opposite the MP, spitting out the words. 'If this is your constituency, why are you letting all this happen?'

Pejeta looked around, jutting out his lower lip. The villagers looked away. Only the teacher stared back, in defiance. 'This? This is normal, Barnes. *Excellency.* The Kalenjin and Pokot have always raided each other. Long before you Brits were here, and long after. I'm afraid it is just our way of life. A rite of passage for our young men. We grow out of it.'

'But not this far south, Pejeta, and not this well-armed. This is different. This isn't boys with bows and arrows, stealing cattle to prove their manhood. This is ethnic cleansing. How many times can these people rebuild? Move on? Can you promise me it will stop once you win the seat again?'

Pejeta paused. Then a loud and long guffaw. His security laughed nervously along. The DC looked at the ground.

Pejeta moved close enough that Barnes could have struck him. A bodyguard stepped forward. Pejeta spat a toothpick onto the dust at the high commissioner's feet. 'Barnes, you people have never understood this country.

This is not about politics any more: you can't blame it all on me. We learnt all this from you. Divide and rule. Use the force you have.'

Barnes had heard enough. 'Then what? Is it our fault again now? Maps we drew on a map when the district commissioner was British? Will it always be about us?'

'Not those lines, Ed, though they didn't help. Not even forcing your beloved multiparty elections on us every five years that drive so much of this conflict. No, it's not really about any of that any more. The Pokot are coming this far south because there is no water any more to the north. Your failures, again. Your choices in the West. But this time it's our water you've taken, not just our land. Leaving us with nothing but prayers, which you've stopped wasting time on in the West. This is on you – the world powers, your airlines, your capitalism, your oil, your entire way of life. And don't say your Jordan conference is the last chance to reverse all that. Fat chance. Why do you get all the water to flush down the toilets of your expensive, polluting cities? Why shouldn't the Pokot fight for survival, for their water, for their place to live?'

Barnes felt his shoulders sag. 'But you're still exploiting it all. You could stop this. You're not an onlooker here, you can lead. You have authority here.'

Pejeta looked resigned for a moment. 'No, I couldn't stop it. If you want to stop the violence for a few days, lock me up. If you want to stop it for a few weeks, send me to The Hague, where there is plenty of water. Let me see the cities you built, on the backs of my ancestors. Maybe that will make you feel better. But if you really want to stop the violence for good, lock up President Hoon, lock up your investors, and the people fuelling the climate crisis. Do something serious for once at the Jordan summit. Look at yourselves before you blame me. It can't always be the fault of the poorest or the least white.'

Ed Barnes sighed deeply. He glanced back at the old man, who stared into the distance, chewing his lower lip in reflection, not understanding and yet understanding everything. He looked at the teacher, disconsolate but fiercely determined. He looked at the priest, his eyes flitting nervously towards the MP, fighting one small battle at a time, saving one life at a time. He looked at Lucy, who was staring at her shoes, the idealism draining from her with every week, every visit, every brush with reality. This wasn't in the development economics coursebook.

And then he looked back at Ole Pejeta. He was loathsome, and he had to be fought. But on one level he was right. His violence was just a symptom, a spasm against the reality of climate change amid a young democracy. People had always fought to survive, whatever speeches Barnes could give about Darwin being really about *collaboration* to survive.

And any project they devised to help this community to rebuild was just a sticking plaster.

Is it the job of a diplomat to hold up a mirror to the world, or try to change it? Maybe he could get Orla to come over, tell these people's story, inject some urgency into the conversation. In Paris he had made his call: try to change the world, not just observe it.

Barnes made his farewells, holding the handshake of the teacher and the priest. He nodded at Pejeta, as civil as he could be, and strode back to the car. It was not enough anymore to hold a mirror up.

10

The Fellow for Free Speech

Like most academics, James Masters despised academics. He also hated groupthink. He was looking for sparks of ingenuity from his students, not regurgitated tosh. And these needles were becoming harder to find in a haystack of mediocrity. The factory education system was churning out second-class robots, not first-class minds.

'Geography has been displaced by the new religion,' he liked to thunder to half-empty lecture halls and full TV studios. 'Like any religion it has its rituals, its gods and its acts of faith. Challenging climate change is the new, heresy.'

It had hurt him more than he could admit when the governing body of his college had voted to remove his fellowship. The convention was that the Fellow under consideration should make their case and then leave the rest to deliberate. Few had expected him to show up for the meeting. But he had swept in, his gown trailing behind him, ignoring the muttering of the historians and the angry looks of the scientists. While the portraits stared down and the dons stared at their feet he had risen from his seat to make his defence. 'This university used to be about challenge, free inquiry, debate. But if you take this course, you are confirming the views of our worst critics: that we have become a madrassah of woke.'

They had done it anyway. The new Head of House – a left-wing baroness who Masters suspected had never opened a geography book – had seen to that. The college didn't want to be defined as the new home of climate change denial. And his face no longer fitted in the new Oxford, where diversity was finally being taken seriously. He had been more wounded than he let on to hear her say in her infuriatingly jaunty monthly e-bulletins – ghastly – that 'Oxford advances one retirement at a time.'

'Diversity in everything but thought,' as he had put it in the thundering *Daily Mail* column that had followed within a week of his exclusion.

And once they had kicked him out, he had felt no restraint in taking his views to the media. The BBC wanted balance, and there were no other professors of geography who would challenge the new orthodoxy. So the invitations flooded in, making him a familiar figure. A pantomime villain with a PhD. US networks didn't want balance: they wanted controversy. And they paid much more and helped him shift more books. US speaking tours followed, climate sceptics fascinated by this owlish Oxford don and his provocative takes. In increasingly rare moments of self-reflection, he no longer remembered what was theatre, and what was authentic. Every academic feared being found out.

To be honest, and only in his private moments, Masters was finding the evidence for climate change increasingly convincing. He continued to read his opponents particularly carefully: he was not like the other talk show guests, all of them paid lobbyists and nutters. But most of those with whom he debated also had the feeblest grasp of the science. They had simply bought into the religion. And it was that lack of understanding that he most enjoyed exposing. Even if he might be proved wrong in the long-term, he saw it as his role to provoke and challenge, just as he had done in tutorials with those fragile students with their mental health lexicon and infuriating sense of enti-tlement. That was how science advanced. Not through saluting the orthodoxy of the day, but through scepticism and argument.

Masters had taken a small flat in London in place of his beloved room in the Oxford staircase with the creaky stairs and the flaking paint. It was still full of papers and books. But there was space to write, a nostalgic bottle of the college's claret normally nearby. He was often lonely, but had set up a corner for the online media interviews that took up so much of his time. His Oxford gown still hung in his wardrobe, and he would occasionally wear it for US television.

Tonight, he was preparing for an interview with a right-wing talk show host. These were easier than the BBC interviews: a sympathetic questioner, no opponent, a friendly audience. It was like playing cricket at one's home ground. He was getting better at hitting his applause lines. 'Free speech needs to be defended at all costs ... ignore the climate change ayatollahs ... the new orthodoxy that wants you to pay more for so-called renewable energy ... the evidence is inconclusive.' They would lap it all up. Where were those sneering dons in the geography department or at the high table now? Unread and unnoticed where it really mattered: in the court of public opinion.

He went to the wardrobe to select a tie and matching pocket square. They liked him to go Old School don, even on Zoom. The theatre was a major part of the performance, and he enjoyed it more than he let on. It conferred more authority and expertise, on a TV station that normally pilloried both. 'The Prof.' He had taken to wearing bright red socks for live events and book signings, to make him stand out. Eccentricity sold. And he suddenly had bills to pay now that he was a normal civilian.

There were two sides to every story.

There was a sound in the hall. A creaking floorboard or radiator. Masters ignored it: this was a city of small sounds, of dilapidated infrastructure. He tightened the bright red tie and ran through his soundbites. He had put the claret out of sight and out of reach. For now. A reward for later. He wondered what they would be eating at high table tonight, but then drove the thought from his mind. He missed correcting the young dons who didn't know that you had to carry your napkin to the second dessert. The duck was better than he had ever acknowledged out loud. He felt the adrenalin of combat, the thrill of the chase.

And then he felt the hands on his neck. Warm, firm, almost a relief. The last image in his head was of his own interview for the undergraduate place at Oxford, waiting nervously outside the room. Had he fulfilled the potential he had hoped they would see?

The assassin slowly lowered his body to the floor and breathed out slowly. For a moment his shoulders slumped. Each death took a chunk from him. He let himself back out into the anonymous London night. 'The Prof' would not be appearing tonight.

Two weeks later the baroness running the college amended the small death notice before it appeared in the quiet recesses of the website. 'Former college lecturer James Masters died peacefully at his home in London.

His controversial views on climate were at odds with the evidence and the science on which Oxford prides itself, but we have always believed in challenge and free speech. Former students may donate in his memory to the World Wildlife Fund.'

The talk show producers removed his details from their contact lists. Other academics emerged to fill the vacuum, but they had less panache, less anger, and – most importantly – fewer academic credentials. They found themselves increasingly outgunned in the debates, and became more reluctant to take them on.

11

Conspiracy of Inertia

The head offices of the *New York Herald* had big glass windows, a statement of transparency and openness. The board held their discussions in the basement.

Orla's editor had agreed to the meeting swiftly, and had not made her wait in the PA's office. This did not seem like a good sign.

They had known each other for a decade. Orla wouldn't characterise Anette as a close friend, but they had always got on well. To be honest, Orla had come to realise that she herself didn't characterise *anyone* as a close friend. They recognised in each other that same passion for the work, commitment to the story, sense of independence. Anette had worn a burka for a month, travelling across Europe, in order to write a piece on Western attitudes to Muslim women. She was a few years older than Orla, and had taken a more conventional route, moving between bureau chief jobs and then rapidly up through the editorial hierarchy.

A brief hug, pleasantries, and into the Manhattan office, overlooking Eighth Avenue. Plenty of glass and light. Sparsely but thoughtfully decorated. A strong coffee for Orla and some kind of green juice for Anette.

Orla had sent the story proposal a week earlier. Anette would have had time to consult.

'I envy you all this freedom, Orla.' Anette was wearing a crisp white shirt, no jewellery, navy trousers. Her hair tied back. Orla wondered if she should have gone more austere herself, left off her own makeup.

'You don't feel it here?' Orla asked.

A shrug, that took in the computer on the desk, the spartan corridors, and the city outside. 'Beware achieving your dreams.'

The coffee was good. Orla took another sip. 'So why not get out on the road again? Get back to your stories rather than editing other people's? That's where I always thought you were happiest.'

Anette chewed her lip. 'There's a generation of us that came up fast, took the jobs that the men had said we couldn't do, did them better. It was always hard to resist the promotion. But we lost something in the process.'

Orla very deliberately turned her head to look out of the window. She would not have taken those promotions for anything. And yet here she was now, waiting to hear from her boss whether her story would live or die. And with it a verdict on whether she had lost even more time in getting to a story that actually mattered. The low hum of the city was ever present. These people were out there, making the choices that enabled leaders like Elizabeth Hoon. Unchecked.

Anette knew her too well to try to spin it out. She took a sip of the juice before glancing down. 'So they're not backing it.'

Orla felt a lurch of disappointment. *They* were the editorial board. She composed herself, noticing that Anette had now looked away so as not to suggest any hint of triumphalism. 'Because it would take too much more time, Anette? Or something more worrying?'

Anette sighed. Orla could see her trying to decide to own the decision or apologise for it. 'It's just the scale of the thing, Orla. We wanted you to do the book on Hoon because we knew you would bring it balance, nuance. We desperately need some more of that in the debate. We can't be part of this polarised narrative. I'd hoped it would surprise people a bit, including me, make us confront our own prejudices. Everything is just so black and white.'

Orla was gathering her thoughts. Fight or flee. 'I'd hoped that too, Anette. But you can't ask me — I can't ask myself — to find subtlety and nuance where none exists. Hoon is as bad as we all think she is. Simple as that. Probably worse, much worse. And that's just not an exciting story. Everyone on one side of the debate has already written it. Everyone on the other side won't listen.'

Anette held her hands up in exasperation. 'But what about the interviews, Orla? You've had great access to staffers too.'

Orla shrugged. Would someone else have done better? Maybe she was losing the knack? 'I... they're hard to open up.'

Anette leant forward angrily. 'You're as good as you've always been, Orla. Please don't think you're not. I think it's something else. We're all struggling to get traction. Social media, the polarisation of politics. It's turned us all into partisans. Made it harder to see the greys. And every day I see the more balanced stories fail to excite the algorithm. They sink like a stone. If you leave the AI to do my job, it will always go for controversy, for the dividing line. Where does that leave us all?'

Orla felt a flash of anger. She couldn't let Anette off this easily. 'Maybe it's not always wrong. It might let me write my story. And this one actually matters. We're not here to please people, to always get both sides. Sometimes we have to expose what is actually happening, shine a light on these threats. These people are destroying us.' She immediately regretted the hyperbole.

'Maybe, Orla. Probably. But not if it was also handling all the humans we have to manage. It's not as simple as just the story.'

Orla watched Anette as she shifted in her seat. There would be no compromise. But she was determined to force Anette to take a side. 'Advertisers?'

A half-shrug. 'It's just that your proposal has too many villains. It's too much for the reader. Everyone knows that political donors are buying something. Why else donate? And everyone knows that Hoon has more of them than her opponents. And these investigations need a smoking gun. Often literally. It seems to me that what you're saying is that these donors are all linked not by something they want, but by something they don't want. It's a conspiracy for inertia. A choice to do nothing.'

Orla sniffed. 'That's about it, sure. And if I hear you right, you're basically telling me that the editorial board are part of something similar. Protecting these people. Stopping me exposing what they're doing to prop up Hoon, how they're benefiting.'

Anette bristled. She rose from the chair and walked to the window. Her shoulders fell slightly as she composed herself and turned.

'Don't make us the bad guys, Orla. You know that's not fair.'

'Then why?' Orla made no attempt to hide the defiance.

'We just can't offer more time, more space, for this kind of story. It takes you out of action for even longer. We don't know where it goes. It manages to annoy lots of people without really hitting any major targets.'

'You sound like *you're* turning into the algorithm.'

Anette gave a wry smile. 'Maybe I am.'

The job wasn't worth the fight. The story was. Orla sighed and stood.

'What will you do, Orla?'

Orla was not going to let her have the camaraderie. 'I'll do what I've always done. What you should have carried on doing. I won't be part of the inertia. I'll follow the story, go where the writing takes me. My integrity...' She choked slightly and composed herself. '...as a journalist. I won't give it up. Not for you, for the paper, not for anyone or anything.' Her voice quiet again. 'It's all I have.'

She knew it had wounded Anette, but took her moment to look away, to avoid any triumphalism.

Anette's voice was quieter now. 'You know we can't give you another period of leave, Orla. You have to choose.'

Orla smiled. She crossed the room to Anette, and gave her a genuine hug of affection and farewell.

Both of them knew what she should choose. Neither of them had doubted for a moment that she would.

12

Out of Shot

The six-seater plane rattled as it flew low over the Kenyan bush. Vast tea and coffee plantations broke up the endless green of the fertile uplands. As they descended over Nairobi National Park they could see elephants below, and patches of zebra and giraffe. It was a landscape that humbled you.

Even before they landed back in Nairobi, Ed Barnes had felt his antennae for danger twitching. At first, he assumed that it was a reaction to the destruction and despair he had seen north of Eldoret, his anger at the hopelessness in the eyes of the kids. But the persistent sense of threat remained with him as they came back into range, and his FCDO-issued phone started twitching.

There had long been a trade-off between the pace and security of communications. Eventually – and reluctantly – the office had made the call, and gone for pace. And so gone were the brick-sized devices that ambassadors had carried around to make their calls secure. Better to have kit that worked. The assumption was now that plenty of intelligence agencies were listening, but that, on most issues, by the time they did it was too late to matter.

Nevertheless, officials had developed a form of language to obscure the detail. Careful half-sentences.

Under pressure, some forgot this, some became more obscure.

Dave, the other half of the deputy head of mission, was one of the former.

'Boss, we have an awkward situation.' Dave had tried to modify the Welsh accent in his first posting but had long stopped worrying about it.

'Awkward?' Barnes was impatient. 'Or threatening?'

'Gunshots at the Lavington Mall. Some sort of siege. Probably a robbery. A lot of Brits up there, for sure. Mostly long-term residents, expats. But plenty of tourists too, probably.'

Barnes winced. Normally he might have corrected *mall*. 'Do we know who is firing the guns? Sure it isn't al-Shabab?'

The intel had been flashing red on potential attacks from the Islamist terrorist group. Barnes had sought to downplay it in the reporting to London.

'Not yet. And nothing for an open line. The media are unsure. Pretty heavy Kenyan military presence around the mall.'

Barnes wondered if they would blame him publicly. 'I bet. You're on top of the update to London? Get it out before they ask for it, even if it's short and sketchy for now. Caveat anything we're unsure of. Don't let them leap to the wrong conclusions yet... even if they're the right ones.'

Barnes heard Dave swallow. He forgave him in advance. 'They'll ask about the travel advice.'

Too right they would. Why had he been so stubborn? 'Hold all that off for now. We don't know what is happening, or why. Tell them we need to focus on getting support in place.'

'Do we want an RDT?'

Barnes could hear the hesitation in Dave's voice. It was the last thing he needed. The rapid deployment teams – RDTs – had been put in place after a Bali terrorist attack in 2004. They were on standby to support embassies during crises. Most ambassadors resisted: too much churn, a sense that the local team on the ground couldn't cope. Surely better to soldier on? Yet most were glad of them once they arrived. However good the crisis preparations, Max Crawford had been right to point it out: no plan survived contact with the enemy.

Barnes hesitated. There would certainly be UK casualties, only a handful if they were lucky, if he was lucky. He was one consular official down because of staff cuts. But either way there would be a lot of media on the story, as so many regional correspondents were based in Nairobi. And he had acquired a certain notoriety after his time in Paris.

Dave would have to deal with it. 'Yes. Ask for a team. Better than having it foisted on us in two days' time. But do all you can to make sure it's a good one. We need a decent press officer with proper credibility in London, but one who will work *with* us, not against us. Some experienced crisis officers, not fragile fast streamers just off a gap year. Meanwhile, pull together everyone at the High Commission without a really good reason to be doing something else. Let's meet in an hour.'

'An hour? Won't you be back sooner?'

'I need to get in front of a camera first. Text me any updates.'

It had been part of the drill for at least a decade now. Embassies had lost media control of crises too many times. So the number two pulled together and led the actual response. The senior figure got in front of a camera fast and projected calm. This was not just about spin: the comms were part of the crisis management plan. You had to show grip.

Barnes ran a hand through his hair, and brushed the dust off his jacket. A light jacket, a bit dishevelled. Not really the look he needed. Orange dust from the drive. He felt it in his eyes and his ears. They would be all over him. Every crisis needed someone to blame. This was on him. He had to own it. When had he stopped listening to anyone or anything but his instincts? He needed to see Stephanie.

'Henry, get me back to the res as quickly as possible. Then to wherever the Sky camera is near the Lavington mall.'

The security team buzzed on their radios as the message was passed. A discreet cough from the front passenger seat. Sam was on duty as the principal BG today.

Sam's voice was firm but respectful. 'Boss, it's going to be a serious scrum up there at the mall. We could get stuck for hours. And we can't guarantee who's around. The terrorists are still in the mall. Army could go in. Could get messy. Can't we just do all this back at the HC?'

Barnes shook his head. You overruled the security team only very rarely. 'Absolutely not. I have to show myself near the scene, to show we are on top of it.'

Barnes could see the raised eyebrows in the front mirror. 'Are we?'

Barnes grimaced. 'We will be.'

At the residence, Barnes swigged two large glasses of cold water, splashed water on his face and hair, and put on a dark grey suit and sober tie. No sign of Stephanie. These were the moments when he most missed Emma.

A quick once-over, a reassuring look, a calm hand on his back.

You've got this.

Sam was waiting outside with the convoy ready. He had been told by the team leader to have one more try at dissuading his high commissioner, but he took one look at Barnes and decided against. He recognised that look. Part of him was glad to see it. And part of him was excited to be heading towards the sound of gunfire. They were through the gate, past the two *askaris* guarding the entrance, and back out into the bustle of Nairobi traffic.

Barnes had asked Lucy to check Twitter. 'The first ten minutes were just a few factual messages. "Something happening at Lavington Mall" etc. Reports of the first shots. Not much. No visuals. Agencies just had it as breaking. But there's been much more in the last few minutes. Some videos of armed terrorists, people on the ground, the army presence outside.'

'Is it running yet on Sky? BBC?'

'Yes. Both have people there now. But it's all quite sketchy, vague. Everyone is waiting for something more definitive.'

Barnes called Dave as they swung between the traffic.

'Any updates on Brits? Or who's behind this?'

Dave was steely and curt. He had done these before. 'Not yet, Ed. Chaos up there. Worth getting your piece done fast and getting back here where we can take proper stock.'

'Then tell the station I need a better update than that on arrival. Their best guess. And if not theirs, the Americans'. I'll hold the public line for now on no speculation.'

'The station' was open-line talk for his MI6 team. Surely they would be getting something decent from the phones by now?

The traffic had slowed as they got closer to Lavington. Barnes felt his frustration growing. He could see the Sky cameras set up about fifty metres ahead. There were people everywhere. Every tragedy drew an audience. They always had.

He reached for the door handle. 'Okay, Sam, let's walk the last bit.'

The briefest hesitation. The earpieces crackled. Better on balance to be moving than stationary. And then the heavy door swung open from outside, and Barnes and Sam were out into the noise and the heat. The media team had seen him coming and swung the cameras his way. There was a rally of gunshots from the building. The air was more humid here.

He recognised the journalists, gave them a curt nod. They had been having a quiet few months in Nairobi itself, punctuated by gruelling trips to the drought-driven conflicts in Sudan and Ethiopia.

The barrage of questions started. 'Are there any Brits inside, High Commissioner?'

Barnes waited a few moments, composed himself. The shot should not look too chaotic, or out of his hands. He breathed deeply, forcing his shoulders to relax. Remember the drill: not just what you say, but how you say it. *We have a plan.* Even if you haven't worked out what it is yet. Steely but not theatrical.

The press office in Downing Street turned the volume up as they watched him on the big screen.

'The British High Commission is monitoring the situation very closely. My first thoughts are with those in the mall, and their friends and families following the situation. I won't speculate on the details for now, as the priority must be to establish the facts and protect those who are in potential danger. We offer our full support to the Kenyan authorities as they respond with bravery and profession-alism. The High Commission is setting up a way for Brits to contact us. Full details on our website. For now, I ask everyone to remain calm and support those leading the effort to protect those inside the shopping centre.'

The journalist could see he was looking to move away fast. There wasn't a clear storyline for them yet. Every crisis needed a scapegoat and a villain. Was the high commissioner both? 'But what is the intelligence telling you about who is behind it? And what about your travel advice, High Commissioner? Did you know of this threat? Should you not have warned that an attack like this was likely? Inevitable?'

Barnes clenched his fists slightly at his side, held himself steady. Yes, probably. But if every bit of intel triggered a warning they might as well shut the whole country down. How long before he was 'champagne-swilling diplomat Ed Barnes, hosting soirees while Brits were exposed to danger'? Or, even worse, would they make him out to be some clueless duffer?

'No further comment.'

A firm hand from Sam moved him swiftly back towards the vehicle. They passed groups of Kenyan soldiers, nervously handling their weapons, sweating in the heat. Anxious relatives had started to gather. He was relieved to be back in the air conditioning of the car.

Barnes sank into the seat. 'Anything more, Lucy?'

She had been scrolling fast. Her cheeks were slightly flushed. 'Masses, but none of it very clear. Lots of speculation about al-Shabab. More videos. Dave just messaged to say that they think there will be thirty-plus Brits inside. They've got the hotline set up for relatives to dial in. It's already swamped. Slow news day in the UK.'

They passed another two lorries of Kenyan soldiers heading towards the mall. Just boys, uncomfortable in their ill-fitting khaki fatigues. Nervous eyes and hands uncertain on the weapons.

Barnes WhatsApped President Obwocha.

> I'm at Lavington. We need to speak. Too many still inside. Situation very unclear. Please don't send in troops.

It risked being a bloodbath if they went in without a plan. He called his defence adviser, who was up in Nanyuki supporting UK/Kenyan military training exercises.

'Carrie, what are you picking up?'

'They're up for it, boss. Special Forces on standby. As you know, they've been looking for a chance to kick the shit out of al-Shabab for some time. Try out some of this new US kit.'

Carrie Taylor was an ex-Queen's guardsman. She had done what a fellow officer once described – with deliberate understatement – to Barnes as 'some pretty effective soldiering' in Iraq and Afghanistan. She was happiest on the range with the Kenyan troops, away from the medals and gin of the Nairobi circuit.

'But surely they need more intel first?'

Carrie was clipped and crisp. 'Too right. We and the Americans are trying to put it together quickly. They reckon twenty-odd terrorists inside. If so, it would be a disaster for the regular troops to pile in. Especially with civvies everywhere. Most of the infantry lack any training for this kind of action. They're barely out of school.'

'I've just told Obwocha to hold back. But he's only thinking about the elections. Needs a bit of drama. How long would you need to put something more effective together up there?'

'Good call, boss. Whatever time you can buy us. It has to be Kenyan-led, of course. Needs as much US intel as they'll offer locally, but without Washington crashing in. The Kenyans have got the right special forces, hard as nails, well trained, disciplined, dangerous, but most of them are here with me in Nanyuki.'

Incoming message. Obwocha. *Your advice is kind, HC, but I believe we became independent in 1963.*

Barnes sighed as he rang off. Count to ten. He called him. Obwocha let it ring. Barnes pictured the phone vibrating on the table, one among many, Obwocha dismissing it with disdain. He called again. This time he picked up.

A strained politeness. 'High Commissioner – Edward – you might have noticed we are dealing with a serious crisis? Can this not wait?'

'Don't do it, Mr President. Hold back. We can help you get it right.'

'People are *dying* in there. Your people, my people. On camera. If we let this happen, they'll do it again, and again. These thugs won't compromise. We won't stand for it anymore.'

Barnes kept his voice steady. 'Mr President. I'm asking you to think about what it will do for your country's reputation if an operation goes wrong, in front of the world's cameras. That's what the terrorists want. You are smarter than them. Gather the intel first. We and the Americans will drop everything to help. Get a fuller picture and then send in your special forces. They have the skills. Your op, your credit…'

'You seem to think this is just about the elections, Edward? Politicians acting without restraint because they want the glory?'

That was exactly what Barnes thought. 'I didn't say that, Mr President. Some commentators will claim it, but I know that you are too wise to act in a rash way for political reasons. I'm just offering our help to get it right.'

Obwocha hesitated, then rang off. Barnes waited, refreshing the screen with his thumb.

Come on, come on. The Americans must be saying the same thing to Obwocha. With more leverage. The WhatsApp came.

> OK, we wait two hours.

Barnes exhaled, and messaged the defence adviser.

> Two hours max, Carrie. Probably less. As much intel as you can gather. Do everything you can to get the right guys running it. And if you have a chance to get on the helicopter yourself, don't ask me, or London, for permission.

> Roger that.

The convoy arrived back at the High Commission check-point. The guards were more alert as the main car swung through the gates. Crisis mode. And a personal crisis for the high commissioner.

> But Carrie. Do me a favour and stay out of shot.

13

To Beat a Conspiracy...

Wayne Cross picked his nose and looked up at the clock that signalled how long was left on the show. Four minutes. Enough time for a final caller, another plug for his speaking tour, and today's closing rant for social media. As ever it would be on climate change. Ratings were picking up since he had made this the new cause, even more than his pieces on migrants. Ideally he got both in.

'Next up, on line two, we have Michael from Folkestone. What's your take, Michael?'

Seaside town, south-east, an angry white bloke. This was Wayne's demographic, his sweet spot.

'Morning, Wayne. Thanks for having me on.'

'My pleasure, Michael.' A glance at the clock. 'What's bugging you about the woke climate brigade? Wind farms? The tax rises they're using to signal their virtue? Compulsory vegan food in schools replacing the decent British sausage? Forcing you to tell people that you're a he/him? What's making you angry, mate?'

There was silence. Cross tapped the table. 'Michael, we don't have much time.'

The voice was gruff. No discernible accent. 'No, we don't have much time.'

Something in the tone made Cross hesitate. A sense of authority. It reminded him of the kids who had bullied him at school, of the entitled overconfident snobs who felt they had a right to run the country. Cross had recently joined a golf club. He had been surprised at how quickly the excitement wore off. Everyone there wished they were at the better one in the next town. There was always another club that wouldn't let you in.

'So who's to blame for the climate nonsense, Michael? The migrants who want to create a sense of panic here while they quietly take over? The Chinese? The liberal elite preaching at us from their second homes in Bordeaux while their kids vandalise Churchill statues? The mainstream media and left-wing academics in their ivory tower universities, taking our heroes out of our history books?'

Another pause. Cross glanced again at the clock. This one wouldn't work for social media. Was the guy too nervous? The producers were meant to weed them out. He took a swig of coffee from the mug with the bulldog wrapped in an English flag.

The caller's voice was flat, but carefully articulated. 'Actually, I blame you.'

Cross liked a bit of argument on the show. Great for ratings. It was what drove his brand: never afraid to shirk the tough issues. The freest of free speech. But something about this caller frightened him.

More hesitant now, but a hint of condescension. 'Why's that, Michael?'

'All this. The polarisation. The denial of science and reason. The use of your platform to reduce the life expectancies of my grandchildren.'

An old fart then. Didn't sound particularly educated, but clearly a Guardianista. 'Sounds a bit OTT, Michael?

I'm not forcing you to agree with me. But the silent majority do. Are you denying me my freedom of speech now? Sounds like someone has been eating too much tofu. Who's going to stop me?'

'I am.' He didn't sound like an armchair warrior. He sounded like a warrior.

Time to end the call and do the rant. But the door to the studio swung open. A man stood there in black trousers and T-shirt and a black balaclava. Strong arms. Cross felt his heart rate increase. The air in the room felt constricted. He looked around for support.

Cross pressed the panic alarm, but no sound came. He swore. 'Listeners, I'm afraid we have an intruder here. Security, please get in here and sort this.'

He turned to the man. Buy time. Get the nutter dealt with. 'What do you want?'

'I've just told you. To stop all this.'

Cross left the microphone live. Even in his fear he had a sense of how to give the listeners some drama. 'Why?'

'We don't have time.'

The man walked across the studio. Cross rose from his chair, and it fell behind him. As the man came in range he threw a coffee cup at him, which he dodged with a small movement of his head. Cross gripped the desk with one hand and reached for a stapler with the other. But the man punched him hard in the face and he dropped it. He felt the blood start to flow from his nose.

A whimper now. 'What do you want? Michael?'

The man turned his head slightly so that the microphone would pick him up.

'Enough.'

The man reached his hands around his neck. Cross writhed for a moment but could not stand. His listeners heard the crack of his neck, and then silence. By the time security arrived, the assassin was long gone. There were a few days of media and social media speculation on the likely killer, centred on whether the motivation was personal or political. By the time a replacement was found, most listeners had found that they didn't need the show in their lives. The ratings never recovered.

14

The Signal Versus the Noise

As a freelancer on her way up, Orla had longed for the legitimacy of a decent paper. Almost immediately she had landed the job she started to want to escape. And now what? The sense of liberation did not last long. She walked for long enough to reduce the risk of bumping into colleagues. *Former* colleagues? And then ducked into an anonymous-looking cafe.

Orla had once had a boyfriend who seemed to think the scenes in his life were all some kind of first rehearsal for a film. It was as though he believed there was a soundtrack playing in the background. She had tired of his sepia-tinged self-absorption pretty quickly. Yet this had something of that feel. A sense of a sliding doors moment. A before and after shot.

She would have to move to a smaller apartment. In any case she had never really unpacked in Washington. Where to base? She didn't want to stay with family or friends. It would seem like some kind of failure. And there would be all the normal crap of their kids and their drama to navigate. All a distraction. She needed somewhere quiet to write, and to think.

Once before, when she'd needed it, Ed Barnes had taken her to his cottage in Wales, away from the noise. She chuckled at the thought of turning up on his doorstep in Kenya. It would be fun to watch Stephanie terrorising the diplomatic circuit. Stephanie always teased her about Ed, liked to suggest there was something there.

By the time she got back to Washington, she knew that this was the wrong way to think about her problem. It wasn't a need to find a refuge that was getting in her way. She needed to follow the story. She opened her laptop and tried once again to join the dots between the Elizabeth Hoon donors and allies. Were they connected, these enablers? Or all just opportunists? What did they really want from the administration?

Media barons wanted what they had always wanted: influence, power, wealth.

Big business wanted what it had always wanted: more big business. Plus the social recognition that offered a fig leaf of respectability.

The big donors were mainly men. They had that in common. Big egos to match the bank balances. She had managed to take a photo of the list of the largest donations to the last campaign. Hoon had made much in public of the many small donations, but they were dwarfed by these. Cameron, the head of a media empire that had employed her, was right up there. Orla had been watching as his group of companies started to splinter. His son had been killed in some kind of break-in. Neck broken. Drug-related.

Another name struck her. She did a quick internet search. Elias Abu Khalid, a former deputy prime minister of Lebanon turned arms dealer and fossil fuels investor who was missing presumed killed while on safari in Kenya. The speculation at the time was that he had been caught up in some kind of clash between poachers and the anti-poaching patrols.

Pretty nasty characters. Not really lamented. She chewed a knuckle as she looked out of the window. She had followed the story the preceding week about the UK airline tycoon who had been found dead at his country house. Also a big donor to right-wing parties.

Where was the story taking her? What connected Elizabeth Hoon and these deaths? She had learnt that you had to stay calm at these moments, try to hear the signal amid the noise.

The book Stephanie had given her was on the window shelf. Orla skimmed books, and was only halfway through. Violent environmentalists. This must be why Stephanie had been messaging her media coverage of recent high-profile deaths in the US and UK. The most recent was a UK talk show host. The story had got more coverage as he seemed to have been killed on air by someone who had called into the show. Grim, but great social media. And another neck broken? Was that a bit of a theme? And a controversial Oxford don, favourite on the 24/7 media round. Masters. She'd seen some of the coverage: tweedy. She recognised him from *Question Time*. Always banging on about climate change.

As ever when she needed to think, Orla put on her trainers and ran. It had taken a while to get through the traffic lights and crossings of downtown Washington and out onto clear ground. But it had been worth it. She had run first along the side to the Washington Monument, and up to the basin to look across at the Jefferson Memorial. And then looped around the Martin Luther King Memorial to Lincoln, where she had dodged the tourists to climb the steps and into the relative darkness of the statue. Americans did grandeur better than anyone.

Orla leant against a wall, and looked up at the figure towering over her. There were moments when Lincoln had chosen liberalism and freedom over democracy. He would not have had a clear majority for ending slavery. She watched as a small group of climate change protesters huddled together at the bottom of the steps. She slowed as she passed them on her way back down, felt the charge of anger and frustration. One man turned to her, eyes blazing. On his placard he had etched the words in black marker. *What will it take for you to listen?*

At what point would these activists realise that their protests were not enough? And what would that mean?

Perhaps Hoon was a distraction. Perhaps the donations were not the story here. Orla had assumed Stephanie was sharing the stories out of curiosity, or because she was worried that Orla was drifting. But perhaps Stephanie was on to something. A series of unexplained and seemingly unconnected deaths. All of pretty unpleasant characters, certainly by the standards of even the NYT editorial board. None seemed to have been killed for money. All seemed to have been killed swiftly and efficiently. Professionally, even?

But all in some way linked to climate change. Someone had decided not to wait for the world to start listening. That was the story that was calling her.

15

Big Flag

Ed Barnes climbed the stairs quickly to his first-floor office. Penny had set up a briefing meeting. But first he needed five minutes of silence. Time to think. A screen in the corner was showing clips from the mall. He switched it off.

He was pretty confident that Jim and Dave would handle the consular and crisis response. It could never be perfect, certainly not in the eyes of the UK media, but they knew their work. His job was to make sure that they had the people they needed, to keep ministers off their backs, and then to stay out of the way. He wrote a post-it note and stuck it to the screen of his computer: 'don't be a control freak'.

What now? He needed to slow President Obwocha down: a badly prepared military escalation risked mass casualties. And he needed to try to get ahead of the situation: what did the terrorists want? And what was their next move?

But first, he had to project calm to the team. It was vital that they kept their heads. He wrote another post-it note: 'be seen to listen'. He then screwed it up and replaced it with a shorter message to himself: 'listen'.

Penny put a head around the door, and Barnes nodded. As they filed in, he was by the window, filling a coffee cup from the machine. He watched their faces. Carrie was still in Nanyuki but would be on the screen. Dave looked relaxed. The head of station, Aiza, was poised. This was her first real crisis, but so far, so good. He gestured them all to the table. He could feel the collective anxiety, but also the sense of anticipation.

'Thanks, everyone. Let's get straight on it, I don't want to keep you too long. Dave: consular first. What about the Brits?'

'Still hazy. There must be thirty in there, at least. Social media suggests several already hurt or killed. We've set up a reception point at the airport, for families and others wanting information. Or trying to leave. We'll get one in place at the closest hotel, the Hilton.'

Barnes nodded. 'Good. Big flag, bright vests, lots of water?'

Dave smiled. 'Yep. London have got the phone lines set up. Calls will go straight through to them. They're using those to reassure families, and to try to get a picture of who might be in there. We'll also have someone at the hospital. RDT on the way, so we'll have the manpower.'

He glanced at Aiza, who had rolled her eyes.

'Sorry, personpower,' he corrected himself. 'The comms team say your clip is getting decent oxygen, Ed, and comes over well. Reassuringly boring. We should take that. There's not yet too much for the media to report.'

'Be careful what you wish for.'

Dave grinned. 'And one other thing. Travel advice…?'

Dave left the question hanging. Barnes had known it was coming. He felt the tension move up a notch around the table, the eyes shifting in his direction.

No hesitation. 'Just give them the factual update. Say what we know has happened, what we're doing. No change yet to the overall threat level. I'll get some flak. No 10 will seize on it, especially if the media do. I'm ready for that. We have to back our judgements.' Should he have said *my* not *our*? Too late.

Barnes turned towards the screen. The picture had cut out a few times, but Carrie was looking eager. Hair tied back, cheeks slightly flushed. 'Carrie, make sure we have a decent line in to whoever is running things at the mall for the army. We'll need to know as soon as anyone comes out, alive, injured or...'

Carrie interrupted. 'Done. I have the number of the guy. Musikari Kianjuri. We've just spoken. He came to the last QBP. Likes a drink, and had a few then. But a good reputation. A pro. He'll take the calls, and he'll get out of the way once the special forces get there.'

Barnes was struggling to picture him. 'Good. What's his thinking on their next move?'

'Your call with President Obwocha clearly worked, for now. Slowed it all down. Kianjuri's grumpy: says any op is above his pay grade now.'

Thank God for WhatsApp. 'Let's hope so. And in Nanyuki?'

'We're taking off in twenty. Right people. Right kit.'

Dave interjected. The defence adviser and the deputy head of mission had a very different approach to risk. 'We?'

Carrie let it go. Barnes caught Dave's eye and gave a quick shake of the head. Better not to know, Max Crawford would have said. Another of his mantras: own nothing, influence everything. Crawford had hated timidity. *The downfall of any nation can be traced from the moment that nation became timid about spending its best blood.* They could do with Crawford now.

He turned to his head of station. 'Okay Aiza, what have you got?'

Aiza gave a small shrug. Barnes could see that she was torn between wanting to impress and wanting to hold back. 'Not much I'm afraid. US all over it of course. Working theory has to be al-Shabab: they have the people, means, motive. And plenty of people, since the tourists stopped coming to Lamu and the coast. Most of their recent recruits come from the east of the country, where climate change has dried it all up, literally. There'll be plenty more to replace those they lose today.'

Barnes nodded grimly, thinking of the kids he had seen in the north. 'And those in the mall. Do they know what they're doing, or just teenagers with guns and grievances?'

'Too soon to say. They'll have some experience, from dust-ups with Kenyan anti-terrorist forces. But probably a fair share of trigger-happy kids too. Many will be as high as kites on khat. Sigint inside the mall sounds Somali, and disorganised. Plenty of shooting and shouting. We know they don't hang around long before civilians start going down.'

The signals intel would be more important in the early phases than the human intel. But at some point they would need a decent source on the inside of the group. 'Stay close to the US. And share as much as you possibly can with the Kenyans. I want to show Obwocha that he's in charge, but that he needs us, and we can help.'

He looked around the table. *Listen.* 'Right, what else?'

But he could see they were all keen to move on. 'Okay. Stay hydrated. Pace yourselves. Dave and I will look at staffing: get everyone rotated, and pull in support for you from other teams. RDT will help. I'll stay close to Obwocha and check in with No 10.'

As they filed out, Barnes pulled out his phone. A quick message to Stephanie. He felt a deep need to know that she was fine. 'All okay? Home?'

He dialled the No 10 switchboard. The usual efficient reply. They could find anyone, anywhere, anytime. 'It's Ed Barnes here in Nairobi. Can I get Hermione?'

Hermione Buckingham was the new PM's chief of staff and fixer. A civil servant rather than political adviser, but she was there because she thought and fought like both. Stellar career, two perm sec jobs already. Ambitious and direct. Ministers loved her. Always underestimated by the mandarins. But most of the old school had now been cleared out. She and Barnes had known each other as young fast-streamers in their early twenties. A few drunken nights. One that had become a morning, which they both pretended to have forgotten.

A pause as Switch tried her phones. 'Sorry, High Commissioner, she must be in with the Boss. Shall I get her to call you back?'

Barnes winced. He had hoped to get to her before she discussed the situation with the PM, before the wrong narrative settled at the centre. They would want to appear decisive, in control. They always needed an action they could take. He needed to focus their attention, and make sure that it was the right one. The last thing his team needed was a long screwdriver from No 10.

'Please keep trying. I'll hold.'

He flicked between screens as he waited. No reply yet from Steph and she didn't seem to have picked up the message. No time for too much protocol: he WhatsApped Hermione.

Two minutes later she was on the line. 'You're persistent, Ed. Nice suit, by the way. Clearly not eating too much of that roast goat.'

In normal circumstances Ed would have been more flattered. 'Thanks for noticing. Under control here, so far. But a likely op in the next hour or so. We could get casualties.'

In normal circumstances Hermione would have teased him again. 'Should the Boss call the Prez? He wants to look active. On the front foot. What can we give him to occupy him?'

Barnes could think of nothing worse. 'Good call. But no, not yet. Let's hold him back for when Obwocha stops taking my calls. Probably pretty soon. We're getting the crisis centres up and running for Brits.'

'There wouldn't be so many Brits if you'd changed the travel advice, Ed.' No banter now.

Barnes winced. She knew him well enough to know that she didn't need to say it. 'Hindsight is a wonderful thing, Hermione.'

Hermione glanced at the colleague taking a note of the call. 'So is foresight. Show some.'

Barnes let it land. Enough to allow her to tell people she had told him off. Not enough to paralyse him.

'Indeed. Anything else, Hermione?'

'The Boss has asked our special forces to be in place. Wants to get ahead of this, just in case. They're straining at the leash.'

Barnes sighed. 'They always are. But surely we're not at that point?'

116

'Not yet. But it's always the part of the toolkit he reaches for. At least if they're out with you we'll be ready to use them if we need to. You seem to have a habit of attracting danger. Always did.'

Once again Barnes wished Max Crawford was there. He would have misquoted Teddy Roosevelt: 'Never punch unless you need to, but never punch soft.'

Deep breath. 'And what will you say in public?'

She had clearly already put the line out to the press officers. '"No 10 in close contact with the high commissioner. Gravely concerned. Watching closely. Full support to Brits. Ready to use all means at disposal." Keep it short and sweet.'

As good as he could have hoped. For now. But enough to chuck him under the bus if it started to go wrong. 'Okay, Hermione. But do me one favour: no surprises. Please make sure they play it straight. I have to keep Obwocha and the Kenyans on side. They are incredibly sensitive to anything that looks like interference.'

The line went dead.

Barnes changed screens to check for messages. At the top of the WhatsApp screen, *Stephanie is typing*. Great, she must be back at the residence, and picking up messages. He messaged Obwocha:

> Thank you for your leadership. Spoke to PM. Full support for your approach. He sends his solidarity and respect. Let us know how we can help you.

Steady the ship. Buy time.

And then Stephanie's message came through. The phone fell from his hands onto the table.

Pops. Don't panic. In mall.

16

The Trade

There was a cold breeze on the hillside above Loule. There were thick ripples on the infinity pool and the purple bougainvillaea swayed. In half an hour the sun would rise behind the cabin and the terrace would start to warm. In an hour the crickets would strike up.

Stephen Raford looked up from the laptop and chewed his knuckles. In the distance the deep blue of the Atlantic. Across the valley the curve of a ridge. He loved the remoteness of the place. Far enough from the golf courses, noise, strip clubs and expats of Quinta do Lago and Vale do Lobo. Close enough to get to them when he needed to. He took a deep breath, stretched his shoulders back and returned to the screen.

He felt most alive in the moments before moving the market. These were seconds of extreme power, when traders and brokers were hanging on his decision. On his fingers on his keyboard on his terrace in his world. He pictured them in Singapore, New York, London. How many would be celebrating tonight? How many would be broken?

They had been wrong again and again, the analysts who had been swayed by the climate lobby. All that emotional bullshit about green stocks, ethical investment, carbon offsets, ESG. Another acronym that would be quickly forgotten. Serious companies knew that the key was to sit out the fads, back the market, avoid emotion. Markets didn't have morals. It should be up in lights above every trading floor. He had doubled down on his fossil fuel stocks when others had got squeamish. And that was why he was in the big house, with the cinema, the swimming pool and the high fences. He took a swig of the coffee.

The trade was set up. He always did the big ones himself. When you stopped doing that you lost your feel, your instinct for the pulse of the market. In one move he would signal fresh confidence in the big oil and gas stocks. Human conflict and human greed had always been bankers. The rest of the market would follow him: they always did. This would be worth billions.

He wondered, what to do with it? The ex-wives, beach houses and school fees were long paid off. He wrinkled his nose. It didn't matter what he would do with it, as long as he had it, and someone else didn't. He was in it for the thrill of combat, and to win.

He looked across the valley. It was more parched this year. They were worried about more forest fires. The bees that had once made this region a honey exporter had died in the heatwaves. He hated air conditioning. Another summer like that and maybe he would have to find some-where new, somewhere cooler. Move north? He would miss the lemon trees, the fresh figs in the morning. Eating his own olive oil. But why take the risk? This arc of Southern Europe was becoming too dangerous. He would always have the resource and agility to stay one step ahead of the rest. Survival of the fittest.

He looked back at the screen, waiting for the perfect moment to execute the trade. 'What if you're wrong, and markets did develop morals?' an interviewer had asked him at his last Davos panel. He had shrugged, genuinely surprised that they still asked the question in the face of so much evidence. 'Then they wouldn't be very effective markets.'

The sun was now starting to come up over the brick wall behind the terrace, and he felt his shoulders relax in the warmth. Was global warming really such a bad thing? Maybe not if you were in charge, if you could stay ahead of it.

He called the concierge for another coffee and a microdose. He didn't hear the birds as they started their chorus. He would feel the caffeine and the mushrooms surge through him as he watched the markets follow him. Bloodsport.

There was no reply. How much did you have to pay to have decent coffee when you wanted it? The curse of the billionaire. He looked back at the screen. Two more minutes. He went into the kitchen and made the coffee himself.

He didn't hear the man come onto the terrace, but he was there as he came back outside. He had closed Stephen's laptop and was looking out over the valley, towards the ridge and the blue of the sea beyond. Dressed in a black T-shirt. Thickset, muscular.

Stephen had recently upgraded the security. There were more migrant workers arriving from North Africa. You couldn't be too careful. 'What the fuck are you doing here? How did you get over the fence?'

The man looked round at him, casually, and shrugged. 'Taking in the view?'

'Well, you can take it in somewhere else.' Stephen had a personal martial arts trainer, and was sizing up the visitor.

The man was older and shorter than him, tough, but the guy didn't look armed. An air of confidence. The safe in the basement could be sacrificed if necessary. What was he after?

The man sighed. He looked pained for a moment, as though he wished he were anywhere else. And then he stood and turned to Stephen.

Stephen squared up. 'I'm serious. Get the fuck off my terrace.'

There was almost a sadness to the man. 'I'm where I need to be.'

Stephen stepped towards him. He had read online about the figure they were starting to call the Assassin. A mysterious chain of deaths, unexplained. This guy didn't look like a serial killer. Or a common thief. But what was the incentive for targeting a trader, if it was not about money?

'What do you want from me? There is no way you'll get past the security on that laptop. You need me if you want to try to get a penny.'

The Assassin took another look at the view and then checked his watch. He wasn't here to start a trade, but to stop one. Stephen followed his eyes out towards the sea. He didn't feel the blow to the back of his neck.

The Assassin sighed as he checked the man's pulse and let the arm fall.

As an old and very dangerous mate of the Assassin's had once said, 'A buddy will help you move furniture, a friend will help you move a dead body.' This was another one he would have to do on his own. He made himself a cup of coffee, took in the view one last time, and put Stephen Raford's corpse over his shoulder.

Another trader would quickly move to fill Raford's shoes. But they would take time to develop the same influence. Maybe over time the market would develop some morals. And eventually, with help, it might heal itself. The Assassin didn't pretend to know about economics, but he knew who the enemy was. And he knew how to kill.

The trade would not be executed today. But the trader would.

17

Too Rough to Plunge In?

Initially, Orla moved between couches as she adjusted to her new independence. But it was as unsatisfactory as she had anticipated. As one friend had gently, but only so gently, chided her, she was almost forty. This was surely no way to live.

So she had taken her laptop home, or close to it, renting a one-room apartment on the south-west coast of Ireland, in a small fishing village called Youghal. Each morning she would walk early along the boardwalk, relishing the taste of the sea air and listening to the gulls. Some mornings she would take a dip, enjoying the feeling of the sand under her feet. She found her mind was sharper after swimming in the bracing cold of the Atlantic.

But the writing wasn't flowing yet. She was stuck again on the 'why'. She was convinced that there was a link between the assassinations. Was the purpose of the project to find and expose this, to find the Assassin? She had started to capitalise it. Or was it to ask deeper questions about climate change? She had abandoned the Hoon project because she had failed to convince herself that she had a way to change the world rather than just describe it. This story had shock value, if she could stand it up. But in almost every case the Assassin – if she was right that it was just one, or a group working together – had done their work too efficiently to leave a story behind. Relatives and police had tried to investigate but come up blank.

One morning, as she dried the cold water off and felt her body tingle back to life, she realised that she had a bigger problem. As Anette had put it, every story needs a nemesis, a villain. And in these stories, if they were really connected, the villains were the corpses. So did that make the Assassin the hero? A killer with a conscience? There had been great literature in which the reader was asked to sympathise with the person committing the crime. But a piece of contemporary journalism that seemed to condone a serial killer?

She still loved the feel of a newspaper. As she called into the shop to pick up the weekend papers, the harder question confronted her more firmly. If she wrote about the links between the murders, was there a chance that they might stop? Perhaps one would say a *risk* that they might stop.

Orla had chatted in the past to the couple who ran the shop, but today they could see that she was pensive as she produced the coins.

'How was the sea today?'

Orla felt the coldness of her swimming costume beneath her clothes. Her face was still flushed. 'It was rough again.'

'Too rough to plunge in?'

Orla scooped the papers under her arm. The headlines were dominated by what one of her editors had called *one day stories*. The quality writing would be in the supplements, the human interest stories, the culture sections. Where were the big stories, the ones that journalists had sacrificed something for? The one that took time and pain? Where were the investigations that mattered? And who, including in her industry, had an interest in ensuring that they were ignored?

Orla smiled. The story was calling her again. *What will it take for you to listen?*

'No, not too rough to plunge in.'

She climbed the stairs to the apartment and opened a window to let the sea air in. She switched on the kettle and looked again at the papers she had stuck up on the wall with blu-tac. Perhaps her mistake had been in trying to work out who the Assassin was, and how he – or she? – had killed their victims. But the dotted lines she had drawn between them all indicated the clear motive. And it was not just that the targets were acting in ways that made climate change worse, or slowing down the effort to counter it. It was not just that their deaths might act as a warning to others. It was that their deaths might make a difference because it made them harder to replace. The Assassin was choosing very carefully. They wanted the deaths to be noticed.

So instead of following the trail of victims, she had to follow the motive, and work out where The Assassin was going next. She felt a wave of anger at the people running the media. They were complicit in the failure to hold these enablers to account. The Assassin clearly felt the same.

If in doubt, follow the money. Where was the money being made that accelerated climate change? Not the companies themselves, but those financing them, trading their stocks. Orla left the papers unopened and started to research the investors running significant funds with the influence to move markets, to set trends.

When the BBC site flashed up the story of Stephen Raford's death in the Algarve, Orla felt for the first time that she was making real progress. The story contained few details of his business interests, but the death had all the hallmarks of her assassin. No evidence left behind. A broken neck. Nothing taken, no claim of responsibility. No harm to people beyond the target. A brief internet search indicated that Raford was up to his neck in trades that were harming the environment.

Orla's great skill had always been her ability to get into the head of her subject, to understand what it was about them that made them who they were. It was her failure to manage this with Elizabeth Hoon that had driven her away from that story. Now she had to get into the mind of someone she had never met, and might never meet. She had to predict his next kill.

What drove the Assassin? Idealism? Surely a dose of that. Frustration? Personal vendetta? But to act in such a methodical way also suggested a terrifying detachment from reality. Was this someone with not long to live, trying to upend the chessboard? Or maybe just a sociopath serial killer who thought that these kind of targets meant that they could kill for longer, get away with more. Orla found herself wanting to be in the engine room as the decisions were taken. How to justify picking Raford and not the hundreds of other men doing exactly the same thing?

She looked at the pictures she had pinned up. The Assassin appeared to only be killing men. She assumed this meant it was a guy. What was his code? And what would it take to get his attention? The game hunter killing looked to be the first in the sequence. A gateway drug.

Orla stood and walked to the window. She had to meet him. That meant either pre-empting the next murder:

surely too hard without a clearer sense of how he selected the targets. Or baiting him with a story, a sense that he had been seen, that he was being watched. And it probably meant a big dose of luck.

Investor. Budget airline entrepreneur. Talk show host. Oxford don. Not yet a politician.

This story mattered to her. Orla pulled out her smart-phone and quote-tweeted the BBC coverage on Stephen Raford's murder. 'Curious about similar methods to recent unexplained deaths of Michael Cameron, Andrew Banks and Wayne Cross. Links?'

Almost immediately a WhatsApp message arrived. Surely no coincidence.

> O, please come: Dad needs you. S

Stephanie Barnes. Out in Kenya. What mess had Ed got himself into now?

Orla messaged back:

> What's up, Steph?

But there was no reply.

She chewed her lip. There was an uncharacteristic urgency to Stephanie's message. On the BBC site she watched as the Raford story was replaced as breaking news by one on a shooting in a Nairobi mall. She felt a jolt of adrenalin and fear. Were they safe?

Somewhere out there, the Assassin was working out who to kill next. She had just as much chance of finding him from Kenya as from Youghal. Especially if that was where he had started. Especially if he wanted someone to make the connections, to tell the story. Ed Barnes might even take his tie off, get that famous contact book out and start helping.

Orla took a long look at the sea. She could taste the salt. The coastline ever-changing in power and beauty. Ed Barnes needed her? She smiled. It was time to see him again.

But first she needed to try something. To follow one more instinct on the story. She looked again at her work on the enablers, and the mapping of the previous targets. She tried again to get into his head, to think like the Assassin. Who would he kill next? Who would she kill if she had the chance?

She booked a flight to Paris.

Part Two

One Story

18

Switchboard

Later, trying to defend himself, Barnes would be unable to recall what happened next. He held the sides of the table for a few moments, trying to steady himself. He walked to the coffee machine, started to prepare one, and then left the empty cup on the machine as he strode back to his desk. He loosened his tie and took a deep breath. Stephanie was in real danger. Hold it together.

His eyes darted to the phone. Another message from Stephanie.

> Long story. They took phones but I hid mine. Chaos.

Barnes felt the message like a further blow to the stomach. His thumbs and fingers suddenly, somehow, too large to type.

> You OK? Injured?

Don't worry Dad.

He could hear Emma in her.

Injured? What's happening?

No. They're checking ID, looking for US?

Get rid of yours now.

How could he have put her in such danger?
No reply.
He tried again.

Steph. You there?

Steph?

The messages weren't being read. Barnes stopped himself from throwing the phone across the office. He felt the floor beneath him unstable. He picked up the framed picture of her on the desk. Black and white. Looking back at the camera. At the photographer. At him.

He placed the frame carefully back on the desk, as if it might shatter. One more time.

> OK Steph?

No reply, but a message from Orla.

> Ed, just seen news. You and Steph OK?
> What can I do?

He didn't have time for Orla now. Carrie and the Kenyan Special Forces team would be in the air, and phones off. It was too late to turn them round. The Americans would have been able by now to map who was still in the mall, and start to take a decent guess at which of them were terrorists and which civilians, based on their movements. But that process would take too long for it to be of much use if the group went blazing straight in.

Every negotiation was about leverage. The point of maximum leverage with the terrorists would be when they needed to negotiate a way out. Their point of maximum leverage with the Kenyan authorities was when the risk to civilians was highest. It was too soon to strike a deal, but they could buy time and lives by trying to work out what they wanted and get the timing right.

He moved fast down the corridor to Dave's office. His DHM was in with the crisis team, setting up the hotel and airport reception areas for Brits. Dave nodded at them to continue and came out to the corridor.

'You okay, Ed? You look really pale.'

Barnes shook his head to dismiss the question. 'Anything more on the Brit numbers in the mall?'

Later, at the public inquiry, Dave would wonder whether he should have been more curious about the high commissioner's uncharacteristic anxiety. But this was a crisis: everyone went through waves of adrenalin. 'Plenty of families contacting us now to say that they have had messages from relatives inside. Definitely Somalis. Not clear what they want. Aiza may have more from the Americans by now.'

'Carrie mentioned Kianjuri, the senior military guy at the site. Can you track down his number?'

Dave nodded. 'What do you have in mind?'

'We need to slow down the Kenyan special forces op. Buy a bit more time. There are too many moving pieces. I think I should talk to the terrorists, try to get a sense of what they want.'

Dave shook his head. 'Surely that's way too risky, Ed. Why put yourself in harm's way? We need to stay focused. It will be chaos up there, especially when they go in.'

He saw the steeliness back in Barnes's eyes. That rebellious streak. 'I'm still hoping they won't need to, Dave.'

Dave found the number for Kianjuri and watched as Barnes called him.

Kianjuri sounded relaxed, too full of bonhomie. Adrenalin at work there too, or something stronger. 'High Commissioner. A pleasure to hear from you. But you know I have my hands pretty full today.'

'I know. I've told the president you have our full support. We'll give you whatever help you need. I'll be back on site doing media in ten minutes. Can we meet?'

A pause. 'I'd rather you didn't come, HC. I need my men focused on the mall, not an *Excellency*. It is pretty tense here. There is more shooting inside. We're trying to convince the Somalis to let the children out. I've got a line to their main guy.'

This was the moment for Barnes to step back, leave the professionals to it. Dave waited for him to ring off. But Barnes persisted. 'What do they want, Kianjuri?'

Dave could hear the man's politeness trump his frustration. 'He's not clear, yet.'

'And which part of Somalia?'

'Somaliland, so it will probably be about independence. Getting their own state. They hate the Somalis more than we do.'

Barnes turned his back on Dave. 'I need to talk to the guy.'

This time Kianjuri was angrier. 'You know I can't allow that, *Excellency*. It will only increase the price they want to extract from us.'

Barnes gripped the table. They didn't have long. Stephanie didn't have long.

'Musikari, you and I know that it will get pretty grim, and fast, if the special forces go in. I can help stall that. Maybe the Somalilanders will be ready to reason with me. They'll see me as some kind of intermediary.'

'No way. I'm sorry, High Commissioner, but this is not your show. We don't negotiate with terrorists. Wasn't it you guys that taught us that? I don't remember much negotiation between the Brits and the Mau Mau.'

Line dead. Barnes waved Dave back into his crisis meeting, ignoring the look of curious concern, and called Aiza as he walked back to his office.

'What do we have on the regional governor of Somaliland?'

No hesitation. This was her first real chance to show she could do this under pressure. 'Decent guy, did his degree at Oxford on a Chevening scholarship. Trying

137

to do the right thing up there. No obvious corruption. Smooth. Good-looking and knows it. Not exactly a dream job: the last three were assassinated. You pretty much have a target on your back. Pro-independence, obviously, but has been trying to convince them all, especially the militias, that he can get more progress via the UN than through violence. He's in a very small minority on that.'

Listen. Focus. 'What does he need from us?'

'Need? A bit of attention, I guess. Some sense that his plan might work. Ministerial meeting maybe. Some help in New York. Not much in the scheme of things. But they're a long way down the list for London. Not really on the radar.'

Barnes nodded: half a desk officer somewhere in King Charles Street might be following Somaliland. Perhaps an annual submission to update whichever minister had rotated in that month. But no real expertise or attention at the centre. 'Maybe they are now. I think it's time to move them up the list.'

From the window, Barnes could see the four Special Forces helicopters landing at the nearby stadium. He called Carrie as he walked.

'Plan?'

'Not much of one, boss. We… they're going to position themselves around the two main entrances to the mall. They've been told not to go in without an explicit President Obwocha instruction, but they're pretty tooled up. Y'know, a lot of these guys have been desperate for a crack at the Somalis. Some have fought up there. They don't like the fact that the Somalis have brought their shitshow… sorry, boss… down here.'

Barnes was back in his office now, and waved aside an update from Penny. 'I think it's more complicated than that, Carrie. Your friend Kianjuri thinks they're Somalilanders. They hate the Somalis as much as the Kenyans do: they've been fighting them for as long.'

'To be honest boss, I don't think that will give the Kenyans enough reason to hold off. They don't really care about that difference. And, y'know, these things tend to get their own momentum.'

'Try to slow things down. Tell them they have more chance of success once they get better data on what is going on inside, and that we and the Americans can get them more of that. I'm going to try to increase our leverage.'

It didn't take the No 10 switchboard long to get the governor of Somaliland. It was not for them to question how far the high commissioner was going off-piste.

'Mr High Commissioner, I don't often hear from you Brits. Are you planning a visit at last?'

Barnes was trying not to think about Stephanie. He made a conscious effort to steady his voice. 'Your Excellency, you will be aware of the hostage situation in Nairobi?'

'I'm watching it on your wonderful BBC, like everyone else.' The governor had been educated at the only private school in Mogadishu. His English had a quaint, 1950s timbre.

'The Kenyans on the ground think they are Somalilanders. Sound likely?'

A brief pause. 'I see. And what happens next then?'

'A bloodbath, probably. No one wins. Unless we can stop that?'

Another pause. 'We?'

Barnes was steely now. Stephanie didn't have long. 'Yes, you and I. You studied International Relations. You know about mediation. You also know that Somaliland involvement in terrorism will be catastrophic for your cause at the UN. Set you back years.'

The governor sounded frustrated. 'I'm hardly making progress now. What makes you think I have any influence with them, High Commissioner?'

Don't give me that crap. 'Just a hunch. They will need a ladder to climb down. Whatever they planned, it will feel different now. We can find something they can show is a win. I can't give that to them direct: the Kenyans won't let me talk to them. And we can't be seen to be rewarding terrorism.'

Barnes chewed his lip for a moment. This was already way beyond what ministers might sanction. The mantra was handed down from diplomat to diplomat: *we don't talk to terrorists*. But if diplomats don't, who does?

Find the leverage. Get to the ask. 'But maybe you can give them something... and maybe we could give it to you?'

Silence at the other end. The governor was curious. But his response when it came was brisk. 'You're going to offer more aid, I guess? By the time it gets past the consultants and development economists, there is not much left for us. And Somalia needs it more than we do. We don't need your aid. We need *recognition*.'

Barnes hesitated. Change of plan. 'Not aid, Your Excellency. Respect. What if I can get you a meeting at No 10?'

Barnes heard the intake of breath. Found it. 'With the PM? Seriously? Why would they suddenly agree to that? They couldn't find us on a map.'

Barnes kept his voice steady. They didn't have much time. 'It would be with the chief of staff. But we would get the PM to drop in for a photo. What we call a grip and grin. That's what you really need, isn't it?'

'That would indeed be a great help. But how do I know you could deliver it? And what do you need in return?'

At last. The odds of delivering it were miniscule. 'Consider it done, Excellency. Now I need to know who's really in charge in the shopping cen— the mall, and what they want. Can you help?' A brief pause. Barnes pressed again. 'Governor, we need to trust each other. Please, call me Ed.'

A longer pause. The governor's voice was quieter, but determined. 'Thank you, Ed. I was taught in your universities to trust and then verify. So let's see. But I'd prefer we drop the titles, too. Call me Ali.'

The governor rang off. Barnes checked his phone. Still nothing from Stephanie. And no sign that she had picked up the last messages. Had they found her? Or was she keeping her device turned off to avoid the signal being picked up?

The television footage showed more troops arriving at the mall. Carrie was right about the Special Forces: they were preparing to move in. This was the moment of greatest risk to the hostages. To Stephanie. On an instinct he replied to Orla's message saying she would help. Later he would wonder what he had hoped to achieve. Maybe he just needed an ally, someone who also cared about Stephanie. *If anything happens to me, look out for S.*

His phone rang. It was Musikari Kianjuri.

'General, thank you for calling. Have you changed your mind? Can I speak to the terrorists?'

'Well, strange as it may seem, and infuriatingly for us, they've just asked to talk to *you*.'

Barnes narrowed his eyes. An opening. The governor clearly had a decent line in. In the worst-case scenario, they wanted him because they had found Stephanie. Serious leverage. But more likely the governor's call to them had got their attention. Either way he seemed to have a way to the group in the shopping centre.

It was a start.

Diplomats are the ripples, not the stone that makes them. He could see Stephanie's bemused reaction to his usual excuse for inaction.

Barnes took a deep breath. The coffee stood undrunk on the machine.

'Thank you, General Kianjuri. Tell them to release the children, and I'll do better than that.'

19

Proceed Until Apprehended

The sky was threatening to rain, dark thunder clouds gathering. The vehicles had ground to a standstill. The BGs were nervous: they hated standstill. They also hated spontaneity: the High Commissioner heading to the middle of a terrorist incident was too much spontaneity.

'Boss, the Kenyan troops won't let more than two of us in, and only with sidearms.'

'I understand. But it's worth the risk. Get Carrie to meet us when we get there.'

They were able to pass swiftly through the military checkpoints, the soldiers recognising the diplomatic plates. Carrie and Kianjuri were waiting for them, and they were moved to a tent. They passed a group of shaken children. There were tables with maps of the mall. Radios crackling and mobile phones buzzing. An air of chaos. The air smelt of smoke and adrenalin.

Kianjuri shook hands solemnly. He was working hard to contain his frustration at the high commissioner's cameo, but Barnes could see that he was seething. Everyone had a tell – Kianjuri's was a double blink. 'The children are out, High Commissioner. Not a bad start.'

Barnes narrowed his eyes as he surveyed the building. 'It's a start. It shows they're willing to negotiate. Any better idea yet of the numbers inside?'

Carrie nodded. 'Twenty or so terrorists, eighty or so civilians. We reckon twenty to thirty of those are international.'

Kianjuri flinched. 'And that matters how?'

Carrie held up her hands in apology.

Barnes moved it on. Stephanie was somewhere in there. He needed to keep the Kenyans on side. 'Musikari, you're in charge. I'm just here to back you up, any way we can. What's your sense of why they asked for me?'

The double blink. 'No idea. But they hadn't been interested in talking on the first contacts, so something changed. They asked for you personally – Ed Barnes. Not just the British high commissioner. The main contact point, we think he's in charge, calls himself Hussein. We've got nothing much on him yet. Probably just another smooth-talking Somali gangster.'

Barnes glanced at Carrie, who knew it was an instruction to consult Aiza, and nodded slightly. Any sense of what drove Hussein might help.

Barnes focused again on Kianjuri. 'Did they say anything about the identities of any of the hostages? Anyone they were particularly targeting?'

Carrie looked at Barnes quizzically. Kianjuri shook his head. They all knew there was a hierarchy of value when it came to hostages.

A message came in from Orla.

Oh Ed. Are you OK? Where's S? Trust yourself.

The negotiation playbook was to wait, to make them ask again, see how much they wanted to talk.

Deep breath. 'Okay, let me talk to Hussein.'

Barnes pretended not to hear Carrie's sharp intake of breath. Proceed until apprehended, as Max Crawford had always said.

Kianjuri passed his phone and pressed the last number dialled. It rang twice.

'What now?' The voice was anxious, clipped. Educated?

Trust yourself. 'Mr Hussein? This is the British High… this is Ed Barnes. You asked me to call. Thank you for releasing the children: that is the right move. We can see that you don't want any further violence. I am explaining that to the Kenyan president and his troops. I'm keen to hear what it is you want. It is time to end this. Can we agree that—'

'End this? This is only just the beginning, High Commissioner.'

Clipped, yes. There was a note of anxiety in his voice, but also a sense of command; a man used to power.

'But what is it you really want? And call me Ed.'

Everything depended on establishing some measure of trust. Hussein's voice was calmer. But Barnes could still hear the nerves. 'We want your attention, High Commissioner. And I think we have it now.'

Barnes had to check his impatience. 'But what for? And why me?'

'Perhaps you will have more reason to help us than other people. Yes?'

Carrie could see Barnes clench his fist below the table. Something was different about him.

'Mr Hussein, we don't have much time. You have my attention. My full attention. I will meet you personally if you release the women.' The line went dead.

The heat in the tent was stifling. Barnes chewed a knuckle. He didn't have enough leverage. His senses were heightened. He flinched at the sound of a volley of gunshots in the building. Kianjuri's hand went instinctively to his weapon.

Carrie gestured to Barnes to step outside the tent. 'You don't seriously plan to go in?'

She could see the famous Ed Barnes stubbornness in his reaction. 'We have to make a gesture. We don't know what he wants. The more civilians we can get out, the more we can hold the Kenyans back. It buys us time.'

Later, Carrie would be carpeted for not making more of an effort to stop him. She had to listen in silence to male officers telling her that she should have been more forceful.

'But once you go in, boss, what guarantee is there we can get *you* back?'

Barnes was pensive. 'I don't think these guys are lunatics. They're rational. They're ready to trade. We've seen that.'

They waited. No messages, no replies to the calls. Barnes paced, hunched, hands deep in his pockets. He needed more intel, more time, more allies. *Head down, Steph. Get rid of the ID. Stay calm. I'm coming.*

Noise and movement over by the main mall exit. Kianjuri was heading in that direction. The door opened. The Kenyan Special Forces outside drew their weapons. Two bodies were thrown out. Males. The corpses slumped by a banner advertising cheap rice. Barnes felt his stomach lurch. Hussein was escalating.

And then a line of women started to exit, nervously at first, with hesitation. Once they reached the military lines, some stumbled into a run. A mixture of Kenyans and expats. Barnes scanned them carefully. Raw fear and relief on their faces. No sign of Stephanie.

Kianjuri came towards him with the phone. His anger seemed to have receded. Some of the bonhomie was back. 'Hussein says he's ready to *receive* you now.'

Barnes was still watching the line of women. Several wore headscarves. 'Has he told you that these are *all* the women?'

Kianjuri looked grim. The double blink again. 'He just said to tell you to come now. He didn't sound like he wanted a debate.'

Barnes glanced at Carrie. She gave a slight shake of the head: this wasn't the protocol. He looked again at the line of women, at the bodies outside the mall, at the Kenyan special forces, checking their weapons, watching and waiting for the chance to go in.

He removed his jacket and gestured at the main BG, Raul, to do so too.

'Leave the sidearm.'

Kianjuri was watching him, head tilted to one side. The BG hesitated for a moment, and then took his weapon off, avoiding Carrie's protest. He moved to stand two paces behind his high commissioner.

The Kenyan military moved aside to let Barnes past. The theatre of diplomacy: he had often told junior diplomats about how to walk into a reception, how to project confidence. *Stand upright, look like you know where you're going. You have to remember what you are representing.*

The cameras were on him, now. Would Orla be watching, and understand that this was the only way? In London there would be fury that he was taking these steps. But Ed Barnes didn't care; he was where he was meant to be.

He stepped around the two bodies on the road, trying not to look at them. The first was badly disfigured. Blood caked the ear, and the side of the head was gone. From the cavity, brain and blood.

As he approached the door Carrie watched him take a deep breath, steady himself. Later, she would say that this was the last moment she could have stopped him. But she knew he would not stop.

And then Ed Barnes was inside.

20

One Man's Terrorist

The doors to the mall shut behind them. It was cooler inside. There were three Somalilanders immediately beyond the entrance. Young, sweating, edgy, trying too hard to look calm. Each carried a Kalashnikov. The first nodded at the other two. One of them gripped Barnes by the arm, checked his trouser pockets, and led him down the corridor. The second told Raul to kneel and stood over him with his weapon drawn.

Barnes settled his breath and shook off the grip of the man. He glanced at Raul to signal that they should show no resistance. The bodyguard looked steady. But Barnes knew that he would be thinking through the options should he need to protect his high commissioner. These were not trained men, but they would be more experienced than they looked. And unpredictable. Barnes could picture Raul's kids, arriving on his shoulders at the Christmas staff party.

'I'm here to see Hussein. We have come with respect, and as representatives of Her Majesty's government. I expect you to treat us *both* with the same courtesy.' Barnes hoped they could not hear the hoarseness in his voice. The man kept a more deferential distance as they went up the escalators to the first floor. More armed men, standing in groups. The mall was quiet but they were anxious, primed. Barnes counted four bodies on the floor.

Not Stephanie. Not Stephanie. Not Stephanie. Not Stephanie.

They passed three shops, and the man slowed to ensure Barnes could take a proper look inside. Each of the rooms of hostages was guarded by two to three Somalis. In each were at least twenty civilians, kneeling or lying on the floor. They had been separated by ethnic group. The first room were Kenyans. The second, Asian expats. The third, white. No Stephanie. Some cried out as he passed. Signs of struggle: overturned chairs, smears of blood on the walls and floor.

The man gestured towards the entrance to a bookshop. Barnes straightened his back and entered. Inside, a slight man was leaning against the shelf. He was unarmed. Denim sleeves rolled up revealing gangly arms. Early thirties, deep-set eyes, skin tight around high cheekbones.

'Welcome, High Commissioner. I'm sorry that I can't make you more comfortable.'

Barnes instinctively held out a hand. *We don't negotiate with terrorists.* The man took it, his handshake weak, fingers bony.

Barnes let his hand go and stood opposite him, close enough to try to read his face. It didn't feel like Stephanie was yet part of his equation. But Barnes had come to the mall too soon: Hussein knew he had the advantage.

Focus. Listen. 'This will do. We don't have long. I don't know when the Kenyans will lose patience, but they won't give me long. When they do, they won't be as diplomatic as me.'

Hussein sniffed. His eyes darted around the room. 'So what do you suggest we do next?'

First job: build trust. 'You've done the right thing in releasing the women and children.'

'Most of them.'

Barnes held his eye, tried to ignore the threat in the other man's words. 'I need to know why you're doing this. What you actually want.'

Hussein narrowed his eyes. He seemed fully present for the first time. 'What makes you think that democracy is only for white people?'

Barnes suppressed his exasperation. 'I don't think that. I never have. Neither, more importantly, does my government. Maybe independence from Somalia for Somaliland does make the region more democratic. But there has to be a proper process. It takes time. Don't get between the dog and the lamp post.'

Hussein scowled. 'The last time I checked we had no lamp posts. When was the last time you actually lifted a finger for democracy in my world? Since 9/11 you have backed whoever you think can suppress terrorism, which to you is anyone who threatens *your* security, not ours. They're never democrats. All I ask is that you give us the same opportunity you give yourselves.'

Barnes tried to hold his eye. 'Look, I don't have time for an academic debate on democracy, Hussein. We've made mistakes, sure. But that is not the issue for you and me. Right now, we have to find a way out of here.'

'Why? We've got nothing to lose. I have been fighting since I was captured by the men who burnt my village and killed my parents. The only difference between me and most of those holding guns in this mall and outside it is that I did some reading along the way.' There was anger in the words but the voice was measured, thoughtful. 'If that makes this all *academic* to you, I can't help it. Perhaps you prefer us when we aren't reading your books?'

Barnes softened his voice, trying to find a connection. 'So tell me, then… Ultimately you want democracy. Great. But what is it that you really want out of all *this*?'

Hussein lifted a book from the shelf. Thomas Paine's *Rights of Man*. 'Same as you. Elections, equal rights, freedom before the law. Democracy is always on trial: and you're losing. The fish rots from the head, and American democracy now is like Gandhi said about British civilisation: a nice idea. I want to help you fight back. Democracy only ever advances through conflict or crisis. So be it. We're willing to do the fighting, make the sacrifices. For democracy. But we need help.'

Barnes was struggling to keep his attention in the room. He glanced towards the door. 'Please, we need to end this. I can't magic up democratic elections for you. Tell me how we all get out of here.'

Hussein nodded at one of the armed men by the door. He calmly brought over a Kenyan hostage and roughly pushed him to his knees, holding a gun to his head. The Kenyan kept his eyes to the floor. He was wearing an Arsenal football top. He was whimpering softly.

Barnes stepped towards the armed man, holding his hands out. The man kept his eyes on him and the gun to the temple of the Kenyan. Barnes turned to Hussein, more urgent now. 'No more bodies. You've made your point. You have our attention. What about *his* rights?'

Hussein smiled. 'How many bodies did it take you – or the Americans, or the French – to gain democracy? And don't you celebrate them? Parades and statues for the terrorists of their day? Musicals and national days? Why don't we get to write our names in history too?'

He nodded again at the man. The Kenyan screamed, high-pitched. The Somali shot him twice in the head. Blood and bone. Barnes flinched and looked away. The body slumped to the ground, a red halo spreading around it, the colour of the shirt.

As he forced himself to raise his eyes, Barnes saw Hussein watching him closely and without emotion. 'We need to make democracy great again, Mr High Commissioner. It's that simple. And that starts with a few new democracies. Including Somaliland.'

Barnes felt time slipping through his fingers. They would have heard the gunshots outside. It was a mistake to have come. He unclenched his hands and tried again. 'So you want a democratic Somaliland. Independence. We can talk about that. But more bodies won't help. They will turn us all against you.'

Hussein sneered. 'You don't think? Then why else are you here?'

Barnes needed to regain some authority. He changed tack. 'I saw you had divided the hostages into three rooms. Why? And are there more?'

'There may be more scattered around the mall. We are checking all the shops now. But it doesn't really matter. We already have enough civilians here to hold your attention.'

She was out there somewhere. 'Not if you keep killing them.'

A hollow laugh. 'Come on. You and I both know the Kenyans will be in long before we run out of hostages. *That's* how this ends.'

'So why? Whatever your message, it will be set back in international opinion by what you've done here. And this will get two news cycles… three at best? You're not going to get statues and a place in history.'

Hussein shrugged. 'A news cycle is more than we get now. We don't have anything to lose.'

Barnes gestured to the armed man. 'And do your men agree? Are you giving them the right to decide their fate?'

Hussein paused, narrowed his eyes. 'Okay, enough questions, High Commissioner. Give me something. Show you can be serious. Let's make some deals. For a room of hostages. What are they worth? Or is each of these rooms worth something different to you?'

Barnes felt the situation moving further away from his control. 'We don't negotiate with terrorists. You know that.'

'Too late for that. You already are. Otherwise, why come? What's the offer? What do *you* want, *Excellency*?'

Barnes felt the barb. He wrestled his mind back from his daughter. Did Hussein know where she was? He steadied himself. Find the leverage. 'Maybe I can try to get you some sort of safe passage out, convince the Kenyans to let you go.'

Hussein sneered. 'Meaningless. They'll kill us all eventually, or someone else will. And what hope is there for these men anyway? A life on the run. Or back to poverty.' He gestured at the armed man to bring forward another hostage.

Barnes held his hands up, stepping between the man and the door. 'Enough. Okay, I can get you more attention for the Somaliland case. Get some levers pulled in London and New York. Maybe get your governor a meeting in London. I can work with him. Why not ask him?'

Hussein cocked his head. He was more intrigued than he wanted to let on. 'The governor is part of the problem. I'll make this simpler for you. I want a statement from your prime minister that you back our independence, our democracy.'

Barnes threw his arms up in exasperation. But this was at least an opening. 'You know I can't promise all that, and that if I did, I could not deliver it. I'm not going to make you false promises.'

Hussein sneered. 'Then let's raise the stakes.'

Hussein called over the man by the door. 'Asia next.' The man grinned. His teeth were yellow. He was chewing khat, giving his eyes a reddish hue. He walked to the door and barked an order.

Barnes stood over Hussein. 'This is madness. Don't do it. Give me time. You have to stop.'

Hussein shook his head defiantly. 'Democracy advances one body at a time. That's how it has always been.'

'But surely these people are not your enemies.'

Hussein paused. 'True. But they got – what's your quaint phrase? – between the dog and the lamp post.'

Barnes sank to his knees as he heard the volley of shots in the shop. The screams turned to whimpers and then to silence. It went on for two minutes. Hussein leafed through the Paine book, pretending not to listen.

Barnes felt the room spinning. The media would be broadcasting every gunshot. Outside, the Kenyan special forces would be preparing to come in. Somewhere, his daughter was hiding. He tried to steady his breath, suppress the waves of nausea.

Hussein scraped some wax from his ear with his finger-nail. He spoke without emotion to the Somali by the door. 'One body at a time. Through the doors of the mall.' He crossed the room, and lifted Barnes's chin to force his head up. 'Shall I let your Kenyan friends know we're not making progress? Or would you like to tell them yourself?'

21

One of Ours

Barnes tried to stop his hands shaking as Hussein passed him the phone. He heard General Kianjuri's voice on speakerphone. Urgent and angry. 'What's happening? All we can hear is shooting.'

Barnes tried to compose himself. 'They're serious, General. And yes, they are killing hostages. I'm... sorry.'

Kianjuri sounded more despairing than before. 'I'm afraid that our orders from the president are clear. No more waiting. Tell them to let the rest of the hostages go, *now*, or we come in. This ends here.'

Hussein laughed. 'You'll come in anyway. The only question is whether you'll wait long enough for the real soldiers to arrive, or whether they'll let your amateurs have a crack at us. Either way, we'll take plenty of you with us, comrade.'

Kianjuri spoke slowly and deliberately. 'Believe me, *comrade*, I can't wait. Enjoy your last minutes.'

Barnes held the phone between him and Hussein. *Focus.* 'Listen to me, both of you. Many more will die unless we find a way out of this. Let me try one more thing. There is a room full of Kenyans. Can we not agree to get them out?'

Kianjuri paused on the line. 'How many?'

Hussein shrugged, feigning disinterest. Barnes speculated. 'Thirty, at least? Just give me a few minutes, General. For your people.'

Hussein took the phone back and ended the call.

'You surprise me, *High Commissioner*.' He was now using the title like an insult. 'I thought you would only care about the whites, the *mzungus*. Okay, I'm curious: what will you give me for the Kenyans? I've told you: I don't plan to leave this mall alive. So it has to be bigger than what we're doing here.'

Barnes chewed a knuckle. His eyes kept being drawn back to the corpse on the floor. 'Can you let me call President Obwocha?'

Hussein looked impressed, briefly. He was intrigued at least. 'Why not?'

He handed the phone back to Barnes, who dialled the No 10 switchboard.

'Switch, Ed Barnes again. I need the Kenyan president, please. It's urgent.'

He could hear the anxiety amid the professionalism in their response. They would have seen the footage of him entering the mall, watched the reactions outside to the shooting. 'High Commissioner, I'll put you through.'

The line went silent as the call was connected. This time, Obwocha came on swiftly. He was watching, too.

'What the hell are you doing, High Commissioner? My men would have finished this by now if you hadn't got in our way. You are putting more lives in danger, including your own. The fact that you are in the mall is the only reason we haven't gone in. Every death from here on is on you.'

Barnes felt Hussein's gaze as he tried to focus on the cards they each held. 'I'm trying to do the opposite, Mr

President. We don't have time. These are Somalilanders rather than Somalis.'

Obwocha sniffed. 'Same difference. And they're all terrorists and pirates.' Hussein sniffed in derision.

Barnes held a hand up to silence him. 'Mr President, they have just killed a roomful of Asian hostages. The Kenyans will be next, and that will start as soon as the first soldier comes in that front door. We have to get as many civilians out as possible. I can't negotiate with terrorists, but you can.' He bit his lip. One last try. He held Hussein's eye. 'I need something from you, sir: to offer to host talks between the Somali government and Somaliland's leaders over devolution of more power.'

Obwocha was angrier now. 'You don't understand how power works in Africa, Barnes. We don't do devolution. We don't do concessions. If you have power, keep it. No one gives power away.'

'I'm learning, believe me. But can you do this? For thirty lives?'

Barnes looked at Hussein as they waited. He was listening intently, his head tilted to one side. This was clearly more than he had anticipated. But they didn't have long.

Barnes looked back at the phone as he spoke, making a deliberate effort to slow down and give Obwocha time. Sooner or later every leader had to imagine their place in history, make themselves bigger than their country. 'Mr President, you can be the peacemaker. You'll save lives here and impress the West. You can help to mediate. There could be a Nobel Prize. Think of what that means for Kenya's reputation. Your reputation.'

Obwocha continued to hesitate. 'And how can you be sure they will make the release?'

Barnes raised an eyebrow at Hussein, who shrugged in response. But he was still listening carefully.

That much quoted line: *a diplomat is sent to lie abroad for his country*. 'I'm very confident, Mr President.' A deep breath. 'These are not crazed terrorists. I understand that now. They have thought this through. It is just that they see no other way to secure their freedom.'

Barnes felt time slow. He wrestled his mind away from Stephanie. How close was she? Had she seen him arrive? Would she be grateful or furious that he had come?

Obwocha paused. 'Tell them that we are coming in unless those Kenyans are released immediately. And tell them that I will offer the mediation. I don't know what you think you can pull off here, Barnes. And I suspect London will agree.' The line went dead.

Barnes turned to Hussein and handed back the phone. The man was looking at him quizzically. Barnes pressed the brief advantage. 'Take the win, Hussein. You can show that you've got something. And it buys us – you – time with the Kenyans. We'll hold him to it. Get the UN behind it. You have my word.'

Hussein leant back, stretching his arms and narrowing his eyes in thought. Barnes could see that he was enjoying the power. He called over the armed man who was standing by the door. A small shrug. 'Let some Kenyans out.'

Barnes exhaled slowly. Hussein left the room, leaving him alone with a single gunman. Barnes wondered what it would take to overpower the guard, take the weapon, and search for Stephanie. But he dismissed the thought. He had to use the skills he had, stay rational, however desperate he felt at the thought of Stephanie. He had much more chance of success his way. He waited, watching the clock on the wall.

There was noise again in the next room. He could hear the fear of those being moved as the gunmen shouted at them to stand. Confusion and terror.

Barnes processed his options. Many of the Kenyans would soon be with their families. But there was still a roomful of expats: his job was to get them to safety. Stephanie was somewhere in the building. And Raul. The Kenyan military might now feel there was less risk in piling in.

Hussein strode back into the room. There was a jaunty cockiness to him again. 'Want to go with the Kenyans, *High Commissioner*? Claim the credit? Hold Obwocha to his promise? You're now more useful to us alive than dying with us in here. And we've found more civilians in the shops upstairs.'

Barnes stared back at Hussein, trying to show no emotion. His stomach felt hollow and his feet unsteady. Every instinct said that they had her. 'I'm staying here until we finish.'

'Good. That makes two of us. And as long as you're here it will ensure that the Americans and Brits aren't part of the assault. Thanks for that.'

Barnes resisted the temptation to share the story of having been under a targeted American attack in Copenhagen.

Hussein was more energised now. 'So, now you know I'm such a reasonable man, who are you going to call next? How about that statement from your PM? Perhaps he'll think the stakes are higher for the roomful of Europeans and Americans than for the roomful of Africans? Surely not, eh?'

Barnes ignored the jibe. 'Shouldn't we now be working on getting you all out without a bloodbath? What about all these boys you have holding the guns? Don't they deserve better than to die in a shootout in a Kenyan mall?'

Hussein sneered. 'They're all well beyond caring, too. Like me, few remember their parents. Or any life but this. We are already dead men walking. The only question is how many of you we bring with us. Why not call your prime minister next?'

Barnes knew he didn't have much more to offer. He might already have done enough to lose his job and any remaining credibility in London. He imagined Angus having to defend the decision to send him back into action. 'I can't get straight through, Hussein, it doesn't work like that.'

Hussein called to the man by the door. 'Kill one more.'

Barnes winced as he heard the shot, and the screams from the room.

'I'll call the PM's chief of staff. Give me the phone.'

Hussein half-smiled. 'Give it your best shot, *High Commissioner*. I'm enjoying watching how diplomacy *really* works. You must be missing the champagne receptions and the glad-handing?'

'Not so much.' Barnes held out his hand. 'The phone.'

He punched in the switchboard number. 'Ed Barnes again. Hermione Buckingham, please. Urgent.'

This time he got straight through. 'Ed, what the hell is happening? We're watching the footage. Saw you go in a few hours ago. The Kenyan hostages coming out. We're getting better intel, and our guys are close by now. Can you talk?'

'Sort of… I have company.'

Hermione took the hint. Her voice changed register, conscious that she had an audience. Designed to influence as well as inform. 'The PM is watching it all closely. We don't talk to terrorists. But he wants a negotiated outcome. And he's ready to send the Kenyans more military support if and when they choose to go in.'

Barnes recognised the tradecraft, but felt crestfallen. What had he got left in the locker? 'It will be too late, Hermione.'

'So what next?' She sounded slightly breathless.

Barnes exhaled slowly, eyes on Hussein. 'Hermione, I'm with Mr Hussein. He's in charge here. He is a reasonable man. He wants democracy for his people. As we all do, of course. I'm not negotiating with him, naturally. But I think it would be a good time for the PM to issue a statement on his support for democracy in Africa.'

'Not enough!' Hussein stood angrily as he spat out the words.

Hermione was guarded, picking her response carefully for his benefit. Was the PM with her in the room right now? Hermione continued. 'Ed, I got your message on the meeting with the governor. Our friends suggest that he and your current host are closer than it appears. Does that help?'

'Maybe.' Barnes glanced at Hussein, whose eyes had narrowed. 'Hermione, how about this statement: the UK welcomes the commitment by the president of Kenya to mediate between Somalia and Somaliland. We hope that the process will lead to a democratic and just outcome that respects the rights and freedoms of the peoples of the region.'

A pause. It was open enough for her but interesting enough for Hussein. 'Let me try, Ed. I'm not saying no.

But this would be a big move. And the PM can't be seen to offer it under pressure. *If* he agrees, will your host accept the commitment to say it at a later point, in return for your release?'

Barnes was holding Hussein's eye as he spoke. 'I'm not leaving, Hermione.'

Her exasperation was clearer now, even knowing Hussein was listening. 'Ed, you've got to get out of there. That's an instruction, not a request. You know what happens next. You are making it harder for us to act. You have responsibilities.'

Responsibilities. 'I still have a roomful of hostages next door, Hermione. One fewer than two minutes ago. I'll leave after they do. Please say again, for my host's benefit, what the PM will say in the coming days.'

Hermione sighed. Why couldn't Ed fucking Barnes be ignored like the other ambassadors? She'd always found him hard to dismiss. 'I have confidence that he will say, at the right moment, that the UK supports the Kenyan mediation, and hopes for a peaceful, democratic outcome. And I'm even more confident that, if you come out in one piece, he will have some serious questions on your decisions today.'

And then her voice softened. 'Good luck, Ed.'

Barnes cut the line and turned back to Hussein. 'Enough?'

Hussein had raised his eyebrows. 'Not bad at all, High Commissioner. I read all about you going rogue from Paris. The undiplomatic diplomat. We've made more progress in fifteen minutes than in the last fifteen years. And you Brits really say you don't negotiate with terrorists?'

Barnes ignored it. 'And so?'

Hussein looked up at a noise at the door. A different gunman this time. He was impatient.

'What is it?' Hussein barked at him.

The man spoke in Swahili. Barnes could follow it. They had found another woman, a European. No passport.

He steadied himself, knowing before he saw her who it would be. He had to show no recognition. Most importantly, neither could Stephanie. Time slowed again. He turned slowly to the door.

Stephanie was now standing there alongside the man. She looked defiant, unhurt. She stared back at her father impassively, not betraying any shock at seeing him there: perhaps she had watched him come in. Barnes felt nauseous. He had to summon all his strength to stand still, as the room reeled around him. It was too much now.

Hussein sighed. This was a distraction. 'Put her with the rest. Maybe one of yours, High Commissioner?'

Barnes nodded, trying hard to stop the room from spinning and his world from breaking apart.

His voice was quiet, and caught slightly. 'Yes.'

He cleared his throat.

'One of ours.'

22

Endgame

Barnes worked hard to hold himself steady. *Focus.* The only way to save Stephanie, and the other hostages, was to focus on Hussein. They were approaching the endgame of the negotiation.

Both knew the limits of what the other had to offer, and what they could not concede.

Barnes tore his mind from Stephanie. Beneath the outward defiance she had seemed cowed, lacking her usual spark. 'It's the best deal I can get you, Hussein. You know that. And this way you also show that Somaliland can be a reliable partner. Part of a serious process. That helps the governor. This can be the start of something.'

Hussein sniffed. A glance at the door: he knew that the bullets would soon be flying. 'I told you, he's part of the problem.'

'So why don't we ask him what he thinks you should do?' Barnes gestured again to the phone. But Hussein shook his head, impatiently, and spat on the floor.

'He would ask for more, too. A UN Security Council statement, backing our independence. That would give our people courage, hope. Maybe an official invitation to your climate summit in Jordan. It would show that we were being taken seriously.'

Barnes struggled to suppress his exasperation. 'You know I can't promise a UN statement. The Americans will try to block it…' He composed himself. 'Look, I can get the UK mission to propose a statement backing the mediation talks, and I can promise that we'll do all we can to bring the Americans on board. Surely that's enough. But one thing is beyond any doubt: they won't do that if there are any dead Americans in this mall.'

Hussein grinned malevolently. 'You seem anxious to save everyone but the Brits. Okay, ten hostages.' He held up his hands, miming counting on his fingers. 'And because I'm starting to like you… you can help me choose.'

Barnes followed him to the room where the white hostages were being held. They were now all lying face down on the floor, hands crossed behind their backs. Twenty or so. The room, a toy shop, smelt of urine and sweat. Several twisted their necks to glance up at him as he entered and then swiftly looked back at the floor. He saw bruises on the faces, one with blood caked around his nose. They were all men, except for Stephanie, who sat in the corner on a chair, staring straight ahead. She looked away as Barnes entered, a scowl fixed on her face. Raul was off to one side, a bruise on his cheek, a streak of blood from one ear. He, too, avoided Barnes's eyes.

'Ten go, the rest stay,' barked Hussein. The Somalis shepherded the group into rows of five at one end of the shop, kneeling to face them. The dolls and toys gave the scene a more macabre feel. 'You really don't want the Brits first, Barnes? I'm beginning to wonder if they'll ever let you back into the embassy.'

Barnes ignored him and stepped forward. How many of those in the room would make it out? He needed them to trust him. 'I'm the British high commissioner. I know that you have all been through a tough experience. We are trying to ensure that you all leave here safely. But it takes time, and I need you to help us. We are building dialogue and respect with these men, who also have families to go home for. Some of us can start to leave.' He surveyed the group. Some held his eye, most were looking down. 'Do any of you have young children? Please sit up.'

A gunman objected but Hussein gestured him to stay silent. He was enjoying the spectacle. He picked a ball from the shelf and started to bounce it.

Eight men sat up, hesitantly. They were mainly in their thirties and forties. Fathers. Barnes nodded at Hussein, who waved a dismissive hand to indicate that they could be taken out, continuing to bounce the ball in his other hand. He made a show of counting theatrically on his fingers as they left the room. Barnes was also counting those left: eleven, plus Stephanie and Raul. He knew Raul's kids, but knew there was no way he would leave.

Hussein threw the ball into a corner. 'Two more then, High Commissioner, and that's it.'

Barnes forced himself not to look at Stephanie. His mind was racing. He had to show no preference for her. And yet would it not be normal for any mediator to ask to free the woman before the men? Would he already have provoked suspicion by not doing so?

Barnes looked round the group. 'Anyone need urgent medical attention?'

A man raised his hand, gesturing to a wound in his side. His shirt was caked in blood and he was shivering with cold. Probably at least one gunshot wound. Barnes nodded to Hussein, who in turn nodded at his men to release him. Ten men left, plus Raul. Barnes looked at Stephanie.

He kept his voice calm. 'Madam, do you need medical attention?'

Just say yes. Make this easy. Don't be stubborn. For once in your life, don't be stubborn.

She looked back at him defiantly, and slowly shook her head.

Hussein was impatient. 'Last one, then?'

Barnes stared hard at Stephanie. 'The woman. She would have been released with the others if you had found her earlier. I know everyone remaining would support that. Let her go.'

Hussein gestured to the men. But Stephanie was adamant. 'I'm not going anywhere. Pick someone else.'

Barnes stared at her, proud, exasperated. 'Just go, please. We are fine here.' *I am fine, Steph. Please, please, please go.*

But she would not move. Their eyes were locked together. She glanced away as she spoke. 'I'm staying until you are all out.' *I'm not going anywhere until you're out, Pops.*

Hussein shrugged impatiently. 'We don't have time. Enough. She stays, then.'

Barnes shook his head with anger, furious at her stubbornness. But he forced himself to stay calm. Ten men were walking out. He gestured at an elderly hostage to leave. No more bodies. That surely bought him more time with the Kenyans.

Hussein did not seem like a man with much willingness to use that time. 'Okay, High Commissioner... last round.'

Barnes forced his mind back to the negotiation. 'Look around. Take the win, Hussein. The Kenyans will surely be here soon. The statements, the mediation, a UN process. This is major progress for your people. The start of something significant. Much more than you and the governor could have expected. And you get to walk out.'

Hussein had now picked up a model car, and was wheeling it back and forth on the shelf. 'I never had a toy car. Statements and communiqués. They matter so much in your world of maps and chaps. But it's all words and empty platitudes, High Commissioner, you and I both know that. No, we'll still need the drama, too. The governor can bank the words, do his thing with them. And we—' he gestured to the two sullen gunmen in the room '—we'll keep killing until you really take us seriously. How many did it take to secure American independence? Or the French revolution? We're done here. You personally can leave, and we will hold you to your pledges once you're out there. Why don't *you* get to walk out?'

One of the hostages tried to stand. Promises of money. He was clubbed with a rifle butt and fell back to the ground, blood oozing down one cheek. Barnes could hear helicopters: the Americans, more Kenyans? They had no more time.

Barnes took a step towards Hussein. 'I told you, I'm not leaving without the other hostages.'

Hussein stared back at him. 'I need you alive, *Excellency*. Out there. Holding your people, and the Kenyans, to what they have said they will do.'

Barnes shook off the grip of a gunman who had stepped between them. 'Then let them all go too. Secure some goodwill. This can be the start.' They stared at each other for a few moments.

Hussein was quieter now, steely, almost sad. 'I can't do that. Democracy advances through violence. We cannot conclude this looking weak. It has to be this way. You can choose to watch. Or go.'

Hussein gestured to one of the men to give him a weapon, and approached Raul. The bodyguard was trembling now, his head turned slightly to look at Barnes, imploring him not to intervene, not to risk his life. But his eyes were filled with terror. Hussein pointed the gun at his temple, and he too looked back at Barnes. Barnes remembered watching him play with his boys in the residence garden, a sidearm in the leather holster at his side. Confident, muscular, but with an uncharacteristic tenderness. He forced himself to hold Raul's eyes as Hussein pulled the trigger. The single shot echoed around the room. A hostage whimpered. The bodyguard slumped. Barnes heard himself cry out.

Hussein lowered his arm, and crossed the room to where Stephanie was crouched. He slowly lifted the gun to hold it at her head. Stephanie held Barnes's eye, imploring him not to move. But Barnes heard himself scream out again as he ran across the room. Two men moved in front of Hussein and held him, arms gripped behind his back.

Hussein chuckled and lowered the weapon. He turned back to face Barnes, and then moved to where he could see both Stephanie and Barnes. This time he aimed the weapon towards Barnes while training his eyes on Stephanie, his head half-cocked. His eyes were red with adrenalin. And this time it was Barnes who held her gaze, imploring her to show more resolve than he had. Her lip trembled.

Hussein looked from one to the other, a smile playing on his lips.

In that moment, Barnes thought of nothing beyond his daughter. In his head, they were playing together by the stream at the cottage in Wales, the water splashing over the top of their boots, Stephanie cackling with laughter.

Could she sense his thoughts? *I will give this everything my cells and soul can offer. But if, and maybe when, that proves to be… not enough… then know that — for me — this, all this, has been enough. And yes, I grieve to my core for what I won't get to see of you. Glorious you. But it is enough for me to know that there is a part of me, somewhere, in your adventure.*

After what seemed like several minutes, but could only have been seconds, Hussein lowered the weapon. There was almost a leer on his face. 'I think perhaps we have established some more leverage in this negotiation. And maybe we have lost some trust? But if this really is your daughter, the price just went through the roof. We can start with that invitation to the climate summit.'

Silence again, except for a deep groan. Barnes realised that it was coming from him. He wrenched his eyes from the corpse, and tried to keep them from Stephanie. What hope now for the remaining nine men, and her? He could not walk out without them. And while he was still inside there was more chance that the Kenyans would have to come in cautiously rather than all guns blazing. Or let the Brits or Americans do it. The time he had bought them meant that they would be on site by now.

Buy more time. 'I can deliver the Jordan summit invitation for your governor. It would need to be some sort of observer status. But why does he want it? You said yourself these conferences were pointless.'

Hussein was now standing over a second hostage, who was whimpering. Hussein curled his lip. 'We'll take the invitation. It is legitimacy. Gives us status. Reminds people we are a country-in-waiting.'

Barnes nodded. 'Okay, give me time. But let's stop all this now.' He had no idea of how he would deliver it. He had nothing left to offer. If he died, would it be Jim or Dave who would make the call, *his* call, to Raul's widow? What would they say about his life, about this failure? Would Emma ever forgive him for bringing Stephanie into this horror? Would she bury them both? He felt the adrenalin recede, and an overwhelming sense of despair and exhaustion.

Suddenly the room went black. Screams from the hostages. Barnes hit the floor hard. Four quick shots, evenly spaced. He stayed down, waiting for death, inhaling the smell of the shop floor. He heard himself murmuring Stephanie's name. And then: more shots in the main hallway, moving away from them.

23

An Old and Very Dangerous Friend

Barnes waited several seconds. The room went quiet again. He wanted to call out Stephanie's name, but forced himself to resist. 'Is everyone okay?' His voice was muffled, hoarse.

Mainly silence. A few murmurs, and – thank God – her voice. Quiet, frightened, but relieved to hear him speak. Alive. 'I'm here.'

Barnes blinked as his eyes adjusted to the dark. 'What just happened? Hussein?'

No reply. Barnes rose slowly to his feet, moved to the door and switched the light back on. The four terrorists were shot, including Hussein. A bullet wound in the centre of his forehead. He had fallen back against a shelf of toys and was lying on the floor with one leg twisted under him.

Even in death he seemed to sneer as the blood spread around him.

Barnes tore his eyes away and looked around the rest of the room. He counted the eight remaining men on the floor. Unhurt. Beside them, Raul's body, the face gone. Some of the men were sitting up, looking dazed. Stephanie was in one corner, curled into a ball. Her eyes on Barnes. Fearful yet defiant. He gestured at them all to stay still and walked out into the corridor. The shots seemed to have stopped. The building was silent again.

A single soldier in black combat kit and balaclava had his back to him, standing over another of the terrorists, checking his pulse. He was bleeding from one arm. Stocky, strong shoulders. US Special Forces? He turned slowly towards Barnes and removed his balaclava.

'I thought you might need a hand, Ambassador.'

Barnes wiped the dust from his face and blinked, his eyes adjusting faster than his brain. It surely could not be him.

Max Crawford grinned back at him. 'I was going to wait to be asked. But "to strive, to seek, to find and not to yield."' He moved towards Barnes, pausing to turn the corpse of a terrorist over with his boot. 'Or, as an old and very dangerous friend of mine once put it, sometimes in a negotiation you just have to kill the guy.'

Barnes shook his head. 'Crawford?... Max?... But you're...'

The grin again. 'Dead? It didn't suit me.'

The room now stank of blood and excrement. The hostages on the floor were pushing themselves off the ground, their eyes moving from the bodies of those who had held them to the wiry man who seemed to have saved them.

Barnes swayed slightly as he tried to find his balance. 'But... Max? Copenhagen? The US attack. Your funeral?'

Crawford was back in efficient mode, moving through the room, checking the bodies of those he had killed, looking for signs of life in the hostages who had not yet staggered to their feet. 'Pretty close, yes.'

Barnes was staring at him, unbelieving. A few more lines but the eyes as sharp as ever and still the mischievous glint. He was not sure whether to laugh or cry.

'Thank you for coming for us. And thank you for getting me out of Copenhagen in time. And I'm sorry if I—' *I'm sorry if I stopped believing in you in Paris, doubted your loyalty.*

Crawford looked awkward, and then gestured at the room of hostages. He raised an eyebrow. 'Not much time for a catch-up. Can the nostalgia wait, Ambassador?'

Barnes smiled. 'Of course.' He looked around to check the condition of the captives. 'All OK?' They nodded grimly.

'Steph?'

He looked around for her. He saw the flicker of alarm in Crawford's eyes.

Barnes was suddenly disorientated. 'Where is she, Max?'

Crawford was by the door, scanning the corridor. 'The threat is neutralised. We need to get everyone out.' He gestured at the first hostages, who started to file out. 'You too, Ambassador. No more risks today.'

Barnes shook his head. 'Not without Stephanie. She was just here. We need to find her.'

'Leave that to me. She can't be too far. You *need* to lead them out. Now. I'll cover the back, in case any of these guys start to come round.' It was an order, not a piece of advice.

Barnes narrowed his eyes. 'What will you do with the bodies?'

Crawford shrugged. 'I've got some Kenyan friends outside. We did some time together on the Somali border. That's how I heard about the siege, and you coming into the middle of it. They'll take them in, and claim the credit for ending it. So can you: your negotiations bought us the time for me to get here.'

Barnes blinked. 'And you? I thought you were dead. I went to your *funeral*. We need to talk. I want to know what's going on, where you've been.'

'Keep the gin decent, and the tonic ice cold, Ambassador. I'll find you once I've found your daughter.'

Barnes left the room and moved to the front of the group, checking them as he passed for injuries or signs of trauma. Their shoulders sagged and there were signs of exhaustion, but the relief was clear. He gestured at them to follow him, and breathed deeply as they approached the exit. He could see the outline of the Kenyan soldiers outside. He paused for a moment before opening the doors: even – especially – at this moment, the theatre of diplomacy. Wherever Stephanie was, he had to keep the focus on the release.

And then they were out, among the cameras and the soldiers and the noise. Kianjuri strode forward, beaming, and shook his hand. It was a good sign: everyone now wanted this to be seen as a success, and to share in that. Barnes ushered the hostages towards the medical tent. He clocked members of his consular team, ready to help, the big flag in place. He ran a hand through his hair, feeling another wave of exhaustion, and walked slowly towards the cameras, pausing for a moment before he spoke. They would be watching in Downing Street, and in the governor's office in Somaliland. A scrum of cameras and journalists.

'My thoughts are with the families and friends of those who died today.' Barnes had always loathed the phrase 'loved ones'. He tried not to think of Steph. But he almost choked at the last image of Raul, choosing to stay at his post.

He cleared the dust from his throat. This wasn't over. 'I am grateful to President Obwocha and the Kenyan authorities for their wisdom, patience and professionalism, and they have our full support as they continue to respond. The High Commission has set up reception points here, at key hotels and the airport for Brits seeking information on their loved ones. Please bear with us…' Only Stephanie would have noticed the way that his voice faltered slightly. If Emma was watching, perhaps she would too. '…as we work to locate everyone.'

The journalists started to shout questions. 'But what really happened in there?' 'Who were the terrorists?' 'What did you offer them?' 'How many dead?'

Barnes shook his head and held his hands in front of him, to indicate that the interview was over. But he hesitated for a moment. Bloody Max Crawford. Back. Alive. Saving his life again. Extraordinary. He thought of Hermione watching in No 10. He would need her on side, too.

He cleared his throat once more, and the journalists went quiet. 'Someone once told me that in every situation, however grim, there are always good people trying to make it better. Often quietly, often anonymously. Willing to take the risks to help. However terrible a situation, look for the helpers.'

He walked away from the cameras. His feet felt unsteady. A bodyguard emerged to grip his arm and lead him towards the convoy. Barnes paused and held his eye. Raul was gone. He could not find the words.

The BG nodded, and placed a hand on his back to push him closer to the vehicle.

Barnes brushed him off. 'Wait, we need to find Stephanie. She's in there, still.'

The BG shook his head. An order, not a piece of advice. 'No, boss, that's it. Non-negotiable. We've got to get you out of here, now. It will be chaos here. And...' Barnes watched him steady himself, but the voice was quieter. '...we're already one man down.'

They opened the heavy armoured door for him, and Barnes sank into his seat. He felt the exhaustion course through him in waves.

Raul was dead. And Stephanie was still in danger. Everyone thought he had succeeded. But he had failed.

24

Paris

Orla had followed the coverage of the mall siege from her favourite cafe in the Marais, Les Philosophes. Her phone battery was low as she constantly refreshed the news feeds. Normally she relished every taste of the *confit de canard*, and the garlic-drenched potatoes. But today her mind had been in Kenya. When Ed Barnes walked out of the shopping centre, he had seemed somehow disjointed to her. Of course, part of this would be the theatre of diplomacy, the drama of the moment. The relief. But there was more. He seemed half of himself, lacking something. It had to be connected to Stephanie.

She would go to them, tap up Ed for more on the dead hunter, try to get some clues on the Assassin. But for now, she was torn between the story and Kenya. She needed to get into the killer's mind, find a way to disrupt him enough to get his attention.

It was a hunch, but all she had to go on. A gathering of Europe's far right leaders. The ironies seemed to be lost on them: a global campaign against globalisation; an international alliance of nationalists; a private, high-level gathering of the populists who were taking on the faceless global elite.

At the heart of their shared project: climate. How dare the centrist parties impose green taxes on hardworking families? Who were the metropolitan elites to tell people where and when they could drive their cars? Why were hardworking families in the West expected to make the sacrifices? We can give you back your dignity, make you great again. Elizabeth Hoon wasn't there in person. But her voice, and her inspiration, were everywhere.

As was Moscow's money. Not openly of course, that would be an irony too far even for this lot. But in the speaking gigs the leaders got, the consultancies for their family members, the board seats in safe but not demanding companies, the quiet but relentless amplification of their social media presence. What was so wrong, they muttered in the corridors, with the way the Russian president led his country? They purred at his strategic vision, his ability to surprise the West while their own leaders tied themselves up in red tape and worrying about rainbow flags. Didn't Europe's feeble vetocracies need a bit of strong leadership too?

Orla had managed to secure access to the venue as part of the media delegation with the French far-right leader, Manuela Guitton. She had followed her on a trip to the north-east, and promised to write a glowing piece on the way that she connected with the real France. But being here was also a chance to get to Sebastian Keys, the UK's latest far-right pin-up.

Keys seemed to be cutting through. He had acquired the American hair, teeth and fundraising skills. But he had held on to a cheeky chappie Englishness. An ability to say the things that others could not. Good on TV and on the stump. He called it authentic, but to Orla it was as synthetic as the controlled soundbites and risk averse policies of those that he was attacking.

And the drive-by attacks were working. He seemed to move faster than the PM, making his opponent look weak and lumbering. Governing required compromise, but campaigning could be about arguments and points of difference. And he had worked out that the biggest wedge, the most effective differentiation, was climate.

Orla waited in the media queue at the venue, an upmarket hotel on the Rue du Faubourg St Honoré. Not far from where Ed Barnes had lived, in the UK's Paris embassy. She had watched him work these rooms as the ambassador, always pretending that he hated it. She had watched him throw all that away to pursue the truth about the murder in his residence. And she had seen him try and fail to come to terms with the fact that Stephanie had been responsible. It seemed years and miles away, and yet so close.

Getting under the skin of these people intrigued Orla. But it was not enough. She scanned the faces around her, looking for the Assassin. She wasn't sure what exactly to expect. Someone ex-military, tough. Low profile. But professional: it took effort to make it look so effortless. If the target was one of these leaders, he would surely put in the work to make it smooth.

Orla had made progress in analysing his approach. The Assassin killed sparingly: if he was taking out a far-right leader, he would select the one that would resonate most widely. He wanted to discourage others from emerging to fill the vacuum.

Guitton was the obvious choice, then. The most effective, the one who had been most outspoken on climate. But, if Orla was right, the other targets had all been men. Her hunch was that he – and she was certain it was a he – would not kill a woman.

That surely left Keys as the next choice. But another Brit? People were joining the dots and the police would surely be ahead of Orla. Other journalists might start making the connections between the killings. But wasn't that what the Assassin wanted?

Orla entered the room for the reception. Europe's strong men and strong women mingled among the donors, media barons, investors. She picked up a glass of champagne from the tray. There was a hum of ambition and hunger to the room. As she circulated, watching and listening, she wondered why the Assassin didn't take the whole place out. But it wouldn't be here. He preferred the silence of the hotel room. No collateral damage. He got to them alone.

Keys had an entourage. Two young female staffers. Tight blouses, short skirts. They were channelling the mixture of fans and funders to him and moving them swiftly on. There was method to the madness. It was going to be hard to get to him.

Orla circled the room again. Guitton was holding court in one corner. Orla got into her eyeline and waved. Guitton beckoned her over. Orla hovered on the outskirts of the conversation with an Austrian industrialist who was angry about pronouns. Guitton was listening sympathetically, nodding along. The man was ushered away.

Guitton was tall. The heels were prodigious. She addressed Orla in French with a mix of condescension and complicity. 'How's the writing, Orla?' She struggled with the pronunciation of the name.

'Superb. You'll like it. Busy night?'

'Every conversation starts with them saying, "I'm probably not allowed to say this but..."'

'And yet they say it.'

'Indeed we do.'

Orla needed to tap into the sense of camaraderie. 'And who do you rate here?'

Guitton scanned the room, her antennae crackling. 'There's a young Finn. She's smart, sellable. Still a few too many red-faced – what do you call them in English? – *jamon*?'

Orla smiled despite herself. 'Gammon. Yes, not much diversity in the room. I guess that doesn't bother you?'

Guitton looked genuinely surprised. 'But it does. We win when we get the second-generation immigrants. We need their money, their networks, their energy.'

'And their desire to pull up the drawbridge?'

Guitton looked confused. *Pont-levis* didn't work as well in French.

Orla changed tack. She didn't have long. 'And Sebastian Keys?'

Guitton snorted. 'He won't last. Narcissist. A chaser of skirts. Can't stick at anything. I give him a few months.'

Orla raised an eyebrow. 'Should I get him to say something for the piece on you?'

Guitton shrugged disinterestedly. She gestured at Keys across the room. He bounded across.

'Manuela, la belle.' An extravagant kiss to the hand. 'And your gorgeous friend?'

Guitton clearly didn't want to try to pronounce Orla's name again, and simply wafted a hand in her direction. Orla stepped in.

'Orla. I'm writing a piece on Manuela. She is a big fan of yours. I wondered if we could speak.'

Sebastian Keys visibly puffed up. 'Well, yes, and I'm her biggest fan, of course. I see her on a future French stamp, one breast exposed, our brave Marianne, trampling the liberals beneath her heels.'

Manuala placed a hand on his arm, beaming. 'Sebastian, you are too generous. We are all marching behind you. England's future.'

Orla clocked them both looking over her shoulder for more interesting targets. She held Keys's eye, gave a slight wink. 'So I can come and see you, Mr Keys, privately?'

Keys smirked. 'Oh yes, by all means. Any friend of our beacon of liberty is a friend of mine. Just as long as we don't have to do the equality and fraternity bits. And hopefully we still get some exposed flesh.'

Orla recoiled slightly, but held his gaze. He was swept away by his minders, and Guitton plunged back into the throng. Orla looked around the room. There were plenty of military types, but none of them who looked like they did more than bore at bars with exaggerated stories of their escapades. He wasn't here.

If he was coming for a politician, it was Keys. She would make sure she was there first.

25

Ice Cold Tonic

Ed Barnes sat on the terrace of the residence, a large gin in hand. It was going down fast. The wash-up at the embassy had concluded. Dave and his team had managed to account for all the Brits whose families had so far been in touch. Some were receiving medical help, but nothing too serious. The call to Raul's widow had been the toughest of his life. He could hear the kids in the background. Barnes hated platitudes, and yet in death everything seemed like a platitude, an attempt to soften something that could not be softened. He had then called President Obwocha to offer condolences for those who had been killed. The president had sounded untroubled.

Now he could focus on finding Stephanie. He placed his head in his hands. Her voice had been clear and distinct after the shooting. Had she staggered out of the room in shock? Or who had taken her? Had Max noticed her go?

He heard a man clearing his throat. He had been lost in thought and looked up. Max Crawford was stood at the end of the table, a light safari jacket, blue shirt, desert boots, fresh scar on one cheek, cleaned up. But one of those jawlines that never really looked clean.

'Max? How the hell did you get in?'

'I've never been that impressed by your residence security, Ambassador. Hope the gin is better.'

Barnes poured the drink, noticing the slight tremble in his hand, and handed it to Crawford, who was pretending not to have noticed, too. Crawford took a long sip and cocked his head, a slight nod of appreciation.

'Yes. Better than your security.' Crawford saw the wince. 'I'm sorry, Ambassador. I know you lost a good man. It never gets easier.'

They sat in silence for a few moments, looking out into the Kenyan dusk. The crickets had started, and the temperature was dropping.

'You didn't find her then, Max?'

A defiant stare. 'I will.'

'You're meant to be dead.'

Another sip. 'Not for the first time.'

Barnes shivered slightly. 'I know. But, seriously Max… We buried you. Your *family* buried you. What's going on?'

'Death turns out to be the best cover yet.' Crawford chewed his lip. He could see that Barnes wasn't in the mood for more evasion. 'Long story.'

'But do they know you're alive? Your boys? I heard their eulogies for you.' Barnes felt his anger rise. Had they been duped too? What kind of monster puts their family through that?

'Of course they know.' Crawford's voice was quieter. He was trying to close it down.

'And the regiment, too? I guess they know? Is this some kind of warped idea of theirs to get you back out there? Did *they* send you today?'

'No. They don't know. No one else. Except the people I'm working with. The close family. And now, you. And that's already more than enough.'

They sat again in silence. Barnes composed himself. He would get the answers he needed eventually. 'I'm genuinely grateful you came. Again. Thank you.' He cleared the emotion from his throat. 'And I'm sorry that I didn't stand by you before, after Paris. It was all so out of control. Copenhagen. I lost my bearings. I didn't know who was really on my side. I didn't know who to trust.'

Crawford took another long sip. 'You know now, Ambassador, and that's what matters.'

Barnes smiled. 'Actually, it's High Commissioner now.'

Crawford nodded. 'Whatever you're calling yourself, Ambassador, it's good to see you too.'

Barnes leant forward, jaw clenched. 'But we need to find her. Were there other Somalis? Could she have been disorientated, tried to escape? I'm worried I've failed her again.'

'You always have been. And she normally gives you plenty of reasons to worry. More so now than ever. But she'll be okay. I think she worries about you more than you worry about her.'

This was more intimacy than they had ever done. But Barnes was shattered, and Max Crawford seemed different. More assured, reflective.

'Can I keep her safe, Max?'

No hesitation. 'We can.'

Barnes breathed deeply before continuing, finding his centre, keeping himself calm. 'And what are you doing now… when you're not saving my life or finding my daughter?'

Crawford shrugged. 'Same as I ever was, really. Killing bad guys.'

'Evidently. Somaliland terrorists.'

'Not usually. They're not really bad enough.'

'Then who is?'

Crawford stared back at him. There was an intensity that Barnes had not seen before.

Almost zeal.

'You told me once that the shits always win. But what if it didn't have to always be that way? Let's just say I've found a new cause.'

'To die for?'

Steelier now. 'Not if I can help it. To kill for.'

Barnes cocked his head. 'And what is it? If it's no longer just for country, or family, or friendship?'

The phone on the table vibrated. It was the Somaliland governor. Barnes raised an eyebrow at Crawford to indicate he had to take it.

'Mr High Commissioner?'

Barnes was back in diplomat mode. Clipped, professional. 'Thank you for your help today, Governor. The outcome could have been worse, much worse. Though I'm not convinced that you were as surprised by the attack as you seemed when we last spoke.'

The governor didn't miss a beat. 'We are not always responsible for everything our families do.'

Barnes paused. 'I've learnt that.' Then, back to substance: 'What next, Governor? Hussein didn't need to die in there. He could have kept going. Couldn't you have intervened to tell him to make the deal? He lost today.'

'We don't have many cards, High Commissioner. And it's not about winning, it's about the ability to keep playing. If he'd been taken alive the Kenyans would have locked him up forever, which would have been much worse for him. Believe me, we know those jails. But we keep playing, and you made him promises.'

Barnes paused. 'I made him *pledges*. But he executed too many hostages and was ready to kill more. That changed everything. You know I can't let my government reward that.'

The governor sighed. 'Like he told you, it was the only way to get your attention. And those were commitments you made. The talks, the statements, the invite to Jordan. We trusted you. But like your negotiation books say, trust and verify. If you are faltering, we will hold you to them.'

Crawford had leant forward as he listened, and his eyes now narrowed.

Barnes kept his focus on the call. 'It will take time, Governor. Any changes in our approach can't be seen as a response to the attack. We don't negotiate with terrorists. I will do my best.'

Crawford was chewing his lip. His face had darkened. Barnes took the cue: 'But, Governor, is that a threat?'

The line was quiet for a few moments. 'I'm afraid it is. We now know more than Hussein did about leverage in a negotiation. We will look after her well.'

Barnes felt his anger rise again. Crawford gestured at him to stay calm. 'Where is she?'

'You are a decent man. And truth is the currency of diplomacy. So we do not believe you will fail to deliver.'

'Governor... Ali, no. She's nothing to do with this.' His voice was quiet again.

'She is now. Two weeks.'

Barnes suppressed a retch. Crawford was alert.

'How do I know you have her, Governor?'

'Because you trust me. Because she is unharmed. And because when I asked her what she wanted me to pass on to you, she said, "Don't worry, Pops, I'm okay." Is that enough evidence for you, "Pops"?'

The line went dead. Barnes took a long sip of the drink. Always the extra shot of gin on the top but now it tasted hard, metallic. He stared across the garden. It was already too cold.

Crawford looked grim. 'Two weeks?'

Barnes exhaled slowly. 'Two weeks, he said.'

'And what did you promise them in there?'

'Enough to make this hard to deliver. Kenyan-led mediation between the Somali government and the Somalilanders. I should be able to get Obwocha to see through on that. Plus a decent UK and UN reaction. Harder, as I'll have to square off No 10 and the Americans. An invite to the climate summit, to give them some status and legitimacy. I'd need to do some hard yards in London. But maybe with all that I can get enough to get the Somilanders to back off, and to leave Stephanie out of it.'

Crawford looked pensive. 'Sounds like your neck of the woods, not mine. I rather like Lieutenant-Colonel Alexander Burnes, who once wrote, as he headed towards Afghanistan – "I must rely upon my languages, charm and politeness – and not my sword."' Crawford could see Barnes was not listening. 'Sorry. How can I help?'

Barnes needed more answers from Crawford. But he needed his support now. 'I don't want the UK system knowing about Stephanie. They'll think I can't run the operation with that kind of distraction, that my judgement will be flawed. I can't have that again, or risk being taken off the job. Can you find her?'

'Maybe that one *is* more my neck of the woods.'

Barnes exhaled slowly. 'It's so good to see you again, Max. But whatever you are involved in out there, this mercenary for hire stuff, it must stop. Now. All I know is that my daughter is a hostage and I have a bodyguard to bury. And the shits do always win, that's the lesson of history.'

A slight shake of the head and a shrug as Crawford stood.

'Then maybe history is wrong.'

26

L'enfer

The Crawford family had lived for three generations in a small town outside Rochester in Kent. Max's grandfather had taught science in the local school. Max's father, Jack, had served for almost thirty years in the military, moving the family from the terraced house in which Jack had grown up to a semi-detached house on Watling Street with an orchard. Jack had loved sitting under the trees with his *Daily Telegraph* crossword.

Max had gone to a string of boarding schools for the sons of officers, never really settling. Constant scrapes, running away, drama. One headmaster had said he had 'a great brain but a terrible mind'. Another had thrown him out for being 'disrespectful and obstinate'. Max had written to a local company that the week of work experience with them had been more useful than his lessons. The head had told him not to send the letter, as it would damage the school's reputation. Max had refused.

When Max had turned up at his parents' front door with another letter – this one informing them that they would have to find a new school – he had expected his father to be furious. But Jack Crawford had asked him to describe the circumstances carefully, not to leave anything out. Max had done so, his voice monotonous at first, dreading the reaction. But as he watched his father's reactions he became more animated, more descriptive.

At the end of his story, he had paused to await the verdict. He feared sorrow more than anger. But his father smiled, hugged him, and simply said, 'I'll talk to your mother. We never liked that head. We'll just have to start again.'

This had been part of what held them together as a family. Jack was away for long periods. Max was a rebellious and unpredictable teenager. Perhaps the only predictable thing was that he would follow his father into the military, though the more conventional regiments had quickly passed him over and moved him on, until he found *the* regiment.

Meanwhile the other thing – the thing that really held the family together – was his mother, Lily. Jack adored her, in a quiet, undemonstrative way. Max would catch him just watching her as she moved about the house. She loved France, having been there once on a school trip. She could be stern with Max, and had plenty of reason to be. But she showed her love for him through food, especially puddings. Custard seemed to solve most family rows. His parents didn't speak of the younger brother that he had all too briefly known.

When Max had found his home in the regiment, earning his promotions, he and his father had brought a small place in France for Lily. Now in her early sixties, she had thrown herself into renovating the old barn, and making it home. Jack, initially less enthused, had found himself pulled along by the joy it brought to her, and Max's cajoling. Max persuaded them to sell the place outside Rochester. He and his father spent a week planting cuttings from his beloved orchard in the new garden. He had never seen his parents so happy.

Lily turned out to be a brilliant linguist, and threw herself into village life. Jack had found an expat group in the market town, where he could play bridge on Saturdays and talk about the cricket. They drank too often, but never too much. 'We're here for a good time, not a long time' became one of Lily's mottoes. Max had it turned into a poster for her on the kitchen wall. Max's boys loved to visit their grandparents there, with Max constantly surprised at the way they were able to open up an entirely different relationship to his parents, compared to his own.

The colours in the summer evenings were constantly changing. Warm oranges and terracottas, sometimes preposterous purples and vivid reds. Jack liked to moan about working harder than at any point in his life. Lily threw herself into French films, art, literature. And they didn't notice, as Max quietly and contentedly observed, how quickly they slipped into calling it home.

When Max somehow survived Copenhagen, he had warned his parents that the official verdict was that he had been killed in a training accident at Hereford. He had told them that this was for reasons he was not able to explain, but connected to the secrecy of his role. They had not questioned the instruction, but Jack had insisted that they could not travel to the funeral, play the part of grieving parents. *We've been to enough real funerals not to need a fictional one.* Max had understood. They had an undemonstrative, British faith. Max hoped they didn't believe in hell. How terrible to go through life believing in an eternity of punishment if you got it wrong?

Two months later, the fire had come. Jack had been in the town, playing bridge and picking up some essentials.

There had been a sense of unease, of fear. People had not lingered over the shopping, hurrying back to their cars. All the talk had been of the higher summer temperatures, but more worryingly of the stronger winds. People had watched the news of forest fires devastating large parts of California, Spain and Greece. The climate crisis was real, but distant. The local council had issued a ban on lighting fires, and encouraged people to clear their land of dry wood. When Max called to check that they were prepared, Jack had been gently dismissive of the drama, of people's desire to live in a soap opera. He had read an article from an Oxford don in the *Telegraph*, explaining how the woke generation were getting carried away. And seen a television debate that made it all sound much more complicated than the irritating people who chained themselves to rails claimed. And anyway, this was south-east France, not the Sahara.

They had smelt the smoke before they saw the fire. They had been sitting on the terrace for a well-earned gin, having unpacked the groceries and put a joint of beef in the oven. They finished their drinks and Jack wondered whether it was too early for a second. Perhaps someone had ignored the instruction from the *mairie* and was burning rubbish. No doubt the fire service would be on it. What were they called again? *Pompiers*, Lily reminded him with mischievous pride. She pottered inside to refill the glasses, without asking if he wanted a refresh.

Jack only felt the first pang of anxiety when he saw the helicopters overhead, buzzing low, carrying water. He muttered to Lily about European efficiency. He wondered if he should tell her that she had never looked more beautiful. Every wrinkle told a story. They had made them together. She held his eye for a moment, but – as ever – pre-empted the compliment. *Must get the potatoes on.*

Five minutes later they could feel the heat of the fire, and see the blaze coming closer. The wind was fiercer. Jack suggested they move inside, avoid the clouds of smoke, focus on getting the lunch ready until the threat had passed. Lily had looked pensive as she chopped the carrots. *Might as well keep busy, love.* He had found an excuse to go back outside to check that everything was under control. Later he wished he had just held her.

When the first sparks landed on the terrace, he had extinguished them beneath the sole of his sandal. But then more had started to fall, fizzing in the air. He had a memory of being under fire in the Falklands. He felt suddenly hot. He moved from spark to spark, but felt them on his head, and smelt the foul odour of burning hair. She had always complimented his hair, still full. He had run inside to suggest they drive away until the danger was over. The helicopters, the firemen, would deal with it. She was already holding the car keys. But then the flames reached them. She was choking on the smoke, eyes filled with fear. Jack gripped Lily's hands, pulled her back out towards the terrace. She reached to grab a photo of Max from the piano. The beams above them were now creaking with the weight of the fire. He saw her glance towards the hobs, thinking even now of the potatoes. He dragged her, more firmly now, towards the door.

Jack Crawford had no memory of what happened next. He would never be able to describe the blaze, beyond saying how quickly it had taken them. He would never be able to describe finding Lily, beneath a blackened roof beam in the foul, sodden mess of their destroyed home. Her glasses melted, and dress in cinders. Body charred.

Face almost unrecognisably burnt. A hand clutching the remnants of the photo.

At the hospital, when he was finally able to speak, he had asked for a telephone. He had felt hesitant, his confidence drained away. His hair had gone and his head throbbed with the searing pain of the burns. It had taken every remaining ounce of strength in him to make the call to his son. A nurse had dialled the number for him, as his arms and hands were heavily bandaged. Max Crawford never answered the phone to unrecognised numbers. But something made him do it this time. He would never be the same again.

Son, I'm sorry. I couldn't save her. The fire. Will you… she was… can you… we need to have a funeral… I can't… it's all gone… over… keep the boys safe.

Max Crawford had seen too much death, spoken at too many funerals. But this grief was crushing. He found moments where practicality took over – quietly burying his mother, working under an assumed name to find his father a care home, clearing and selling the ruined property. At other times in the dark he wept through it, fought it, ran from it, screamed at it, eventually gave into it.

And then felt it forge within him a cold, unrelenting, violent fury. And a desire for revenge.

27

Shades of Grey

After an unsatisfactory breakfast at the Oxford and Cambridge Club, Ed Barnes checked out, and turned right onto the Mall. It was a crisp autumn morning. He never stayed at the Travellers Club: too many diplomats. He crossed St James's Park and approached the back of Downing Street and the Foreign Office with the palace behind him. The air smelt of pine and bins.

To get Stephanie back, he had to get the basics in place on the Somaliland commitments. But he was increasingly conscious that he was now part of something bigger, and he wasn't going to let that go. His trip to Eldoret, and the lives devastated by climate-driven conflict. The conversations with Hussein about the retreat of democracy. Stephanie's persistent pressure for genuine action on the climate crisis rather than more diplomatic conferences. And now Max Crawford pitching up. Orla was right: he needed to trust his instincts. And an increasingly strong instinct was that he needed to see Orla.

Where was she now? After their adventures in Paris she had once again disappeared.

The prize for investigating the conspiracy had been collected on her behalf by a colleague.

Stephanie always teased him that he pulled his stomach in when she was around. He'd messaged her on occasion, to try to coax her to Kenya. The romantic in him had wanted someone to show those sunsets in the bush. Perhaps there was something there. But she hadn't sparked. Maybe a new man? Maybe just the work.

What was she doing now? He pulled out his phone and searched recent investigative journalism that had cut through. If she was writing, it would be anonymously. There was much less of it around now. Cuts to budgets, the pressure for the quick over the important. Fears over security of journalists. Lawsuits and trolling. Citizens breaking their own stories. He scrolled through the main pieces: mostly political exposés: the usual mix of mistresses, corruption and conflicts of interest. He searched under stories written by an anonymous investigator. Nothing of significance. Certainly nothing at Orla's level.

Had she become a journalist without the investigation? Passing stories off under a byline? Keeping it simple? No, that wasn't Orla either. Much more likely, she was doing the investigation without the journalism. Working for organisations that needed her skills but didn't need to publish the results. But that didn't track either. She wasn't motivated by money.

He paused to message her: *Stephanie needs you.* And then deleted it. What did he really want from her?

He climbed the steps by the statue of Robert Clive. He had walked past it so many times in his life, but only in recent years had he started to wonder whether it should still be there. Clive had been one of the imperialists who laid the foundations for the Raj. Like many of his generation, Barnes had studied a glowing version of his life at school, barely lingering on the Bengal famine between the dashing exploits and battles won. Great adventures and patriotism, yes. But for what cause? And to what ends? What was the message the statue sent to future recruits for the Foreign Office? And to the tourists who passed?

He turned left at the end of King Charles Street, glancing right towards the refurbished facade of the Elizabeth Tower at parliament. Already Whitehall was full of morning bustle: tourists, buses, civil servants hidden inside a parallel world by their phones and earbuds. Ministries on either side of the road, their architecture designed to keep the public safely away from their work.

At the gates of Downing Street, a small group of tourists were clumped, waiting for something to happen. Maybe a car to pass or – as was happening increasingly regularly – a prime minister to exit. Barnes nodded at the policemen on duty who stood aside to let him pass through the security checks. As usual, he was travelling light. And then on to Downing Street itself. He had done it hundreds of times, but the sense of excitement at this proximity to power never wore off.

The black door swung open, and he walked into the lobby, with its checked floor, Churchill's chair and quiet power. To the left, the corridor down towards No 11 and the press office. Bustle and adrenalin. The worst-designed leader's office in any serious country, with its warren of corridors and dank, impractical rooms. Barnes took his place on the small sofa and waited.

He had known Hermione Buckingham since they started together as fast streamers thirty years earlier. She had been at the posher end of their group: academic private school, but one that made you work at it. At Oxford she already had the clothes, friends and an accent that told you that she fitted in. People, especially men, wanted to please her. He had found her slightly intimidating in meetings. Hungry and ambitious, but more perceptive and emotionally intelligent than many of the men who she quickly overtook in the hierarchy. Over time she had grown into herself, and found a different register. She had stopped pretending she wasn't clever. Ministers loved her. *She gets shit done*. But an unconventional streak too: four studs in her left ear. And now here she was in the most powerful, unpopular and precarious civil service job: chief of staff to the PM.

Barnes was pleased to see that she came to greet him herself. After the drama of Paris, he was never sure whether he was someone to be seen to know, but he also knew that many of his peers quietly admired him for having found some backbone. Hermione had stayed in touch throughout. Someone had told him it was one of her mantras: *reach out when they are down*.

Hermione gave him a grin of solidarity as she approached. They stood awkwardly for a moment, unsure of whether to shake hands. It had been so long since that drunken night together in Balham, when they were unwrinkled and unscathed. She rolled her eyes and hugged him. 'Oh, come on, Ed, we're not that decrepit yet.'

Ed noticed that she had an extra earring. She looked less burdened than most people in the role. But there was still the sense of urgency, influence and raw energy that you carried in Downing Street. He followed her along the main corridor, up the stairs by the portraits of previous prime ministers and into the Yellow Room. There was a tray of coffee laid out by the fire. Decent-looking coffee,

Barnes noted with approval, not the usual tepid tap water in metal flasks.

He nodded at it. 'You're clearly making a mark, Hermione.'

She rolled her eyes. 'Drinkable coffee, Ed? What a legacy for the first woman to be chief of staff. Maybe the tea next? Some decent cakes? Glad to have such an impact. You can pour. And I see you haven't settled for a quiet posting after all?'

He had wanted to resist that nagging urge to impress her. 'I tried. Drama seems to follow me.'

Hermione chuckled. 'You don't need to pretend to me that you don't love it. Everyone's very jealous. All the right people are moaning.'

They settled into the sofas, appraising each other. Hermione knew him well enough to notice the extra worry lines. Something more. She knew him well enough not to mention that too.

'You've got the glint back, Ed. I was worried that your adventures in Paris, and the last foreign secretary, plus a bit of hostage drama, might have combined to knock that out of you.'

She was looking older, too, he thought. 'You never lost yours. How's the PM?'

'Eager, hopelessly idealistic, increasingly overwhelmed. Probably not long for this world. He's probably too decent a person to do this job. Too good at the analysis to actually make a clear judgement.'

Roland Campbell had been elected the previous year with a very narrow majority. Barnes liked him: clearly hardworking, effective communicator, genuine if intense, asked the right questions, bit of a hinterland. But he was seen in Whitehall as an inconsequential lightweight and in Westminster as dangerously naive.

Barnes nodded sympathetically. 'I guess he sees too many shades of grey in a world that wants it all to be black and white. He'd probably make a decent diplomat. Give him my solidarity.' *Tell him I still exist.* 'And you? Relishing it all?'

'It's bonkers, but I wouldn't swap it for being back running a ministry. The adrenalin counts for more as you get older. It's just… changing so fast. I genuinely thought I was the one breaking glass ceilings. And Kenya?'

He remembered how hard it was to pin her down before she deflected it back. 'Likewise.'

'I'm sorry about your BG. That must be tough. I lost one in Basra. Have never really forgiven myself.'

They let it hang between them. Barnes felt suddenly unsure of his bearings, trying not to betray his fear. Straight to the point, or consolidate first? He watched her narrow her eyes as she observed him.

Shoulders back. 'You must be flat out. I don't want to take too much of your time.'

She didn't seem hurried. 'You know how it is. The US and Russia are escalating again. And the Home Office are worried about a series of murders. An airline exec, talk show host, hedge funder. No obvious link beyond the fact that most are wealthy, many are party donors, and none are particularly pleasant. Most had some sort of security. All seem to have been killed pretty swiftly and efficiently. Nothing taken, no clear motive.'

'I've seen the media. You think they're linked somehow?'

'No obvious evidence. And it's only just starting to get media attention. But that's what the Home Office and Thames House think might link them: no obvious evidence. No note, no claim, nothing ever stolen. And they've all been killed by professionals. We may have a highly trained serial killer with a taste for killing rich, influential men. That's what they like to accuse me of.'

Barnes held her eye. He'd seen some of the press coverage. 'And these rich men, aren't they all in some way associated with climate change?'

A slight sigh of exasperation. She hadn't asked him to play detective again. 'I guess so. Some more tangentially than others.'

'So your vigilante has a cause, the skills, and – if I'm right – no shortage of targets.'

Hermione Buckingham had known Barnes long enough to notice when he was holding something back.

'Here we go again. You have a theory?'

Barnes lied. 'Not really. But I do think we are danger-ously off-track on climate.'

Hermione sighed. 'Don't we all? The PM is determ-ined to get some decent outcomes at the Jordan confer-ence: he ran on climate, but he's getting trashed in the polls for inaction. We all know how much this summit matters. We always say it is the last chance, but this time all the analysis backs that up. The challenge is that it's polit-ically harder to get enough done here. Our main rival on the right, Sebastian Keys, is seeing to that. We're neutered at home. And so we lack the credibility to ask India, China and Brazil to do more. And the whole international system is overloaded. Can't function, let alone save the world. We're screwed unless we can change the script for Jordan. But we're all too distracted, too tactical. Hang on, don't put me off the scent. What's your theory on the murders?'

Barnes was trying to process his theory, and was not ready to give it any oxygen. 'This is the problem: we're always drawn to the tactical, the immediate. But the Nairobi meetings are almost criminally negligent. And I'm meeting real people whose lives are being shattered as a result. Look at the areas getting hotter. Millions will be uprooted, divided, on the move. And they're coming your way. I was looking again at the statues around here that we should tear down. But our grandchildren will be ripping down our statues.'

He heard Stephanie's voice in his words and steadied himself. Channel Stephanie – don't become shrill.

Hermione noticed him recalibrate. 'But you know our politics can't cope with another wave of migration. The far right will slaughter us. Sebastian Keys is just waiting for his moment to get the debate back onto security, the boat crossings, Britain is overwhelmed. The *Daily Mail* write about nothing else. Stoke up that sense of malaise and failure, with the scapegoats lined up.'

Barnes shook his head. 'Of course he is. So will people who think like him in every country. But you don't have a choice: this is going to happen.'

They sat in silence for a few moments. Too many years now as diplomats to ever have a real argument. They could always see the other's point.

Hermione turned an earring in her fingers as she appraised him. She knew she still had it. 'So what do you suggest?'

'Offence and defence. I'm already the rep to the UN climate organisation in Nairobi. Make me your full climate envoy, and get me to work on the Jordan deal. And meanwhile, you get better at neutralising Keys. Play the man, not just the ball.'

'Neutralise? We would love to do that. But there's nothing on him. And he has a powerful voice in the party, especially in the constituency associations. That's why he's able to water down or drown every initiative the Boss tries to take on climate. Makes it all about fracking. Calls us tofu-eating wind farmers.'

Barnes looked around, pensive. The clock was ticking on the mantelpiece. 'Maybe I can help. Give me the space to do this Somaliland stuff. It won't cost the Boss much. And then let me have a crack at this climate deal.'

Hermione was irritated now. She sat forward. Her face was stern, slightly flushed. 'Okay, well while you find more ways to distract me from my day job, let's get the bollocking done. You know you had no right to charge into those hostage negotiations. If they hadn't worked out, we'd have hung you out to dry. You're already seen in the media as a complete liability. Too much recklessness, again. You're lucky to be alive. This job is not an ego trip, you surely know that by now.'

Barnes nodded, suitably sombre. He needed to show her he felt slightly chastened, so that she could report that she had done it. He probably did feel slightly chastened. And she was probably enjoying that. But he knew her heart wasn't really in this.

Hermione continued, softening slightly. 'But look — the PM is genuinely grateful that you got the Brits out. All the intel we picked up on the Somalilanders suggested they would go down in flames, and take as many of you with them as they could. Despite ourselves, none of us can quite work out how you pulled it off. No medals, but...'

Barnes refused the bait. 'The usual, I guess. A bit of tradecraft and a lot of luck. Plus some promises, which we now have to see through.'

'Here we go again. Surely those fell away when Hussein lost?'

Barnes winced. He thought of Stephanie. He leant forward: serious, intense. Where was she now? Hermione felt him change.

'No, Hermione, they did not. Look, I'm not asking for the moon. You and I both know that Somaliland would *already* be independent if we had the time and energy to work on it. If you didn't change Africa ministers every few months. Why shouldn't they have their freedom? And the big democracies need to start standing up for democrats again. All I need is some action at the UN in support of the mediation process, a bit of US attention, and something public from the PM. An invite to Jordan. None of that needs to bother you. Our word used to mean something in diplomacy.'

She glanced at her watch. 'I'm not sure the world agrees. And you know he can't be seen to be responding to terrorism. We don't do that.'

'Come on, Hermione, save that for the media. The IRA? Al Qaida? Islamic State? Gadhafi? We have always responded to terrorism. We've just used different tools for different situations. Sometimes force. Sometimes concessions. Usually both. The Americans and Kenyans will be hitting these guys hard, so we have some space for negotiations. I can handle it all if you help me with these three things. Give me some capital, some means of building trust.'

Hermione grinned mischievously, trying to lower the temperature again. 'So let me get this right. You're planning to simultaneously save the planet and bring peace to East Africa? Shouldn't *you* maybe prioritise?'

But Barnes refused to respond to the gentle teasing. 'I don't have time. We don't have time. What's stopping you?'

Hermione sighed. Bloody Ed Barnes. Stubborn and self-righteous as ever. And less fun today. 'You want the truth, Ed? I've told you. Keys is. We can't be seen to be making international concessions, negotiating, listening to our opponents at a time when he is calling for tougher, more belligerent foreign policy. We can't always look feeble. The public wants clear answers in a world that is not clear. It's crippling Roland. As long as Keys is there, we need to be just as tough.'

Barnes sighed. 'But you know that's not how diplomacy works.'

'And you know it *is* how politics works. I'll think about the climate gig, and I'll talk to the PM. But forget the climate summit invitation: the US won't let that happen. And seriously, Ed, don't get too messianic with all of us again. It's just… exhausting. The world's not black and white. We really are trying our best.'

She smoothed down the front of her dress, annoyed that he didn't notice. Meeting over. They rose and walked back down the stairs. Some small talk about partners, kids, holiday plans.

She hugged him again at the door. She seemed deflated for a moment.

A look of solidarity and genuine concern. 'Stay safe, Ed.'

He caught her eye and looked away. 'You too.'

Barnes had arrived feeling an excitement at the proximity to power. He left frustrated, feeling the lack of it. Diplomacy was easier when you were a country on the up.

He didn't have time to go at their pace. Sometimes it was not enough to do your best.

But he also left with a nagging instinct that Max Crawford had already decided that. It was time to find out. He dialled the No 10 switchboard again. 'Get me the regiment at Hereford.'

28

Go Low

Barnes took the overnight British Airways flight back to Nairobi. The Foreign Office had stopped flying its ambassadors in business class towards the end of the twentieth century. Other ambassadors chuckled a bit at the fall in Britain's opinion of itself, and there was usually surprise from the other passengers when an Excellency settled down between them, but he had long stopped resenting it. He had stolen a few hours of sleep between the bustle, loud crisp munching, quiet flatulence and other people's toilet breaks. But even those few hours had been restless. Thoughts of Stephanie as a child. Stephanie as an adult. Stephanie as a captive.

Yet, as they landed his mind was clear. The Somalilanders had their leverage with him and they knew it. The path to her freedom started with delivering two things that were tough but maybe not impossible: the Kenyan mediation and No 10's support for it. Both required him to do something different, to change the game.

He watched the sun rise as they approached Nairobi. Huge, orange, and pulsating with promise, hope and danger.

At Heathrow he was one traveller among many, part of the throng. He had his systems for moving as fast as possible through the crowd. But as soon as he got off the plane in Nairobi, he was the high commissioner again. He ran a hand through his hair and brushed down the front of his jacket and shirt. A BG met him at the door of the plane. The nod. No mention of Raul: it would not help either of them. They were taken swiftly through the diplomatic channel and into the cars.

No wait for baggage: he was travelling light. 'You always do,' as his ex-wife Emma had always said. She didn't mean the luggage.

Most of the time, she was right. Not today.

As the three cars moved away from the airport, they switched positions, standard procedure for the BGs. They hated the airport run: too predictable, too few options, too much danger of getting stuck in traffic, too big a target. They weaved the cars expertly through the morning rush hour traffic. The city was bustling with street children, pedestrians, cyclists, energy.

Barnes called Penny. She was brisk, focused. The staff would all be a bit more attentive, a bit more nervous since the hostage crisis. They would sense that they were at the centre of something significant. Good.

'Put in a formal request for a meeting with Obwocha. I need briefings from Aiza and Lucy first.' He paused. 'Separate.'

Intelligence, and the aid budget: stick and carrot. And whatever he said about the need to fuse the different elements of the team, there were times when he didn't need the right and left hand to know too much about what the other was doing.

Barnes texted Obwocha. The more formal request would take days, maybe weeks. It would be faxed to State House where it would decay on the desk of a functionary. Obwocha was a twenty-first-century auto-crat: he preferred to exercise his power by WhatsApp.

> Mr President, thank you again for your wisdom and restraint over the hostage crisis, and my condolences for your losses.

Straight back, even the ironic epithets gone.

> What is it you want now?

Barnes didn't mind. The protocol and platitudes would only get in the way.

> Can we meet, Mr President?

Straight back.

> Wait in line. I'm not giving the Somali terrorists another inch, whatever your games, or the instructions from our former masters.

> I've just been in London. No 10. I have vital messages from the PM for you, personally. I need to update you.

A pause this time. The bait settled. President Obwocha had long grumbled about neglect by London. Barnes had too, arguing unsuccessfully with the Foreign Office to get the president more than an occasional half hour with the foreign secretary, let alone time with the PM. That photo by the black door, or at least the prospect of it, fuelled so much British diplomacy. Upcoming leaders showing they were seen as a prospect; new leaders keen to show they had arrived; leaders in their stride showing that they commanded respect; and leaders on the way down trying to prolong the descent. Obwocha had been seen as too risky.

Barnes knew how little of substance actually took place in the meetings themselves. But he also knew that wasn't why they mattered. The French were better at the pageantry.

He could feel the resentment in Obwocha's message, but also the neediness. *OK, come after lunch.*

The imprecision was deliberate. It allowed Obwocha to change his mind. 'After lunch' could mean a long time after lunch. Maybe not even today.

Barnes instructed the BG to take him home first, to freshen up. Mostly he wanted to see Max Crawford if he was around, get an update, make a plan. At the residence he jumped down from the vehicle, showered, changed and went out onto the terrace. The chirping of the crickets had started, and there was a ponderous heat in the air. He asked Samson for eggs and lots of coffee. Strong. Was the guest still here? Good.

He didn't have to wait long. Crawford planted himself opposite him at the table.

Straight to it. 'Anything on Steph yet, Max?'

Crawford looked slightly crestfallen. He hated not delivering. 'I'm afraid not, Ambassador. I'm not getting anything from my Kenyan friends. You need to make sure your guys aren't stomping around: the Somalilanders will see that coming a mile off. I could head over there, try to pick stuff up, but it is still too high-risk.'

Barnes raised an eyebrow. 'Getting more risk-averse in your old age, Max?'

Crawford sighed. 'Not to me. To Stephanie.'

Barnes felt his stomach lurch. 'Being a father doesn't get any easier just because they reach the point where you can't demonstrate how much you care.'

Crawford nodded. 'And yet that's when it matters most.' They sat in silence for a moment. Crawford leant across the table. 'Ed, she knows how much you care.'

Barnes had never heard Crawford use his first name before. He felt the emotion well up. He steadied himself and nodded. 'In any case, I may need you more for something else. In London. But first, I need answers.'

Crawford shifted uncomfortably in his seat and then straightened himself. He took a forkful of egg and chewed it slowly. Barnes watched him buy time, refusing to look away.

It was Crawford who broke the silence. 'Does it really help you to have this conversation, Ambassador?'

Barnes sniffed. 'Probably not, but we're past that point.'

'But why make this all more complicated than it needs to be?'

Barnes placed both hands on the table. Once he had heard, he would not be able to unhear it. But he was pretty sure he was already beyond that point.

'Max, I called Hereford. Told them I had a message for your parents, wanted to thank them for you saving me in

Copenhagen, and to pass on my condolences for your... death. They told me about the fire. I'm sorry.'

For just a moment, and for the only time, Barnes felt Max Crawford shrink.

'Is that why, Max? Keeping busy, you said. You're the one taking these guys out in the US and UK? No 10 are up the walls. No leads. A professional. I can't believe it took me so long to connect the dots.'

Silence for a few minutes. Barnes resisted the urge to deal with the awkwardness by moving on.

Crawford sighed. 'I'm telling you: it won't help you or Stephanie to waste energy on this.'

Barnes felt his anger rise. 'So you're a mercenary now, but whose mercenary? Your own? I think we both know what that is called.'

Crawford was riled too. 'It's not that. I'm killing to save the planet.'

'And to avenge your mother? What the hell, Max? You're playing God? Choosing who to kill?'

'I'm not playing, Ambassador.'

Barnes shook his head, eyes blazing. 'What gives you the right to do this?'

Crawford clenched his fists. 'What gives me the right not to?'

Barnes felt his intensity. He retreated. 'Okay then, let's make this a hypothetical discussion. Hypothetically, who decides who dies?'

Crawford hesitated, then shrugged. What was the point of holding out? 'They do, through their actions. Truth is, some bad people just need killing. We call it hard power.'

Barnes was trying to process the confession. 'What motivates you? Just your parents?'

'Hypothetically? I'm also doing it for my kids, and their kids. Sometimes violence is necessary to move forward. What about von Stauffenberg? Was he wrong to try to kill Hitler? Was it not better to try? The other side are too strong, too organised to defeat using the normal tools. It's too urgent.'

Barnes was exasperated. 'Now you're sounding like the Somalilanders. It's not a conspiracy.'

'Then maybe they're right. It normally *is* a conspiracy. And sometimes to beat a conspiracy you have to become a conspiracy.'

Barnes felt his anger growing. 'Max, I know more than anyone how frustrating all this is. The incremental change, the evolution of policy, the endless meetings and conferences and summits and talk. But we're getting somewhere, slowly. We're trying. And we don't have a better idea.'

'Maybe we do.'

'We?'

Crawford was silent again.

Barnes waited a moment. 'Max, I know you've never been one to play by the book. God knows I've needed that. But surely there has to be a moral dimension to this. Otherwise it's just… murder. What happened to "when they go low we go high"?'

A shrug. 'That doesn't seem to be working so well. I'm going low for a while.'

'And what happened to the rule of law? Patriotism? Ethics?'

'Influence everything, own nothing. I'm already a dead man. And I'll make my own judgement on all of those. What use is the rule of law or patriotism on a burnt planet? Where are the ethics in sacrificing generations to come because we couldn't get our shit together?'

Barnes raised his eyebrows. This was a new Crawford. Something had changed in him.

'Who would have thought it: the SAS protecting us from climate change?'

Crawford was gruff again. 'Who else will do it?'

They sat again in silence as the coffee pot was refilled. Barnes had got rid of the white gloves.

'Why shouldn't I turn you in, Max? Stop all this, for your sake. Put it down to trauma, PTSD.'

Crawford drained his coffee. 'You won't.'

'But when will you stop?'

'Soon enough. The killing is the easy part. Preparing for it… that is harder. And living with it after that is the hardest. That's why most people can't do it. Good. Every time that you kill, you lose part of yourself. I want to stop while there is something of me left. But for now, I feel the ends justify my means.'

Barnes sighed. How had he become so immune to shocks? Was he also suffering from some kind of moral PTSD after Paris? 'I don't buy it, Max. But for now we have to focus on what's urgent. I need to get Obwocha to kick off this mediation, and to take it seriously.'

Crawford looked brighter again, less burdened. 'And me?'

'London. If I can help No 10 with their politics, we can get them behind us. We need them on the Kenyan track. If this is really how you work, I need you to help deliver something that will make life easier for them.'

Crawford looked curious. 'And what if I walk away, Ambassador?'

'You won't. And if we square No 10, I get the climate envoy role for the Jordan summit. Maybe I can show you that my way works after all. We might be fighting the same fight.'

Max Crawford leant forward, alert. 'When was I ever not fighting the same fight as you, Ambassador.'

29

Win/Win

The convoy turned into the gates of State House. After the potholes of Nairobi, the road was smooth, freshly creosoted. Barnes felt the vehicle unclench. Like his predecessors, the president only drove on smooth roads. Barnes was ushered into the main waiting room and served tea – sweet with mint – while he waited. Through the window he could see a small army of gardeners. Sprinklers throbbed quietly. The lawn was lush green.

Ten minutes' wait. Standard. Conscious of the scrutiny of Obwocha's chief of protocol, Barnes did not look at his watch. He leafed through the Kenyan press on the table: more climate-driven clashes, funerals in the aftermath of the hostage crisis, another corruption scandal, pages of commentary on the prospects of Obwocha securing a second term. An opponent facing a corruption trial. Barnes wondered again whether to tell Hermione about Max Crawford, or someone, anyone. Was he, Barnes, now himself somehow an accessory?

But not yet: he needed Max too much right now.

The protocol chief ducked out, and returned smiling. Surely the most tedious of all diplomatic jobs. Endless small talk. Dealing with all the monstrous egos, quick to take offence. Being treated like a lackey. The gossip and the intrigue. The constant effort to blend into the background. Always tidying up the mess of human interaction. 'The president is ready for you now, High Commissioner.'

Barnes tightened his tie, buttoned up his jacket, tugged at his cufflinks and – carefully unrushed, pausing to pretend to look at a photo on the wall – followed him into Obwocha's study. There were photos with world leaders, including US President Elizabeth Hoon. The furniture was dark, masculine, well made. Photos of the president on campaign: massive rallies, long convoys of Pajeros, supporters in blue, a blue baseball cap. He always looked happiest on campaign. Governing was less fun.

'Mr High Commissioner, our new hero and saviour, welcome!'

Barnes ignored the sarcasm. Obwocha opened his arms as though offering an embrace, but as the gap between them closed it became an awkward fist bump. He gestured to a low chair and planted himself in a much larger one, looking down at Barnes.

Barnes wondered if the president hated any other envoys as much as he evidently despised Barnes. 'Thank you for seeing me, Mr President. I know how busy you are.'

Obwocha rolled his eyes and gestured for him to get to the point.

Barnes again let it go. 'I'm sorry that we couldn't get everyone out. And I appreciate the professionalism of your men. Your special forces saved my life. You have our full support: the PM has personally sent you his thanks and condolences, and is looking forward to speaking soon.'

'That it? You got all but one of yours out, HC.'

Barnes nodded gravely. 'President Obwocha, we've known each other since I first came to Nanyuki to see you. Forty years ago?'

A hint of a thaw. Obwocha rose and beckoned Barnes to follow him into the garden. The gardeners scattered. 'You've aged better than I have, Ed. Less *nyama choma* and *ugali*.' A trademark guffaw. Barnes grinned, despite himself.

'Perhaps I eat less well, Mr President.'

Obwocha paused by a bush of abundant red roses, mellowed by nostalgia. 'I remember you bumping along the roads in that Land Rover of yours. We were more idealistic in those days, remember? Before we had convoys. We sat up late talking about democracy. What I could do for my people. We wanted to save everyone. Sometimes with you I even believed that was why I was in politics.'

Barnes smiled, indulging him, rebuilding trust. He pretended to admire the roses. Obwocha had long stopped being a democrat, and long stopped caring who knew it. 'You haven't done so badly, Mr President.'

Obwocha clicked his fingers above his head, and a flunky shot across the lawn with two glasses of iced tea. Obwocha didn't break stride as he downed his own drink. 'I've helped my people. Not everyone. But time is too short. Speaking of which, HC, I am hoping that you have more than that from No 10? Do we have a bit more of their attention, or are you here to reminisce?' He threw the glass into the bushes.

Barnes sipped his drink, relishing the moment. He knew he was winging it now. 'Yes. An invitation. To visit. The works. Six months *before* your next elections. It doesn't get much better.'

Obwocha nodded approvingly, not hiding his satisfaction. 'It does, for the US president. But I'll take it. In return for the talks, of course? You know they'll cost me much more. I'll look weak. The Kenyans want maximum strength from their leaders in the face of the terrorist threat, not compromise. Just like your people do.'

'That's why we don't leave these decisions to the people, Mr President. Democracy has its limits.'

Obwocha chuckled. 'You're beginning to sound like a dictator too, Ed. I thought you normally gave speeches and interviews saying that I needed to *share* more power, consult more.' So he *had* read them. And then he was fierce again. 'I'll need more. What happened to all those development projects you promised in Nanyuki, forty years ago? We're still waiting. The people are impatient.'

Barnes shook his head. Lucy had not given him much to work with. 'You seem to have directed plenty of state resources their way. No, the aid budget can't be part of this. I've explained that. We don't use it politically. We can't.'

Obwocha whistled through his teeth. 'You're the only ones who think like that. Do you reckon the Chinese ambassador has any hesitation in connecting these big infrastructure projects to Chinese debt? To the cobalt they need for their phones? Of course not. Let alone the Russians, even the French know where to focus their money. *Everything* is connected. The Brits used to get that.'

Barnes shrugged. 'Not our style now. The PM is clear.'

Obwocha turned to bar his way down the garden. He was wheezing slightly from the effort. 'So, what else do you have for me then?'

Barnes had been briefed thoroughly by Aiza. He drew breath, savouring the attention.

Carrot swallowed, now for the stick.

'I'm glad that we are away from your officials. This is just for you, sir. The clashes before the last election. People driven from their homes. Let's be in no doubt. The evidence of your role is increasingly clear. The Americans will have it too.'

Obwocha's eyes narrowed, and he clenched a fist in his hand. 'Lies and slander from my opponents. Nothing has been proved.'

Barnes did not flinch. 'You know we could. I've visited those areas. I know which MPs were most involved. And there are many in London who think we *should* be tougher, even if it creates further chaos. But you're here now. And we also have a greater interest in the fighting not recurring. I've seen for myself how the climate crisis is also driving instability. Families displaced. Villages ransacked.'

Obwocha gave a theatrical groan. 'Violence is part of our lives. You taught us that. And so?'

'We've looked at the maps, the new constituencies. When you were the challenger, the clashes helped you. Constituencies where the ethnic balance was too close were shifted your way. Now that you're in charge, you need to stop them. Stop your opponents doing the same thing. So, on that at least, I figure we share a common interest. We'll spend money, in line with our aid criteria, where we can help reduce violence. You can redeem yourself, in the eyes of the international community, as a peacemaker not a warlord. Fewer Kenyans will die.'

Obwocha took a toothpick from his pocket, and chewed it slowly. 'A win/win, you would say?'

Barnes sensed his advantage. 'More than that, Mr President. You'll also have the international plaudits for the Somali mediation. Think of this as a sliding doors moment: choose the other way and you have a lifetime of tribunals, ostracisation, increasing unpopularity at home. Sooner or later, someone hungrier, more energetic comes along. The old lion is displaced. The new one drives him out. Survival of the fittest.'

Obwocha scowled. 'Spare me the African wildlife analogies, HC, this isn't a Disney film.' And then a broad grin. A nod. He gestured at Barnes to resume their walk.

They had reached the largest tree in the grounds, its trunk thick. The canopy offered the relief of shade. Obwocha seemed to mellow. 'You know, HC, I think I'll enjoy working with you on being a peacemaker.'

Barnes hid his relief. 'Thank you, Mr President, the PM will be appreciative.'

'And this is all really from him? It is really what *he* wants?'

Barnes didn't think of it as a lie. 'It comes from the *very* top, Mr President. I'm just the messenger.' A theatrical pause. 'When will you announce the mediation, Mr President?'

Obwocha chewed his lip for a moment, and smiled knowingly. 'I'll do it on the steps of Downing Street.'

30

Accomplice

Hermione was in the PM's outer office when the head-line flashed up on the screen. The room was bustling with adrenalin and proximity to power. She gestured at the duty clerk to turn the volume up. Breaking news: Sebastian Keys found dead at his home in Chelsea. She went straight into the PM's office, interrupting a meeting with his economic advisers.

They had started to leave before she barked the order. 'Everybody out.'

The PM looked at her, intrigued, as she closed the door. He raised his hands and shrugged. 'What's up, H?'

'It's just breaking, boss. Keys has been killed.'

Genuine shock. 'Ooof, any reason why?'

'Plenty. But nothing so far. I'll get an update from the Met. You need to be out and about, visible: we'll sort a hospital visit. No statement from you but I'll get the home sec to say something suitably grave about the investigation.'

The PM looked pained. 'This is awful. We must find who did it. I loathed the man, but we can't have this. I need to message his family.'

A brief moment of silence while they both pretended to be sad.

Hermione broke it first. 'The tone to all the reactions has to be sober, concerned: police matter, thoughts with families, not a time for politics. But this will, of course, finally lift some of the pressure, allow us to get back to your agenda again.'

The PM nodded, holding her eye. He exhaled slowly. A break after months of swimming against the tide: sometimes in politics you just had to wait for one to come along. Hermione walked to the door. 'Anything else, PM?'

He had his head cocked, processing the news. 'Yes. I've finally made that decision on commissioning the wind farms and halting the drilling rights in the North Sea. We should be bolder. Future generations will thank us. And maybe it's good politics too. Let's go ahead.'

Hermione walked out, settling her features again. The team were gathered around the screen. She opened her phone and started to pass on instructions.

A message from Ed Barnes:

> Formal note on the way but can we do that PM/Obwocha meeting sooner rather than later?

He always picked his moment. But Hermione paused. She had a sense of possibility that she had not felt for some time. The far right would assemble, pretty fast, but they would struggle to find someone with Key's reach beyond Westminster, panache and comms skills. It would be wrong, of course, to feel celebratory, but this was politics: it normally took just a few seconds to move from hearing of an opponent's setback to wondering what it meant for you. And Keys going meant that they had a major critic silenced. She glanced at Ed's message again, remembering how she had moaned to him about Keys. *Who will rid me of this turbulent priest?* Barnes probably wouldn't shed any tears for him either.

She messaged back, feeling lighter.

> Busy here. Big news day. But yes, OK, have a meeting then. And you can have the climate gig. We're feeling bolder. But that's it: no more from us. Don't screw it up. x

She wondered if the kiss looked out of place. But then the press of advisers and action was once again all around her, and she was back to the Keys response. Sober, grave, shocked.

–

In Nairobi, Barnes smiled as he picked up the message. This would be enough to get traction with Obwocha and the peace talks in place, and therefore some capital with the Somalilanders. It should surely be enough to get Stephanie out. The kiss was uncharacteristic.

He glanced at it again, curious.

And then he flicked onto the BBC news site. What was the news they were dealing with in London?

It was leading. 'Climate change–denying politician killed at his home.'

He lurched, feeling the shock in the pit of his stomach. What the hell had Max Crawford done? Barnes had wanted him to find a way to threaten Keys, to get him to tone it down a bit. Not take him out. Did this somehow now make Barnes an accomplice to murder? And how could he now conceal Crawford's identity? He cursed himself for having lost his sense of judgement. He should never have got Crawford involved in this. He should never have let himself get involved in this.

Angrily he punched a message to Crawford, for once not thinking of the risks it might be read by others.

> Max, where the hell are you? Please tell me the SK situation was nothing to do with you. This is all out of control.

A few moments.

> Of course, Ambassador. Don't worry. Nothing to do with our discussions. Purely coincidental.

Barnes breathed a sigh of relief.

> This wasn't because of our conversation about him? Me saying that he was the obstacle for No 10?

> Consider any benefit to you a bonus: he had it coming.

Barnes was less reassured now.

> What do you mean?

> It doesn't matter. You aren't connected. A happy coincidence. But more important: I've seen more old friends in London. Stephanie is now in Jordan. We need to talk to them.

Barnes put the phone on the table and steadied himself. What had he become involved in?

But what mattered most was that Stephanie was somewhere out there, in danger. He could not just pitch up in Amman. Why Jordan? The Somalilanders had no obvious links or presence there. The climate conference was a fortnight away. He wondered if it was time to tell the FCDO, get the professionals looking for her. But there was a danger they would take the climate role away just as it was given, keep him to one side. They would assume he couldn't take objective judgements while his daughter was in play.

And in any case: whether he wanted it or not, he had a professional on side. And he needed him.

Barnes texted Crawford back.

> Max: meet me in Geneva.

Orla Fitzgerald was also following the news concerning the assassination of Sebastian Keys.

She was less surprised by the death than Ed Barnes or Hermione Buckingham. Keys had been the person she had identified in Paris as now likely to be highest on the Assassin's list. He was prominent on her list of 'Enablers', a big political ally of Elizabeth Hoon, and the most outspoken and effective climate denier in the UK. Tick. Tick. Tick.

So, making sure that he remembered her from their brief meeting in Paris, she had swiftly lined herself up a meeting with Keys. The promise of a good profile piece for him too had got her in the door, and a well-chosen blouse had meant she got more time than his team had promised. More importantly, she had managed to leave her recording device behind in his office, under the leg of the sofa, just in case. If she got lucky, she might get crucial intel on the Assassin. If she was found out, she could protest that it was in error, 'a blonde moment', as she had successfully claimed when caught once in the past.

Two days without any surprises. Keys with his secretary, Keys with a young political adviser: demanding, and getting, what he wanted. Favours, gossip, sex. Keys attacking the PM, restlessly plotting with friends and allies. Keys trying to get a higher rate for his *Daily Mail* column. Keys farting and belching when he was alone in the room.

He disgusted her, but she kept listening. People seemed to give him what he wanted.

And then, with brutal efficiency, it happened. Keys alone, watching what sounded like porn on his laptop. He had spluttered with anger and embarrassment at the presence of someone else in the room. The Assassin had been terse as Keys tried to cajole, bribe, threaten him. *Why, because it needs to happen.* The brief confrontation. The sound of the neck being broken. His calling-card. For once, someone didn't give Keys what he wanted.

Then the door closing behind the Assassin. And silence.

At first, she had felt guilty, voyeuristic, ashamed. Twice she had left the house to take the recording to the police. But then returned, confused. How could she explain herself? What chance of the police not making the evidence public, in the hunt for the killer, and selling their media the detail of their source? What chance of them finding the Assassin? Keys wasn't the last of these bastards. Did she really want the Assassin stopped?

But what really held her back was that she now felt pretty certain she *knew* who had killed Sebastian Keys.

Because this time the Assassin had failed to cover his tracks as well as he had in the past.

This time, for whatever reason, he had rushed it. Failed to check the room properly.

On one level she had been stunned to hear his voice. She played it back again and again. Authoritative, firm, refusing mercy to the politician as the man begged for his life. He was meant to be dead, killed – so the plaque at Hereford said – on a training exercise. And yet it was as if she had always known that he was still out there.

And now that he was still killing.

Orla did not agonise for long. The only person she could tell was Ed Barnes. She had warned him in Paris not to trust his defence adviser. He might be relieved to know that Max Crawford was alive. But surely he would be horrified that his former friend and ally was a serial killer.

Hadn't he always been a serial killer?

Ed would at least know what to do with the information.

And Ed needed her help: Stephanie was still in danger. It was time.

She messaged him.

> We need to meet. Urgent. Anywhere.

An immediate reply. No sense of surprise. No questions.

> Geneva.

Within half an hour she had packed and was on her way.

31

Geneva

There was an air of battered decency to Prince Omar. Partly jet lag and years of the debilitating wade through undrained swamps of bureaucratic treacle. Partly bearing witness to the worst of humanity.

As a junior UN official in Bosnia, he had been profoundly marked by the sight of the skull of a child as a trophy on a warlord's car. But the weariness was also something deeper. This was a man who had watched his worldview come under relentless assault.

Omar had been a global citizen before the idea went in and then out of fashion. He was also an outsider before he became an insider. An Arab who took up rugby to survive his English private school. A Hashemite prince who struggled through military service and grew a beard to appear less European in the royal court.

And now he was seen by the Chinese, Russians and Americans as a liability. They hated his speeches. Elizabeth Hoon was guilty of 'state-sponsored child abuse'. Islamic terrorists were creating a 'harsh, mean-spirited house of blood', while the response from Arab regimes was 'trying to put a fire out with petrol'. At this rate he would be the first UN Commissioner for Human Rights not to be re-elected, something he regarded as a badge of honour.

Barnes embraced his old friend. Omar felt brittle, exhausted.

'You need a serious break, Omar.'

'That's what they keep telling me.'

'Who? The xenophobes, populists and racists?'

Omar grinned. 'To be honest it is mainly Alice.'

Alice was his British/American wife: glamorous, loyal, an activist for the rights of girls. She encouraged the air of mischief and disruption that had made Omar such a divisive and effective figure. A fellow insurgent, she was as comfortable discussing the detail of Congolese girls' education policy as being a princess or hanging out with Hollywood A-listers. In New York, they would often slip away from the diplomatic speed dating of the Four Seasons to an Irish bar, 'somewhere we won't meet anyone'. At home in Harlem, Omar swapped the diplomat's suit for hipster trainers. 'The one place his beard is fashionable,' Alice liked to say. They joked that he might set himself up there with a kebab van once his time as the world's conscience ended.

When Omar first took the job with the UN, no one expected him to become a warrior, campaigner, target, or hero. Activists were aghast that a Jordanian prince had been appointed to take on the world's elites. Was this really the right figurehead for equality and human rights? The world's powers saw a UN insider who would tread softly. His diplomatic career – ambassador to the UN in his thirties and to the US in his forties – was based on discretion, charm and tact.

'The list of places where we can holiday is getting shorter,' smiled Alice. But Barnes could see that the isolation and abuse were hurting him more deeply than he let on. 'No one takes this job to win a popularity contest.'

They looked out from his window at Lake Geneva, the fountain and the stillness of the mountains beyond.

'What's still driving you, then?' Barnes knew the answer, because it was his motivation, too.

He saw the fire burn in his friend's eyes. 'I remember flying over Weimar in 1994, the home of the German enlightenment. And then through the cloud, the remains of Buchenwald. In 1933 the Holocaust was unthinkable. Chauvinistic nationalism… the demagogues and authoritarians weaponising intolerance. If we have learned anything from history, it is that scrambling only for our own kind will scramble it all, sometimes horrifyingly so.' Barnes was always staggered at the way Omar's anger drove his eloquence.

'And what if Hoon gets back in?'

Omar groaned. 'Four more years of retreat for everything we have tried to build. They'll leave the Human Rights Council, and that will create more space for the autocrats and despots to jam it all up. Human rights violations are the sharp zigzag lines of a seismograph flashing out warnings of a coming earthquake. And they are shuddering faster and higher.'

Barnes nodded grimly in solidarity. He clocked Alice's look of concern towards her husband.

Omar pulled himself together. 'But I don't need to convince you of all this. I'm sorry to bang on as usual. It's good to see you, my friend.'

Barnes smiled. 'It's not banging on, Omar.'

'You've come in a hurry. What is it that you need, Ed?'

Barnes knew he must have been looking impatient. 'I need your help.'

Omar smiled benignly. 'Anything.'

'It's Stephanie. She's been taken hostage.' Barnes gestured at them both to skip the exclamations of horror. They didn't have time for the theatre. 'Somalilanders. Looking to get independence back on the agenda. I have to find a way to get her back.'

Omar nodded. 'We saw your latest adventure in the mall. I had thought congratulations were in order. Is this connected?'

'Yes, that's when they took her.'

Alice gasped. 'But why's that not in the news? What are the Brits doing to help?'

Barnes grimaced. 'They don't know. It's better this way. But that's why I need your help. No 10 have made me the climate envoy, so I've got a bit more freedom to travel.'

'Why congratulations, *Excellency*.' Omar faked a bow, grinning.

Barnes smiled back. 'I have a lead. Long story. But she's pitched up in Jordan. I need to find her. But without ruffling any feathers.'

Omar looked troubled. 'We must find her.' Silence.

Alice intervened. 'The problem is, Omar is not exactly popular at home right now. He's been far too outspoken, for too long, on Arab dictators. The rest of the royal family kept getting it in the neck from them. They tried to quieten him down.' A smile of complicity. 'But you know how he is.'

Omar was pensive. 'We need to get you to Jordan. But make it not about me. It should be a UN invitation. Connected to the climate conference. I'll get to them behind the scenes. My brother runs the intel there, as you know. I'm soft power, he's a bit further towards the harder end of the power spectrum.'

Barnes nodded his thanks. 'I know someone a bit like that.'

'I'll get you all I can.'

Barnes looked at the floor awkwardly. 'And while we're on the subject of invitations.'

Omar raised his eyebrows. 'Aha? There's more?'

Barnes knew he was stretching it. 'Can we get the governor of Somaliland into the Jordan summit? Some kind of observer status? Something with a bit of visibility, but in a way that won't get vetoed by the Americans and Europeans?'

Omar whistled through his teeth. 'I guess this is you not negotiating with terrorists? Okay, Ed, I'll try. But there will be some serious costs. From the Somalis themselves. And from every country with a breakaway province. Are we going to invite the Catalans? Scots?'

Omar could see the way Barnes's shoulders sagged. He could see the fear. He held up his hands in mock surrender. 'Okay, I'll find a way. But this is way off-piste.'

Alice was watching Barnes anxiously. 'But, Ed… how will you stay safe?'

Barnes sighed, pushed his shoulders back. He was not going to give up on Stephanie. And whatever vendetta Crawford was involved in, he was loyal.

'That's the one part of all this I'm not worried about.'

32

Wolf Warrior

Yang's instructions were simple: say no.

As the Chinese climate envoy, he liked to tell people that his natural habitat was airless rooms full of airy words. The airy words were mostly from his European counterparts. Each newly appointed envoy would hector and corral him across the conference table about China's industrial strategy, as if anything they said would make any difference, as if they hadn't flown in on planes or built their economies on fossil fuels, and as if he had any actual influence in Beijing.

After a few years of this he had decided to make it more fun. At first this had been about using his interventions to point out their glaring hypocrisy. The bottled water on the tables. The air miles in their accounts. Their own coal-fuelled industrial revolutions. Their fossil fuel-fuelled politics. It was too easy.

But this had become boring, too. And so he had been delighted when the invitation had come from Beijing for some envoys to become 'wolf warriors', which allowed them to use social media in more creative ways. Most had not applied: there were too many risks, too much exposure. And it was not the Chinese way to publicly criticise their host governments. It all seemed a bit undignified and risky. But as a climate envoy he had no single host bar the UN, and who cared any more about them? And besides, diplomatic life was otherwise unrelentingly boring.

Yang had gone home for the month-long training and assessment process to see if he could be trusted to use his Twitter handle in more aggressive ways. The rules were still rigid: he had to clear a list of targets and themes with Beijing; and he was not to engage with people below a certain level of influence or rank. Risks were permitted but mistakes were not. He was encouraged to study Western diplomats with high numbers of followers. What were they doing that was effective? He had thrown himself into the research with relish, eager for combat.

He quickly worked out that the answer to winning Twitter was pleasingly simple: picking arguments. The algorithms did the rest. Yang started to experiment more creatively. He would compare a tweet making a positive case with one attacking a weakness in the argument of his opponent. The first would sink like a stone, shared only by the sympathetic, official accounts that churned out platitudes. The second, however, would go viral, picked up by allies or opponents alike; reacted to; chewed over; shared; amplified. There would be howls of anger and screams of solidarity. It would cut through and take on a life of its own.

The first few times he tried it, he felt a frisson of excitement and fear as he watched the retweets mount. The barbs against European climate envoys that he had used in the conference room now spread fast, shared by climate sceptics in their own countries. The echoes loved an echo chamber. The market for pointing out hypocrisy was huge: people in the West seemed to like to discover that they couldn't trust their representatives. Yang was swimming with the tide of distrust.

After a while, and once he had picked up a decent reputation as a tough social media adversary, he realised he had to work much harder. So he dialled up the rhetoric against prominent European climate activists, picked more fights, started to expose more hypocrisy in their capitals. To his satisfaction, and more importantly the contentment of Beijing, his tweets were widely shared by right-wing activists and climate change sceptics across the West. One US TV network regularly invited him on as 'the straight-talking Chinese diplomat sticking it to the libs'. They didn't want facts and stats, just the red meat of the arena. There were rarely questions about China's policy. After a while he was able to dictate it as a condition that there wouldn't be.

Of course, none of this was noticed much at home: only a few licensed colleagues in Beijing were on Twitter to see and celebrate his success. And even they continued to view it all with some distaste. But in Europe it was making him notorious. With climate change becoming more divisive as governments were forced to impose tougher policies, the group he had learnt to call 'the bunny huggers', had a visible face of Chinese obstruction; and 'the realists' (he preferred this to 'climate change deniers') had another spokesman. He was no longer just a protagonist in China vs the West. He was a protagonist in the West's increasingly febrile war on itself.

Of course, around the summit table, the other diplomats continued to hector and lecture him. But he turned up to the meetings less and less frequently now. That was for his deputies, the small people. He could have much more impact outside, in the louder, shoutier forum of social media, than in the room with a bunch of tedious diplomats. The conference often provided no more than the photo to accompany the line, or a short piece of recorded speech, carefully curated for social media.

Yang was at his keyboard tonight. He had ordered room service. Partly to avoid bumping into the other climate circuit diplomats at the Geneva hotel that was always full of them. Most regarded him with suspicion. Earnest Scandinavians normally thought they could somehow talk him round. Good luck with that. The new Brit, Ed Barnes, had seemed curious about him, ready to engage. But that wouldn't last long once he had experienced Yang saying no a few more times. They would soon lapse into sullen antipathy. He pushed the plate of inedible Western hotel food to one side, barely touched, and returned to the more comfortable world of Twitter.

Topically, tonight's Twitter target was the UK and its new, more idealistic prime minister, who had spoken on campaign of the need to stand up to China on climate. The words would not have reached the Chinese public behind the walls that Beijing built to keep the internet out: they knew its dangers. But his leadership knew that they had been disrespected, and they wanted to see a response. Yang looked through the accounts of Campbell's critics. One journalist had written a piece suggesting that he had taken campaign finance from an airline exec. Yang retweeted it approvingly. The Western public also loved a bit of hypocrisy.

He then turned to the activists. He checked a few of the more prominent accounts. One NGO had dialled up the criticism of China's human rights record. He lingered for a moment, but this was not his argument. Stay on-piste.

There was no gain in drawing fire in areas where he had less to return. He searched on. An academic had written a new study showing that only by changing Chinese policy could global warming be kept at below three degrees. It had got some traction among the intelligentsia, but not enough to justify a slap-down. Why draw further attention to it?

Instead, Yang focused on an actress who had given a long interview on climate change. Very little mention of China, but that wasn't the issue. She was the star of a film set in a dystopian climate future. The usual cloying conclusions and self-righteous posturing. Climate was a subject that only the rich could spend time worrying about. There were some in Beijing who were claiming that a deal in Jordan was in their interests: Yang was determined that this view be dismissed.

Yang searched for photos of her. It didn't take long: an Instagram post of her on board a private jet. He copied it into a tweet and added: 'I wonder why Lucy Keeling didn't mention climate until she had a film to promote?'

His rule was always to wait a few moments before pressing send. A tweet could be halfway round the world while the truth was still putting its boots on. He paused, running through a mental checklist of those who might object to it. None included Beijing. He pressed send.

Yang thought he heard a sound from the bathroom but dismissed it. He clicked on the tweet so that he could watch it go viral, the numbers of retweets and likes beneath it spinning like the dials on a slot machine. It was exhilarating. The first few shares were from climate activists: perfect.

'Unbelievable that a Chinese government envoy has the hypocrisy to criticise Lucy.'

'Beijing should watch this film, not pick on an actress with the courage to speak her truth.'

These quickly triggered the ripostes. A prominent talk show host: 'Let's be honest. Pampered Princess Keeling needs to drop the private jet if she wants to be heard. Shame it took a Chinese diplomat to tell us that.'

Back and forth it went, but all the time the photo was being shared. Yang wondered at what point the actress would get a call from her publicist.

You're trending, Lucy. *Great*. Um, not really so great.

He grinned. This was too easy. The problem with democracies was that they gave their opponents the means to destroy them.

Yang first saw the man's outline in the reflection on his screen, and lurched round. He was wearing all black. A thief. His arms and torso were strong.

Yang felt strangely calm. 'What do you want?'

The man said nothing. He didn't look like a thief.

'The safe is over there in the corner of the wardrobe. I can give you the code, but there is little of value. Take it and go.'

The man shook his head. He casually picked a pillow from Yang's bed and walked towards him. Yang stood quickly, eyes darting towards the door. He knew that there was a fire alarm.

His voice was higher-pitched now. The man looked determined. Another try at deflection.

'Please, tell me what you want?'

And then more desperate, the voice almost a squeal. 'I have diplomatic protection here.' Still no reply.

The last thing Yang saw was the pillow that enveloped his face. He struggled ineffectively against the man's grip, screaming silently into the pillow as he gasped for air. After a minute the struggling stopped, and he slumped lifeless to the floor.

His assassin looked briefly around the hotel room, checked that Yang's pulse was dead, tossed the pillow back onto the bed and walked out.

33

Hard Power

The next morning, Ed Barnes was finishing his breakfast at his Geneva hotel when Max Crawford walked in. Max looked fresh, like a man who didn't lose much sleep. Barnes nodded towards the buffet. Crawford took a detour. A few minutes later he was siting opposite Barnes with a huge plate of fresh scrambled eggs, a bowl of figs and a large pot of coffee.

Barnes nodded approvingly at the eggs. 'You got those made fresh?'

Crawford nodded. 'Too many nights sleeping on rocks to put up with eggs from a buffet.'

Barnes grinned. 'Thanks for coming, Max. I've been pursuing the Jordan lead. I know their UN envoy, Omar. I saw him yesterday. He can get me an invite to Amman, from the UN. Maybe even one to the summit for the Somaliland governor. I'll do some climate business, all part of the preparation for the summit. Maybe he can also get us some info on where Stephanie is. I trust him. I want to get there as quickly as possible. Can you come?'

Crawford had an expectant look. 'Can't think of anywhere else I need to be. But what's your plan?'

'Omar's brother is the intel chief. Omar got the suave internationalism and the conscience; he got the muscle.'

Crawford had swiftly finished the eggs. As he laid down his cutlery, he said, 'Sounds like you and me. And why do you think she's in Jordan then?'

'No idea. I'm worried that the Somalis might have sold her on. Her value to them was limited, and they got what they wanted. She would be worth much more to some other part of AQ.'

Crawford looked up from the figs. 'So why not get London on it? My former colleagues. Get some serious resource.'

'Seriously? You of all people need to ask me that? Too much noise. We don't know who we can trust. And they can't know we're coming.' Crawford nodded grimly. 'But, Max, first can you promise me you weren't the one who killed Sebastian Keys? All I wanted was that he could be taken down a peg, give No 10 a bit of space. Not something this… final.'

Crawford winced, glanced around the room and leant forward. 'After the nuclear leaks in Fukushima, two hundred Japanese pensioners volunteered to face the radiation instead of the young. They reckoned the cancer could take thirty years to develop, meaning they didn't need to worry about it. The old boy who organised them said their decision was not brave, but logical. The question is whether you step forward, or you stay behind and watch. So… what's your real mission, Ambassador?'

It seemed like a confession to Barnes. 'We call them objectives in diplomacy, Max. To get Stephanie back of course.'

Crawford nodded. 'Of course. That's my mission too. But beyond that? This climate gig? What do you want to do with it, really?'

Barnes paused. He thought of the Kenyan village, smouldering as the temperature rises drove the conflict for water into previously peaceful areas. The millions who would be displaced in the future by climate change. The conflicts coming their way. Lives ruined. The apathy and inertia of Western governments.

'The Nobel Peace Prizes of the future will be for people who reduce the threat of climate conflict. That's something to get out of bed for.'

'And that's really it, Ambassador? A Nobel Peace Prize?' Crawford was quiet, looking down at his figs.

Barnes was riled. 'Of course not. I'm just saying that all the work in my world will soon be about climate in some way. Maybe I can do something, maybe use the skills I have. This climate envoy job is a chance to make a genuine difference. No more pontificating about it all, glad-handing and hosting receptions. Real impact at last.'

Stephanie's voice again. Weren't kids supposed to resemble their parents as they got older, not the other way around?

Crawford still looked sceptical. 'And you really think diplomacy can somehow do this?'

Barnes shrugged. 'What else do we have?' They sat in silence for a moment. 'And Max, you still didn't answer my question. What about Sebastian Keys? What did you mean on the phone by "*a coincidence*"?'

Crawford stared back at him. Barnes saw a resolve in the other man's expression that hadn't been there before. A sense of purpose.

'I don't need to answer it. You don't want me to answer it.'

Barnes sighed. 'But seriously, this is out of line. It can't go on. I can't let you carry on. What the hell is it really about?'

Crawford was steely. 'You said it: the planet.'

Barnes couldn't hide the exasperation. 'But how does any of this really help? How can you possibly justify...'

'Like you also said: maybe I'm just trying to use the skills I have. The key point is that we are working for the same thing. You know that. And think of all the deaths in history. And all those that will be caused by the climate crisis. Think of the horror of being burnt alive in a forest fire. These deaths are nothing in comparison. They are easy deaths to take.'

Barnes shook his head. 'And easy to carry out?'

Crawford shrugged. 'Practically, of course. But no... not easy to carry.'

'And how have you been selecting your—'

'Targets.'

'—victims?'

'Careful research. Thought through carefully. These aren't innocent bystanders. Precision strikes.'

Barnes felt his anger rise again. Who was Crawford working with? 'Thought through by you?'

Crawford drained his coffee. 'If it's any consolation, Ambassador, and purely hypothetically, Sebastian Keys was already pretty high on the list. You just... bumped him up.'

Barnes stared back at him. Who was Max working with? Why did he not feel more disgust? He could end all this today. Turn his old friend in. Surely that was the only path. But what then about Stephanie? And was he ready to answer the questions they would ask?

'This can't continue. No more surprises?'

Crawford grinned, and chewed on a fig. 'Only good ones, Ambassador.'

Barnes saw Alice from across the breakfast room, before she saw them. He beckoned her over.

She appeared uncharacteristically flustered. 'Ed, I've been looking for you. Omar has sorted your official invite to Jordan. You can go today, whenever you're ready. Some token meetings set up as cover. But meanwhile everything is kicking off here…' She stopped herself, looking suspiciously at Crawford.

'Sorry, Alice, you haven't been introduced. This is an old friend.'

Max smiled but didn't offer his name. 'The ambassador and I share the same mission.'

Alice looked curious. 'You're also in diplomacy? You don't look…'

'Not exactly. I'm a blunter instrument. But we're all working for the same outcomes.'

Alice nodded. It was enough to place him: a spook or military advice type. Plenty of them on the conflict prevention circuit around Geneva. They knew how to stop one because they knew how to start one. She turned back to Barnes.

'Omar has had to go to the UN building. The Chinese are furious. They're blaming the US, threatening to bring down the climate talks, maybe leave the UN altogether. It's all escalating fast. And he's… he's so… exhausted.'

Barnes was confused. 'Wait, what are you talking about?'

She looked stunned. 'You haven't heard? The Chinese envoy was assassinated late last night. In his hotel room across the square. It broke publicly about twenty minutes ago.'

'Yang? The wolf warrior? I was only with him yesterday afternoon. My God.'

Barnes glanced at Crawford. *Surely not.* He was examining the last of the coffee granules in the cafetiere, deciding whether to get another. The slightest shake of his head.

Alice continued, flustered. 'Yes, but none of that matters now. What matters is to find the killer, fast. Before the Chinese make public accusations that they cannot walk back from. And before Hoon and the US start firing off responses. Let's hope it's a freak coincidence and nothing more. Can you help?'

Crawford was now wiping a piece of bread around his plate, hoovering up every last piece of egg. 'You really think these climate talks can make a difference, Ambassador?'

Barnes shrugged. 'They're the only ones we have.' And they seemed to be the only way to get Stephanie back.

Crawford shrugged. 'Then I guess saving them is part of the mission.'

34

Statecraft and Streetcraft

Barnes waited with Alice outside Omar's office, watched closely by his secretary. After a few moments they stopped pretending they couldn't hear the phone call through the door. In any case Omar wasn't saying much, trying calmly to placate the person on the other end. Alice listened pensively.

'We are looking into it urgently... of course you have all of our condolences... no, I don't have any further information at this point... yes, I will speak to my American colleagues, but they say they are in the dark... no, I really don't think those kind of accusations will help us. We all need to take a moment – calmly – to establish the facts.'

Eventually it was clear that the call had been terminated. Alice strode to the door without waiting to be gestured in. Omar was sat behind a large desk covered in papers. He had his head in his hands, but smiled briefly when he saw them enter.

There was despair in his voice. 'This will blow it all up. All that careful, cautious confidence building. Years of behind-the-scenes work to develop some trust, some sense that we could find a way to a deal. Of course, Yang was no great ally. But he was all we had, and there were moments when I think we were genuinely getting through to him. I used to hold a monthly trilateral with him and the US ambo too, finding ways to help them see common interests. Or at least to put the pin back in some potential grenades.'

Barnes looked grim. 'And now the Chinese are blaming the Americans for this assassination. Do you think they actually believe that?'

Omar shrugged. 'It doesn't matter what they really believe. The rhetoric will dial up. The US will defend themselves. Hoon will wake up and start tweeting. They'll all say things that they can't take back. And we will be starting afresh with a new Chinese envoy, with his instructions to be even tougher than Yang. Months, years lost. Summit a write-off.'

Alice was standing by the window. 'So, who had a motive to kill him?'

Barnes joined her, looking out over Lake Geneva. In normal moments it took your breath away. Today, he didn't see the beauty. He wasn't getting closer to finding Stephanie.

'The starting point has to be why he was killed. And this matters to me.' Barnes paused, thinking of Crawford demolishing his plate of eggs. Was Max lying to him? Would he really take on China? He ignored Omar's quizzical look. 'Omar, are you saying that the main impact will be to make climate talks harder rather than easier? So that it is *less* likely he was killed by some kind of renegade climate activist?'

Omar nodded. 'Yes, if they knew anything at all about the process, the negotiations. The NGOs hated him, but they're hardly assassins. I understand that he was pretty tough online, but that's not enough of a motive, even for his enemies there. Are you saying this might have been designed to crash the negotiations? Our opponents really will sink to anything.'

Barnes nodded. He felt reassured, at least that Crawford might not have been the Assassin this time. He wondered for a moment whether to ask Omar when killing was justified, ethically. UN declarations talked about the right to kill in self-defence. Surely killing to save the planet was the ultimate act of self-defence? But he wasn't sure he was ready for Omar's answer.

Stay focused. 'Maybe. And so, assuming it wasn't a freak case, we are probably looking for someone who didn't want the talks to succeed.'

Alice turned to him, her head cocked. 'Like who?'

Omar sighed. 'Sadly, that is a pretty long list. It probably includes several UN members, including most of the big ones.'

Barnes interjected. 'And, let's be honest, there are plenty of senior figures in Beijing and Washington at the top of it. We better get started.'

Omar raised his hands in exasperation. 'Started?'

Barnes nodded. 'We need the Chinese to stay in the negotiations. We need to avoid a US/China escalation. And, whatever we all thought of him, a diplomatic colleague has been killed. You need to work the phones, keep trying to keep the temperature down, allow the Chinese some controlled explosions. I plan to find out who did it.'

Omar smiled. 'But since when have you been a detective, Ed?'

Barnes turned back at the door and grinned. 'Long story. But I've been trying to give it up.'

Alice followed him out. As they waited for the lift, Barnes felt her gaze, slowly assessing him.

When he turned to her there was mischief in her eyes. 'You're trying to give it up? You don't seem to be trying that hard, Ed.'

35

My Enemy's Enemy

Ed Barnes stood alone by Lake Geneva. Autumn was coming and the first leaves had started to fall, orange and brown. The air was crisp but not yet too cold.

Where did this leave everything?

He had to find Stephanie, and save the climate negotiations. He now also needed to know who had killed the Chinese envoy. That was surely key to rescuing the summit. The problem was that he couldn't be seen to be directly investigating. He was already straining London's patience, again. And he really needed to get to Jordan, to find Stephanie.

Who was with him? Crawford was an ally on both, in theory. He certainly wanted to help get Stephanie back, and Barnes would not doubt his loyalty again. And while he might see the negotiations as secondary to everything else he was mixed up in on climate, he clearly saw the case for trying. The Chinese envoy had reportedly been smothered with a pillow: that did not seem to be part of what Crawford was starting to call the Assassin's 'ways and means'. Either way, Barnes had to fly under the radar. He couldn't be seen charging around Geneva investigating a murder, especially one this sensitive.

Who else could he trust? Omar and Alice were allies. But Omar was going to get pushed around, submerged by diplomacy. And this was a moment when diplomacy was on the back foot. He seemed spent, frail. Alice would be tougher, and would protect Omar like a lioness. But she could not be seen to be too involved, to avoid drawing Omar into controversy.

No, he needed someone else he could rely on. It couldn't be anyone from the Foreign Office, or the High Commissionin Nairobi. He had already landed Jim and Dave in enough hassle by charging off to Geneva. And Hermione was too swept up in the daily firefighting of No 10. He would need her to protect him there.

He thought again of Orla Fitzgerald. One person who had always understood Steph. Those tentative messages during the hostage crisis. She had wanted to help, but he hadn't known what to ask. *Trust yourself*, she had messaged.

What was now on her mind? It sounded urgent from the messages. Would she really come? He wanted someone to discuss the case with, someone who cared about Stephanie. But once in, she wouldn't be able to walk away from the intrigue and the drama: she was addicted to it.

Maybe she could make sense of all this? Max Crawford had said that his targets were selected on the basis of research. Someone was doing the investigations that identified the climate criminals. He toyed with his phone, wondering whether to get her take.

Instead, as he watched the fountain across the shimmering surface of the lake, Barnes called Crawford.

'Max. Everyone wants to complicate this. We need to keep it simple. If we want to save these negotiations, we need to get the Chinese something on who killed their envoy, before they destroy any remaining trust with the Americans. If I can help the Chinese on the assassination, maybe I can get some leverage with them. And then we need to get to Jordan and give me space to find Stephanie, and to do the deal. Somehow it feels connected, like all roads are leading there.'

Max sounded alert. 'We can't be in two places at once, Ambassador. And you can't be seen in the wrong ones.'

'I know. And you can't be seen in any places at all. Not even the right ones.'

A pause. 'And so?'

'Max, I asked you a question at breakfast. And then Alice arrived. I need an answer now. The information you, um, act on. You are clearly confident about it. You're not doing all this on a hunch. Who's it coming from?'

Crawford was silent.

'Max, I know you won't like it, but I'm going to ask Orla Fitzgerald to help us.'

Crawford sighed. 'I didn't trust her in Paris. I don't trust her now. We need to move fast and lie low. She slows us – you – down. And she's a hack. How does that help? She can't know about me.'

'Stephanie trusts her. I trust her. Her instincts are good. She reads people. And we aren't exactly overwhelmed by friends right now. Anyway, she's on to something. I feel it's connected. And she's coming our way, whatever.'

'My enemy's enemy is my friend?'

'I don't know about that. But we need all the friends we can get right now.'

'Maybe, Ambassador. But first we need to find who killed the Chinese envoy.'

'I've got an idea on that.'

Max Crawford chuckled. 'Good. So have I. Let's see whether soft or hard power gets there first.'

36

The Ambassador and the Princess

Barnes and Alice arrived at the hotel through the front lobby. There was a strong police presence, and no access to the sixth floor, where Yang had been murdered. The porters and reception staff were on edge. The lobby smelt of detergent and damp carpets.

Barnes asked to see the duty manager and waited in the reception. There was a brief delay and he had to ask again; this time as a UK ambassador.

He grimaced at Alice. 'I hate having to do that'.

Alice smiled. 'At least we didn't have to play the princess card. Not easy for me as a republican…'

A heavy-set hotel employee eventually arrived. German accent. His name card said 'Volker Wilhelm'. He apologised for the absence of the duty manager. 'You can understand that he is a very busy man today.'

They fired questions at him, unsure which might help. He was edgy and uncommunicative. But Alice had a UN badge and said that she had been sent to report back to the UN authorities, which seemed to be enough to make him feel he had to at least appear to be helpful.

They worked hard to extract as much as they could, Barnes being more aggressive, Alice stepping in to ease the tension. Wilhelm recounted that Yang had been killed late at night. He had ordered a meal at roughly eight p.m., which had been delivered by a catering employee at 8:22 p.m. They had provided the police with the signed bill, putting it on his room bill. The envoy had been found the following morning by a cleaner, of Kenyan origin. She and the waiter were being questioned by police. No colleagues or guests had come forward with any information on anyone else who had been seen entering or leaving the sixth floor. There were an American couple next door who had been in their room most of the evening, but they had heard nothing. It was their proximity that had led to the Chinese accusations of US involvement.

He scuttled away officiously. Barnes and Alice sat in two chairs to the side of the reception, watching the life of the hotel carrying on. Alice chewed a strand of hair as she thought. There was something childlike about her. And Barnes could see she was enjoying this more than she would have wanted to admit.

'Not much to go on, Ed?'

'Not much.' She could sense his frustration.

He saw again the flash of sadness. There was more going on. 'Alice, is Omar okay?'

She put a hand on his arm, more to steady herself than him. 'Ed, I've been waiting for a moment to tell you. Omar… it's just that…' She was uncharacteristically inarticulate. Barnes gestured to her to continue. 'He's not well, Ed. He doesn't want you to know. Or anyone really.'

Barnes winced. 'How bad?'

Alice looked crumpled for a moment. 'Let's just say that this will be his last summit, whatever happens.'

'Can I talk to him about it?'

She shook her head firmly. 'You know what he's like. He needs to focus on this deal. He needs *you* to focus on this deal. And you need to get Stephanie back.'

Barnes nodded grimly. 'I'd like to find the Americans, and the Kenyan cleaner.'

'Nothing to lose. Let's give it a go.'

Alice went back to the reception desk. She was glad to see that a new receptionist had taken over. The woman looked her up and down as she approached the desk. Alice was wearing a smart cream summer dress, below the knee. She moved with natural grace. Minimal but expensive jewellery. Confident and crisp. This was clearly enough gravitas for the receptionist not to need to ask any further questions.

'Can I help you, ma'am?'

Alice dialled up the grandeur and the English accent. 'I'm meeting a friend. An American friend. But they are late, and haven't sent a message. Are you able to check their room?'

The receptionist went pale. There was clearly more anxiety than usual about guests going quiet. 'What name?'

Alice didn't hesitate. 'Patty Cox.'

The receptionist started to look through the system. She wouldn't find a Patty Cox. Alice leant across the desk, conspiratorially. 'But I think she's probably travelling a little, erm, discreetly. You understand, I'm sure? Probably under her partner's name. And I'm not sure what he's called. She told me sixth floor, I think?'

The receptionist looked sceptical for a moment. Alice fingered her necklace, flicked back her blonde hair. The receptionist shrugged. 'We only have one American couple on the sixth floor. Mr and Mrs Krause.'

'Can you check their room?' Alice's tone was brisker now, commanding.

'Who shall I say is asking for them?'

Alice paused theatrically. 'Tell her it is Princess Alice.'

The receptionist raised her eyebrows and swiftly made the call.

Minutes later, the Krauses were sat with her in reception, looking intrigued. Alice had spun them a story about a mutual friend who had insisted that she seek them out during their time in Geneva. If she had been unwilling earlier to play the princess card, that hesitation was long gone now.

Barnes meanwhile had gone in search of the Kenyan cleaner. He took the lift to the lower ground floor where the staff had their offices. One passing waiter asked him officiously if he could be of help, and Barnes said he was looking for a bathroom. He found the staff cafeteria and entered. Two porters were sharing a coffee at one of the tables, and looked at him warily. But then they returned to their gossip.

Barnes walked confidently to a coffee machine and made himself a drink. He glanced at the notice board and saw the list of shift names and times. There had been only one Kenyan cleaner working this morning: a woman by the name of Stella Nyangala.

Was it worth seeking her out? What could she really add? But they had nothing else to go on. And finding the killer was the quickest way to stop the collapse of the talks and get to Jordan and find Stephanie. Barnes found a quiet corner of the room and waited.

Staff came and went. They were absorbed by their discussions, taking quick breaks, heading back out. None looked Kenyan. Nyangala was a Kisii name: Barnes had often visited the region.

When she walked in, Barnes had no doubt that it was her. She looked tearful but resolute. Late twenties. A sharp jaw, short hair and defiant brown eyes. The two porters in the corner both noticed her come in. Presumably quite the hotel celebrity now. Barnes waited for her to start making her drink and crossed the room to join her. Her hand was trembling slightly as she added the warm milk.

'*Chai ma maziwa?*' Tea with milk.

She looked at him, startled. The Kisii drank a sweet tea with plenty of milk and cardamom. Barnes introduced himself. She was from Machakos, and surprised to find herself talking to the British high commissioner. But she was not surprised that he wanted to know more about the guest in Room 616.

37

Room 616

Twenty minutes later Barnes messaged Crawford, who joined them in the lobby as they compared notes.

Stella Nyangala had described the hotel room when she found Yang at just after eight a.m. His laptop had been open at the desk. It had been swiftly taken away in the morning by the local police and a Chinese investigator. The bed had not been slept in, but one pillow was in the corner of the room. There was a plate of half-eaten food on the table. An empty bottle of sparkling water. Yang's body had been spreadeagled in an armchair, his head slumped forward, one arm over the edge of the chair. There were no signs of injury, and at first, she thought that he might be drunk. But once she approached the body, she had no doubt that he was dead.

Meanwhile, the Krauses had clearly been starstruck by Alice, and impressed by her UN credentials. They had shown little hesitation in sharing what they knew. They had heard Yang enter the room at seven p.m. or so, and the food being delivered just over an hour later. They had ordered something at a similar time, having decided to stay in because she had a migraine. He had been in the bathroom adjoining Yang's room roughly an hour later, during an ad break in the television series they were watching. He had thought that he heard voices, or at least one voice. It had struck him as strange that the guest next door seemed to be talking to himself. They had then heard nothing more until the scream of the cleaner in the morning. Mr Krause had gone immediately into the corridor. Her trolley was outside the room, and she was stood at the door. He had called reception and then all hell had broken loose.

The Krauses had now requested a move from Room 614. They were upset by the noise, and the sense of such a horrific tragedy having taken place so close to where they were sleeping. Alice had pressed them on what was making all the noise. Surely the room had been cordoned off?

Krause said that there had been a large group of Chinese security officials in the room for several hours, looking for any evidence on how Yang had died. And Krause had twice seen the assistant duty manager, Herr Wilhelm, in the corridor. He seemed to be managing the hotel's handling of the incident.

Alice chewed her lip. 'So still not much to go on?'

Barnes nodded. 'He was clearly smothered with the pillow after nine p.m. or so. And the body was then discovered pretty early the following morning. Whoever murdered him was well away by then. Would there be much to help us in the hotel room, Max?'

Max glanced at Alice and back at Barnes. 'I'm obviously no expert, Ambassador. But it sounds like a professional job. No evidence of a fight, so the assassin must have either been known to him, or pretty swift and efficient. If the former, maybe a colleague, or possibly a staff member? If the latter, probably a stranger. That would make more sense based on Krause's description of the one-way conversation. A pro would have got in and out pretty quick.'

Alice was on her smartphone. 'And Yang last tweeted at 9:16 p.m. at the actress, Lucy Keeling. He seems to have had quite a vendetta against her.'

Barnes nodded. 'All in a day's work for a wolf warrior. He wanted to make the West look hypocritical on climate change. Take the heat off the Chinese in the negotiations. But I'm convinced that whoever killed him did so to blow up those negotiations. That rules out climate activists, I hope.' He held Max's eye.

Alice shrugged. 'So what next?'

Barnes was pensive. 'I don't think we get much more from Stella Nyangala or the Krauses. Could we get into the room?'

Max Crawford grinned. 'Where do you think I was while you were both crashing around down here? I felt we needed something a bit more… direct.'

Alice rocked her head back with shock and then laughter. Barnes joined in, shaking his head. 'And so?'

'Not much to add, I'm afraid. No obvious evidence of the killer. The pillow has gone, presumably as evidence, so I'm sure that the police won't challenge the conclusion that was how he was killed. Body gone, of course. They'll have done a postmortem by now. Not that it will add much. The "how" is the easy part here. The "who" is the problem.'

Barnes nodded. 'So what do we do now?'

'I'm assuming you don't want to wait for the official investigation, Ambassador. It will conclude that he was killed by a professional, which will only boost the conspiracy theories, especially on the Chinese side. So we have two options. First, make sure whoever did it knows we've been sniffing around. They might then seek us out. That would mean you or I had to act as bait, and it could get nasty. Or second, follow the trail of whoever is removing the evidence.'

Alice and Barnes exchanged a startled look. 'What do you mean?'

'I got into the hotel security system. The staff have master cards that swipe in and out of the rooms. You can pretty much track their movements. There is plenty of data on the days leading up to the murder. But as of this morning, nothing on who was on the sixth floor last night.'

Alice cocked her head. 'But surely that makes it even harder?'

Crawford grinned. 'It would do if the person who removed the data hadn't logged in under their own name.'

'And?'

'And so I've taken the liberty of organising another meeting for you and I with Herr Wilhelm.'

Barnes was stunned. 'And where is he now?'

Crawford was almost breezy. 'On the third floor.'

Barnes and Alice stood. 'Well, let's get to him before he moves.'

Crawford rose more slowly. 'Oh, don't worry about that, Ambassador. He's not moving anywhere.' He turned to Alice. 'And with the greatest respect, *Your Highness*, I suggest that this is a meeting you do not want to know about.'

38

Article 15

The German was tied to a chair in Room 304. Crawford had fastened his legs to the piece of furniture and his hands behind him. He had a gag around his mouth. He was sweating heavily.

Barnes shook his head. How had it come to this? 'Seriously, Max? Does everything have to get violent?'

Crawford shrugged. 'Nothing has got violent here, Ambassador.' A stern look towards Wilhelm. 'At least not yet.'

'And it is not going to.' Barnes found himself wondering again what Omar would say. It was as though he needed his validation. He shuddered at the thought of his friend's reaction. This one was more categoric than self-defence. Article 15 of the UN Declaration of Human Rights: no one should be subjected to cruel, inhuman or degrading treatment.

He had to stay focused on why they were here. 'So what next?'

'That depends on three things, Ambassador. First, whether Herr Wilhelm cooperates. And second, if he doesn't cooperate, how fast you need him to be more helpful.'

Barnes sighed. 'And third?'

'Ah, well, hopefully it doesn't come to that. But there may be a moment where you need to decide *how* much you need me to make him more helpful...'

Barnes stood in front of Wilhelm. The assistant duty manager's eyes darted around the room. His upper lip was moist with perspiration. Barnes could smell the fear on him.

'Are you willing to tell us who killed the envoy?'

Wilhelm shook his head defiantly. Barnes looked at Crawford, who shrugged.

Barnes tried again. 'Please, Herr Wilhelm. I don't know how you got involved in all this. I'm sure that there is an explanation. I'm not really sure I know how I got involved either. But we need to get answers fast. My daughter is in Jordan, a hostage. And I need to be there. But I can't get there until we know what happened here. As a parent, I'm asking you to help.'

Wilhelm bowed his head slightly. There was less defiance now. But, again, the shake of the head.

What was the cost in human life compared to the failure of the climate talks? Or the prospect of a US/China conflict? Barnes felt they were at a crucial moment. Diplomacy had a narrow window in which it might still operate, maybe even succeed. Beyond that, they would lose control. And this man might hold the information that could keep that narrow window ajar. He was their only chance.

But did that justify violence against him? Crawford had clearly long crossed that line. He was prepared to kill for the planet. But what gave any of them the right to decide when that was justifiable?

He turned again to Crawford. 'Max, I can't do this. We have to find another way.'

Crawford was gruff now. He didn't like having this debate in front of Wilhelm. 'We don't have time. Sometimes we have no choice. This man knows who killed the envoy. That information saves the negotiations on which millions of lives depend. I don't see that as a difficult philosophical dilemma.'

Barnes held his head in his hands. Crawford removed the gag from Wilhelm, who breathed heavily.

One more try. Barnes moved a chair opposite him and sat close enough that he could feel the heat on his breath. 'Herr Wilhelm. My friend here is, I'm afraid, a very dangerous and violent man. At this moment, I fear the consequences of that even more than you do. Let's start somewhere. We can help you. Were you blackmailed to help?'

Wilhelm swallowed hard, his eyes swivelling to watch Crawford, who was rolling up his sleeves. He nodded.

'And what if we can protect you? Guarantee your safety if you testify?'

Wilhelm, finally, stuttered. 'You can't.'

'Would you be willing to at least brief the UN team? You could do so in confidence. We would not be there. Anything that could help us show that this was not a US assassination could have huge consequences.'

Wilhelm was pensive. But, again, the shake of the head.

Barnes threw his hands up in exasperation.

From today's perspective it wasn't enough simply to have not participated in slavery. The expectation was that you would have fought it, had you been alive. Would it have been right to kill to end slavery? So what would his grandchildren think of a generational apathy towards the climate catastrophe? Would they think that the marginal results of all those conferences and relationship building were enough to show he had fought? What gave him the right to decide when violence was justified, and when it was not? Or who had the right to use it. States had always used force in support of their objectives.

He sighed, avoiding Crawford's eye, rose and left the room. He could hear the protests from Wilhelm as Crawford refastened the gag. He did not look back.

Outside in the corridor Barnes retched. He had to regain control of the situation. At least, influence what he could: do that his way.

He first messaged Hermione at No 10.

> I need that date for the Obwocha bilat with the Boss. Can we make it this week?

She replied almost immediately.

> Done. Fix it for Thursday. And we can do your statement supporting the Somali talks. x A thumbs-up emoji. And a kiss again. The absence of Keys was clearly keeping No 10 on side and in a good mood.

Barnes messaged the Somaliland governor.

> Your announcement is set for Thursday. Please now be true to your word. Let her go.

There was no sound from the room. Taking a deep breath, Barnes opened the door, dreading what he might find.

Wilhelm was still tied to the chair, but the gag was off again. His eyes looked through Barnes. He did not appear to be hurt but the defiance was gone. Crawford was standing over him.

'We're done here, Ambassador. And I've got some more targets to attend to.'

'Done?'

'He's agreed to testify to Omar. He'll go with Alice. You and I were never here, he's agreed to that.'

'And who did it?'

Wilhelm cleared his throat. His voice was quiet, as though every word caused him pain. 'The man was Russian. He was working for a Russian fossil fuel company. They told me they only wanted to meet Yang privately, so I gave them access to the corridor. The hint was that it was over some kind of business deal. It's not my job to ask questions. I never knew any of this would happen. Afterwards they told me that I was an accomplice, told me to remove the data. Threatened my kids.' He tried to steady himself, but started to sob.

Barnes looked at him with distaste. 'They clearly wanted to kill the deal. And you'll tell Omar all this? Put it on record? We'll ask the UN to protect you.' Wilhelm looked again at Crawford, who was refastening his cuffs.

And nodded, his eyes cowed.

Barnes felt his phone vibrate again. News of Stephanie? It was a message back from the Somaliland governor:

> Congratulations. Fast work. And the UN have been in touch with my invitation to Jordan. I'll deliver my side. Let's meet in Amman.

Barnes felt the relief surge through him. Whatever had happened here, they were back in control. Omar could deal with Wilhelm and the Chinese from here.

Another message from the governor.

> But bring Orla Fitzgerald. She can tell our story.

This must have come from Stephanie, somehow. What was she up to? At least she was up to something. That enough gave Barnes a sense that they were back on track.

And Orla Fitzgerald again. He pictured her in Paris, sharing confidences in the residence garden. Vibrant, curious, sceptical. Asking the right questions. It was time.

39

FOMO

Orla Fitzgerald touched down in Geneva in the early evening. She loved the crispness in the air. She was feeling energised, excited. This was where the story was leading her. Would Ed Barnes be able to help her confirm that Max Crawford was the Assassin, maybe even track him down? She wanted to understand what was driving him, how he picked his targets, what the endgame was. She wanted to support Ed and Stephanie, whatever danger she was still in. And, she was no longer kidding herself, she wanted to see Ed. Would the end of his marriage have changed him? Yes, she hoped. But not too much.

Max Crawford had slept deeply in the afternoon. 'When you've spent three months in the Bora Bora caves looking for bad guys, anything softer than a rock is five stars.' He had shut down the brief and unconvincing attempt by Barnes to ask him what had happened with the German night manager. The ends sometimes justified the means, surely even Barnes could see that now. He was relishing the fight, and happy to do what he needed to do to land the Jordan deal, and find Stephanie. After that, who knew. He was weary of killing. But the work was not complete. As he shaved in his hotel room, a nagging concern: what now of Orla Fitzgerald? Barnes was convinced she could help: fair enough. But he didn't trust her.

Ed Barnes was alert as they waited for Orla, an hour later. They took a taxi to a boutique hotel on the Place du Bourg-de-Four. Yellow fronted with green awnings, overlooking the shady park. Barnes paid the driver as Crawford unloaded the bags from the boot. Crawford also travelled light.

The foyer had African art, an old gramophone, deep cream sofas and small two-person coffee tables by the windows. The receptionist was exceptionally pale, with a weak beard.

They were sat at a table in the park opposite, outside the kiosk. The waiter had brought them two beers and a plate of small green and black olives, bitter and full of juice. They waited in silence for Orla to arrive.

Ed Barnes was feeling more confident with the sense that Stephanie was surviving. He was intrigued as to what it was that was bringing Orla back towards him. Maybe she was selecting and justifying the targets: the climate crisis oligarchs who were funding, exploiting, selling, defending the crisis. Orla had always liked a good story, but here she would be a participant, not an observer. Crawford had never been an observer, but here there was a sense that he was working for himself, not following instructions. It would be a pretty impressive combination. A lethal combination. It would explain her low profile, and his reluctance that she join Barnes. No, his wariness of her was genuine. Either way, Barnes knew he needed her help in finding Stephanie. He needed to see her. And he wanted to see her. In Oxford there had been a moment when he had wondered if a younger version of himself would pursue her.

And there was another piece missing. Why was Stephanie trying to bring Orla back into the picture?

He looked across at Max Crawford. What was Max prepared to do for this cause? Nothing he had not done for less urgent ones. He would never ask him again what had happened to Wilhelm in Room 304. Or to Sebastian Keys.

Maybe Max was right that the ends justified the means. Perhaps taking out the people preventing action on climate change was a more efficient way to succeed than endless summits and campaigns. Fewer people might die than via Barnes's slow and uncertain path of negotiation. But these were the skills he had. He was not an investigative journalist. Or an assassin.

Barnes did not recognise her at first as she emerged from behind a group of tourists. She had paused to let a *tuk tuk* past, head down. She was wearing a broad-brimmed sun hat, her hair beneath it shorter, the curls gone, dyed black. He remembered her in Oxford: threatened, hunted. Now she had her confidence back: upright and moving with grace. Ed Barnes had gone through much of his life not noticing what women were wearing. She wore white sneakers, narrow cut jeans and a crisp white cotton shirt, two buttons open at the tanned neck. She looked fresh.

He felt himself sit a little straighter.

She sat down opposite them and gestured to the waiter for another three beers. Barnes watched her try to suppress the initial surprise at seeing Max Crawford. A brief nod to him and a curt nod back. Barnes could see that the mutual suspicion was still there. He had been wrong to wonder if they were somehow working together. And wrong not to warn her to expect a surprise. What was it about this combination of people that made him less trusting? She cocked her head and appraised Barnes. He ran a hand through his hair, self-conscious, but held her stare. She glanced away and then back at him. A moment of complicity.

She made him feel younger just by her presence. 'Orla, it's been much too long.'

He was clearly tired but looking good, in his element. 'Maybe. I needed to get away from Paris.' A sip of the beer.

'Me, too. Career change?' Barnes felt the need to move tentatively.

'Life change.' There was a distance to her.

Crawford was making his way through the plate of olives.

Orla shrugged. 'And now here we all are again. And somehow, against the odds and the public record, Max Crawford is alive?'

Barnes leant across the table. They couldn't have this argument now. 'Orla, thank you for agreeing to help find her.' Why could he not say her name?

Orla chewed her lip. Did Ed Barnes know what Max was doing? How long? 'I'm not doing it for you.'

Barnes hoped she could not see his shoulders drop. 'For her, then?'

'She had already asked. The day of your mall drama.'

Barnes could not hide his surprise. 'But that's when she was taken. There must be a reason Stephanie reached out and asked for your help. We need to know why.'

'We?' She looked intently at Max, who nodded.

Orla turned again to Barnes. 'Loyal to a fault, that's always been Max Crawford's problem. And what makes you think Steph wants to be rescued?'

Barnes winced. 'Seriously?'

'Maybe she is exactly where she needs to be.'

'Orla, she was taken by the Somalilanders after the mall siege in Nairobi. She's now in Jordan, with the Somalilanders. God knows what they are planning. But they have asked for you. I think they want someone to tell their story.' He choked through the words.

Orla softened. 'Of course I'll help, Ed. I should have come earlier. I'm sorry. I hadn't taken her message seriously enough. And I was too distracted by a story I was working on.'

Barnes felt the mood shift. 'I thought you'd been quiet recently. What are you brewing?'

Orla took a deep breath. 'That's what brought me to you. I've been tracking a series of assassinations, I think connected. A budget air company founder, a talk show host, right-wing television producer, fossil fuels investor. My sources in US and UK intel think they're connected too. They're hunting someone who has found a way to operate off-grid, without an identity. A pro. The methods of execution. The quiet skill of it all. The lack of an obvious motive. Willing to kill. But not indiscriminate.'

Barnes glanced nervously at Crawford, who had focused his attention on a second bowl of olives. 'What are you saying, Orla?'

She had cocked her head, trying to think while she spoke. 'I've been hunting him too. I want to hear his story. Maybe it's not just the Somalilanders who need me to help tell their story. I thought you might help me find him?'

Barnes swallowed hard. 'Can't we focus on finding Stephanie instead?'

Orla ignored him and turned to Crawford. 'After the trader in the Algarve, I knew it was about climate change.

I tried to work out where he was going next. Tried to get there first. And in the case of Sebastian Keys, I did.'

Max continued to focus on the bowl of olives, but Barnes felt him tense. He avoided Crawford's eye. 'And?'

Orla took another long sip of the beer. 'And I'm not sure that the killer is really the villain of this story. Perhaps they are the hero? Maybe that's my story?'

They sat in silence. Crawford cleared his throat, but then said nothing.

It was Orla who spoke first, feeling more in command again. 'So help me think this through. I think I have a motive. Eh, Max? And I'm pretty certain that we are right on the profile. Niche military background. And the ability to move around undetected.'

Crawford signalled to the waiter for three more beers. Orla was watching him carefully. He was a dead man with skills. But a climate change warrior?

She was not ready to press it. How had Ed Barnes got caught up in this? 'FOMO again, Ed?'

Barnes was confused. 'Fear of missing out? I don't think I ever had that.'

She smiled. 'Oh, I think you always have. Why else would you be involved?'

Barnes had wondered what to tell her about Max. It appeared he need not have worried. 'In what, Orla?'

She paused and smiled. 'I don't doubt you'll do anything, work with anyone, make any compromise, to protect your daughter. You did that in Paris. You let her get away with murder. But this?'

Max signalled to the waiter to bring the bill. 'Enough. We all need to be in Jordan.'

40

The Right Thing?

Barnes and Orla arrived together in Amman the following morning. Crawford travelled separately. He didn't feel the need for Orla to see more of his craft, yet. And he wasn't ready for her questions. She and Barnes had settled into an uneasy pattern of small talk and shared concern for Stephanie, neither yet ready to confront the big questions on Crawford.

Once they had reunited at the hotel it was not long before the message came from the Somaliland governor, with a liaison point. They agree that Crawford would go ahead to check the venue and be sure that Stephanie was safe.

So Barnes waited anxiously with Orla at their hotel, watching the coverage from London. The governor would not turn up unless he got the right outcome.

President Obwocha beamed as he was greeted by the PM on the doorstep of 10 Downing Street. Barnes could see the distraction in the PM's face, but he seemed to be doing his part. Half an hour later Obwocha emerged, looking equally victorious. He announced that Kenya would host peace talks between the Somali factions, including the Somalilanders. A UK statement supported the initiative, and hoped for the expansion of democracy and economic prosperity in East Africa. It alluded to efforts in New York to ensure wider international backing for the process.

Smiles all round. There was no mention of the siege. But Barnes wondered if Hussein would think that it had been worth it. This diplomatic flurry was more than he had seemed to expect, and granted the Somaliland faction a genuine moment of recognition and status. Was an invite to a conference really worth those lives in the mall? Worth killing for, dying for? It would all seem a pretty incremental series of steps to many. In reality it had not cost the Kenyans or the UK too much. Everything now depended on how much effort and resource they actually put into the talks. Whether the factions turned up seeing an opportunity. And as ever a certain amount of luck.

Barnes messaged Jim and Dave to get the reactions telegram sent. He had asked that it focus on the positive reactions in Kenya. Everyone had to see this as their win. He sent Obwocha a congratulatory text message and received an immediate response on the poor quality of the prime minister's coffee.

I told him to serve only Kenyan in future.

A good sign. And a message of thanks to Hermione for seeing it through.

A swift reply.

No more favours for a while Ed. But it went well. Maybe we all did a decent bit of old school diplomacy here. Might give the PM more interest in doing more of it.

We'll need him to hold that thought for the Jordan conference.

Don't worry. He's fired up. Politics much easier now on climate. He knows how much Jordan matters.

Neither mentioned Sebastian Keys. His murder was still prominent in the news. Unexplained and inexplicable. The major investigation launched by the PM continued to produce no leads.

Barnes paced the room. The handover of a hostage was always the point of greatest danger. He was glad to have Orla there.

'You've seen hostage victims. Do you think she'll be changed, Orla?'

Orla smiled reassuringly. 'She's going to be doing fine, Ed. The thing about Stephanie is that she'll always be fine.'

Ed felt his shoulders relax. 'I know, I know. But I can't always take that for granted.'

Orla stood in front of him and held his arms to stop him pacing the room. His eyes were a lighter blue this close up. 'She's not yours to mould.'

Barnes exhaled. 'I stopped trying to do that soon after she could talk. I just wish that somewhere between the instinct and the action there was a moment of debate, of self-awareness. She would get further if she slowed down.'

'I wonder where she gets that from.' He didn't seem to hear. She had not seen him this anxious.

Orla released him, and he continued his nervous circuits. She tried another tack.

'Is this where it ends? Get Stephanie to safety, then simply get back to Nairobi? Keep your head down? Get back to doing the job? Or are you really going to put everything into this climate deal? Didn't you always tell me that your vocation can destroy the lives of those who get too swept up in it? *Pas trop de zele?*'

Barnes grinned. 'Like yours?'

Orla ignored him. 'I've seen what it does to you diplomats. Pressure, long days and flights, endless paperwork, the merciless scrutiny from my world. That's why so many of you become divorced alcoholics.'

'High-functioning ones at least. But it's not all that, really.' He paused in front of her. 'What destroys diplomats is the sense that when things go wrong in the world, it is somehow our fault. There's no objective standard against which to measure what we do. That's why we end up obsessing over the size of our office or whether we get into the right meeting.'

She sensed him wrestling with himself. Had he ever not been? This was displacement activity, but would help him through the next hour. He continued. 'You know I've been asking myself: what is diplomacy without all those trappings? The protocol, the smug insincerity, the theatre?'

Orla was unsure whether he wanted her to try a reply. It was out before she was ready. 'And all you have left is—'

Ed interjected. 'Everything.'

Orla finished her sentence. '—nothing.'

They let the silence sit between them. Ed resumed his pacing. He sighed. 'My point is, only by taking that crap away do you get the real essence of it all.'

Orla smiled. 'Sounds like another resignation?'

'No, it's why I'm going to carry on. It is why, once Stephanie is safe, I'm going to get this climate deal. I can see it clearly now. That's why I'm here. Stephanie showed me that. And, in his way, so did Max.'

Orla preferred him when he was less grandiose. In other circumstances she might have said that, teased him a bit, got him laughing at himself. But she felt his intensity. Was this also why Stephanie had brought her here?

He noticed the way she had clenched her fists in front of her. 'Are you and Max working together on these assassinations?'

Barnes laughed. 'Seriously? I thought you were working with him.'

Orla relaxed. A grin of complicity. 'Oh, Ed… when did we become so distrusting. At least that's two people I can cross off the list of his accomplices. But seriously, what's the question to which Max is the answer?'

Ed Barnes hesitated, scratched his chin. 'Maybe more than I thought, much more. It all feels complicated, ethic-ally. Like you said, if they are the villains, doesn't that make the Assassin the hero?'

Right on cue, Crawford messaged to say that everything was ready at the handover point. They would meet in the hotel reception. There were plenty of people around, so he thought it as good a place as any. He was confident the Somaliland governor was not going to pull any more stunts.

> Is Steph OK?

Crawford messaged back immediately.

> When is Stephanie ever not OK?

Barnes felt the relief flood through him as he crossed the hotel lobby for the car. He and Orla set off in a Land Rover Crawford had rented. The UK embassy knew that he was there, as part of the preparation for the Jordan conference. But he did not want them anywhere near this, and had shaken off the third secretary accompanying him.

Despite the reassurance from Crawford's texts, Barnes felt strangely nervous. He was desperate to see Stephanie, but would she not have changed? Would he not have changed? The messages with the governor had not hinted at any mistreatment. She seemed to have been looked after well. Crawford would have warned him if she was injured in any way. But surely even Stephanie would have some emotional scars.

When she walked into the hotel lobby, the governor smiling awkwardly by her side, he finally felt his anxiety dissipate. She strode confidently towards them, showing no sense of any injury. Light on her feet. The governor fell a step behind, almost struggling to keep up. He had a kind face. She gave Barnes a smile, raised her eyebrows just a little. They embraced, and he held her tightly for several moments. She stroked his back, and he felt the tension ease.

They sat for a few moments, taking each other in.

'Steph, you…?'

'It's all okay, Pops. But you look tired.'

'I wanted to get them the talks. Get you out.'

How much of the situation would she have been following? She put a hand on his arm. 'Dad, you're doing okay.'

'We have so much more to do.'

'Yes, but for now okay is something to acknowledge.'

Barnes shrugged, but she could see he was taller again. She had seen her mum do this in the past when he needed reassurance. He still needed it.

She embraced Orla. 'Thank you for coming. We need you for the next act.' Orla grinned back, relief coursing also through her too. She was struck that Stephanie seemed to feel in control of the situation, with the governor almost deferential.

Crawford was scanning the lobby, alert as ever. But Stephanie hugged him too, with genuine warmth. 'Oh, Max, always there for us. Getting us out of these scrapes. Thank you.'

Amid the relief Barnes noticed that she didn't seem surprised that Max was there with them. That he was *alive*.

They sat with the governor. Barnes had expected to feel more anger towards him. But something in the rapport the man had with Stephanie stopped him. Almost a complicity between them.

The governor's voice was quieter and milder than on the phone. Yet a firmness that was hard to challenge. He would be effective in the negotiations. Barnes warmed to him. 'High Commissioner, you kept your word. These talks are a start, at least. And the invitation to the summit. They will give my people hope that the world will see us differently from the rest of Somalia. And they will help me to show the armed factions that my way can get results.

What is it your Churchill said when he was not smashing us all up? "Jaw jaw is better than war war"?'

Barnes caught Stephanie's eye and suppressed his frustration. 'But Governor, you've allowed at the very least – more likely, sanctioned – a certain amount of violence. That can't be part of the toolkit. They are still burying Hussein's victims from the mall. I had to bury a good man.'

The governor interjected. 'And I've also had to spend time with the families of our martyrs, including my own family.'

Barnes bit his lip to contain his exasperation. This was not the time or place for this row. 'But the difference is that Hussein and his men chose that path. The civilians in the mall did not. How can you justify that?'

The governor looked pensive. He was younger than Barnes had anticipated. Mid-thirties? High cheekbones and a handsome, angular face. Thin but muscular. A regal grace. Barnes noticed that he too looked for a glance from Stephanie to calm him. His voice softened. 'I know, I know, this is hard. It is hard for me. But we had to get your attention. And sometimes violence is the only way to do that. Sometimes the ends do justify the means.'

Orla sat forward, her eyes fierce again. 'I think Max agrees, don't you Max?' Crawford ignored her. But Stephanie did not. She looked angrier now. 'And Max would be right to agree, Orla. The governor would never have got his negotiations without the action Hussein took. And it has always been that way, especially for those without a voice. Every democracy has needed sacrifice to establish itself, and sacrifice to survive. Why do you think we have armies? Who decides whether what Somaliland has done is less justifiable than what the US said it was doing for democracy in Iraq? The only difference is that the US does the violence at a much greater scale.'

Barnes had heard her speak on similar lines before, often across one of his dinner tables. And normally when a US diplomat had braved the occasion. Stephanie's reputation had started to precede her. But the difference today was her vehemence in support of the Somalilanders. Orla had also clearly been struck by it. A bit of Stockholm Syndrome?

He wanted to end the meeting and get her back to safety. As ever, diplomatic platitudes might help. 'Who decides? Well, that's why we have the UN, Steph, you know that. We've given them that function because the twentieth century showed we can't trust ourselves with it. It's why the Somalilanders want a UN statement supporting the talks, to be among the leaders at the summit. It's why my friend Omar has such a hard and lonely job. And that's why this climate summit matters.'

Stephanie softened slightly. 'So Omar gets to decide what is right and wrong?'

Barnes started to interject. In a way, Omar did. Better him than anyone else. And yet his code was already shattered. He had crossed lines that Omar would never cross.

But Orla was not letting it go, either. The release of anxiety over Stephanie was coming out of them all in different ways. 'And what about climate change, then? If it is right to kill for democracy in a just war. If the Somalilanders can justify violence in the service of their independence. Then what about the rights of future generations? Don't they deserve violence in protection of their existence, their freedoms, their security? Once you've crossed the Rubicon on the use of violence in pursuit of justice, why wouldn't you be using it in defence of the planet, and of our descendants. Eh, Max?'

Crawford shrugged. He was not ready for this argument. Neither was Barnes: it was the argument he had been having with himself since he had realised what Crawford was doing. Yet Orla's anger seemed to be with herself for having been slow to understand. Sure, she was trying to goad Max into telling her more. But for her this was a great story, not a challenge to her entire worldview.

It was Stephanie who closed the discussion down, glancing sternly at Orla. She stood and shook hands with the governor. 'Thank you, Ali, thank you for everything. You are doing the right thing. And I know that Orla will be in touch with you. She'll help tell the story. She is the best. That's why we needed her to come.'

The governor took her hand in both of his. Held it. Orla was watching them carefully. 'And you, Steph, I wish you courage for what comes next. You two are doing the right thing.'

41

Confessions

Barnes and Stephanie sat close in the Land Rover as Crawford drove them back to their hotel. She placed her arm in his. It was evening in Amman and the calls to prayer began to sound across the city of endless roundabouts. By the standards of the great capitals of the Middle East, Barnes had always found it a dull and functional place. Tonight, he looked at the shopping malls and restaurants with affection. He had his daughter back.

But something wasn't right. It had all been too easy, too comfortable. And as for Stephanie, Max, Orla. Glad as he was that they were all here, none of them were being completely honest with him about *why* they were here, and what they wanted. Even Stephanie.

Back at the hotel, they ordered a meal in the hotel restaurant. The dishes came quickly: fresh hummus, tabbouleh, crisp fattoush salad. Plenty of olive oil, lemon juice and garlic. They drank the local Petra beer. Barnes found an appetite he had not felt for days. They relaxed as the second round of drinks arrived. But Barnes felt the list of unanswered questions growing, and the tension between Max and Orla.

He had always been the one to fill the awkward silences. 'This climate summit can still be saved. The PM is up for playing his part. We can get a decent deal. Max and I are going to get stuck in.' He flinched slightly at his own expression, but he wanted Stephanie to see that she had got through to him, that he got it. And there was something here that seemed to bring them all together, but he could not take it for granted.

'You need time, Steph. Why not head back to Nairobi? You too, Orla. You can use the residence to write. Stay as long as you need. It will be good having you around.' He hoped she would say no, stay here in Jordan for the next chapter.

Orla looked interested. She had enjoyed being around Barnes again, even in these circumstances. And it would be good to spend time with Stephanie. Her main mission was to get Max Crawford's story, assuming that he was the Assassin. If she could get him to open up, anonymously, she had an extraordinary scoop. And the sense of affinity between them, the way Crawford seemed to see his mission as protecting Barnes, meant that being close to Barnes looked the best way to get close to Crawford.

Stephanie shook her head firmly. She was increasingly in charge, the person to whom none of them could say no. 'No, Pops, we're all staying here with you.'

Barnes looked surprised. 'But I'm fine. This is my world, now: summits, diplomacy, negotiations. I believe in what we're doing here. Maybe I get to show you all that what I do *can* make a difference on climate change. This deal is a long way off. But it's gettable. We put the pin back in the hand grenade after Yang's murder. I now have to get the Chinese back in the room. Move the undecideds towards a deal that works for them. And find a way to keep Hoon and the Americans on the reservation. You know them as well as anyone, Orla: you can help with that.'

Orla shook her head, thinking of Brad Curtis's warning. *That the greatest threat to US national security is our own president*. And, she realised, not just to American security. 'It won't be that easy, Ed.'

Crawford had been eating quietly, and reached for another handful of pitta bread. 'It won't. And we know that those who want to kill the summit are less squeamish than us. The Chinese envoy won't be the last. There is too much at stake. But this is where we are all meant to be.'

Orla saw her moment once again. 'But it's not just what the other side are prepared to do, is it Max? It's what *you're* prepared to do. What you've *been* prepared to do. When do we get some honesty on that?'

Barnes raised his hands to calm the discussion. But again, it was Stephanie who intervened.

'It's me who needs to share some honesty, not Max.'

The three turned to her, curious.

Orla leant forward. 'What's going on, Steph?'

She took a sip of her beer. 'This deal is everything. And we can only get this deal if we are all here. Pops, you need to do your thing in the room. Find a way to nail down some kind of agreement. Orla, you need to find ways to make the public case. Tell the story. Help us understand how to win in the information space. Maybe even help us with Hoon. And Max? Well, we all know what you can do. You need to protect my father, and carry on dealing with our opponents.'

Crawford nodded, chewing another mouthful of pitta and hummus. 'I'm where I need to be.'

Barnes felt the room spinning. 'Let's get this straight, Steph. You set us all up so that we would be here? You got the governor to insist that we meet here in Jordan rather than Nairobi or Geneva.'

'Maybe I saw the chance to get you focused – seriously – on these climate talks. Ready to throw everything at them. Do you understand that?'

'And so you faked your own kidnap, knowing what that would do to me?' Barnes was staring at her with fury. Could she not just ask for his help? Why always the drama? He had surely given her all his attention, as much as he could. She held his eye.

'God no, Pops. I'm not that manipulative. But they treated me well. I like Ali. He's kind, always respectful. I never felt I was in real danger. And I knew that you'd find a way to give them a ladder to climb down, something to justify my release. I never doubted you. So, I got to know them. Got to know *him*.'

Barnes stood. 'But did you not think what that would mean I had to risk? And that's before you knew what Max was doing?'

Max interjected. 'We had no choice.'

'Why not?'

Orla placed a hand on his arm. 'Would you be here otherwise, Ed?'

'Here?' Barnes steadied his voice.

'Yes. Right where you need to be. The climate envoy. In Jordan for the most significant summit of our lifetimes. The attention of the Chinese, Jordanians and UK. A sense of genuine mission.'

'And what if I walk away? What if I decide I can't put up with this deception?' Barnes pushed the table away in disgust and stood. 'I'm not going to be part of this game.' But his voice faltered now. 'What do you think you're doing, Steph?'

His daughter was silent. But Orla interjected, defiant. 'Saving the planet.'

'That's a bit grandiose.' Barnes still felt his world spinning.

Orla softened her voice. 'Then call it something more diplomatic. You're the ambassador.'

Barnes slammed the table. 'I'm the only person here who hasn't been lying.'

Orla placed a hand on his arm. 'Really?'

Crawford leant across the table. 'Have you ever asked yourself what it means to be a good ancestor, Ambassador?'

Barnes turned to him angrily. 'We don't have time for this, Max.'

Now it was Crawford who stood. 'We do have time for this. We must make time for this.'

Barnes sighed and sat.

Orla gestured at Crawford to continue. 'So what do you mean by a good ancestor, Max?'

He held Barnes's eye as he spoke. 'It's about more than a climate deal, Ambassador. It's about whether we choose to accept the world as it is. Or whether we try to change it. I learnt that from you.' He gestured around the table. 'All three of us did.'

Barnes leant back in his chair. 'And I'm trying to change it. You all know that.'

He felt some of the anger pass and the adrenalin rise. The negotiations were a long shot, even more since Yang's murder. But this was quite a team. Perhaps Stephanie had a point.

Orla knew that it was now her turn to calm it all down. She leant forward, a conspiratorial glint in her eye. 'Don't be too angry, Ed. It's like you told me earlier: you're up for it. I get the sense that you are starting to believe in all this again.'

Stephanie smiled. 'Dad never stopped believing in it. Whatever he liked to claim.' Barnes could see the defiance was still there. Good. But her voice was softer again. 'I'm so sorry, Pops. But don't we now have to get this climate deal, make it worth all that?'

Barnes felt his anger recede. He hated the sense of being played, but he would forgive his daughter anything. Especially when she was right.

He knew when he was beaten. 'Okay, okay. We're here now. Let's make it all worth it.'

Stephanie sat forward, smiling again. The glint of certainty. 'Pops, I know I've not been a great daughter these last few weeks. But Max is right. And I'm also trying to be a great ancestor.'

'Can you not be both, Steph?'

'From here on, yes, I promise. But this was the only way to get us all together, focused on what matters. And nothing matters more than this. Maybe nothing ever.'

Barnes was thinking about what he needed to do to save the deal. 'I hear you. But why us?'

Steph turned her head away for a moment and then gave him a look of utter certainty. 'Who else?'

42

Dead Sea

Crawford stopped the car at the top of the canyon. They had been driving for almost two hours and sunset was coming. Barnes bought two cups of strong, sweet tea and they drank them in silence, watching as the reds, oranges and pinks began to spread over the rugged landscape.

Sand, limestone, more sand. Crusader castles, dams and spectacular panoramas. A landscape etched by history. Roads empty, with the muezzin's call to prayer echoing soulfully over the mountains.

Barnes drank it all in. He had felt the worst of the tension leave him after seeing Stephanie, despite it all. 'Stunning, eh Max?'

'Not when you've seen as much sand as I have.'

Ed smiled. It was good to be here with him. He pointed out the plateaus where the dead had once been left. 'Been to any good funerals recently?'

Max grinned. 'Only my own.'

But Ed then felt him detached, somehow distant. His usual lightness was gone.

'Max?'

Barnes felt Crawford wince. He wished he had not asked. 'Well, one more, but I'm dealing with that.'

Barnes felt again the confines of male communication. 'I never really asked you about your mother. When do you know you've dealt with it?'

Crawford was staring hard across the valley. 'You never deal with it.'

'I'm sorry, Max.'

Crawford was silent a while. The wind swept through the valley, and they shielded their eyes for a moment from the dust. 'Just get that climate deal, Ambassador.'

They drove on in silence for a while.

It was Crawford who spoke first. His voice was gruff. 'It's like that John Donne poem. We are all smaller after a death. Because it takes away those moments that only you shared with that person. There is no one else left who remembers those fragments.'

Barnes saw for a moment the weariness in him. He had always thought that Crawford killed with ease, that was why he was good at it. And yet now he felt that he could see every death marked on his face.

Crawford blinked the dust from his eyes. 'Ask me whatever you need to ask.'

Barnes sighed. 'Who has been helping you with the targets? I need to know. As a friend... and maybe as a father.'

Crawford sniffed. 'You don't need to know, Ed.'

Another silence. Barnes knew he was right. 'And ask me what you need to ask, Max.'

Crawford stared ahead through the windscreen. 'You told me once that none of this mattered. These summits—'

'I lied.'

'To me?'

'To myself.'

The route of the highway they had taken today was over five millennia old, from Amman to Aqaba and the Red Sea. It had been a trading route for Nabateans and Romans. A pilgrimage route for Christians heading to where Moses had seen the promised land or the baptism sight of Jesus. And for sixteenth-century Egyptian Muslims heading to Mecca via Syria.

This was no pilgrimage. But they were trading.

Barnes knew that there was no deal without the Chinese. And that the Chinese would not come to the table while they still believed that the Americans had assassinated their envoy. So Omar had set up the meeting with their assistant minister, safely away from the conference delegations at a hotel on the Dead Sea. There was probably a metaphor there, but Barnes did not have the time or patience any more to point it out. Without a breakthrough there would be no climate deal. And who knew what Hoon was capable of, if it helped her to get re-elected.

And if she somehow won, how many more would die from climate change?

The Chinese diplomat made them wait, perched on cushions of the hotel rooftop bar.

As an Arabic student Barnes had enjoyed a similar view from a rooftop bar outside Petra, watching the sun set behind the dry Wadi Musa mountains. The Nabateans had carved it their impenetrable mountain city in the third century BC, and set themselves up for centuries as highwaymen with class, shaking down spice traders on the route between Damascus and Arabia. He had seen Petra for the first time, then – the massive citadel tomb carved into the rock – and the world had seemed to make more sense. If he had any wisdom now it was in learning that it didn't make sense.

Then, he had been covered by orange sandstone from climbing under an unflinching sun – he could taste the heat at the back of his throat – to 'The High Place of Sacrifice', and then took several hours to work through the maze of tombs, temples and theatres. Every now and again he had stopped to drink a sweet tea with one of the old Bedouin women scattered across the acres of ruins. But there was simply too much to take in. He had been left humbled by the scale of what they built, and marvelling at being so close to the very distant past.

Now there was a deliciously cool breeze, coming up from the coast off Aqaba. No one else was up there except Crawford, sat discreetly on a table at the far end of the bar, and he had persuaded the barman to turn the music off. Every sip of Barnes' beer was hitting the spot in his very dusty throat.

Eventually Ling came, accompanied by a colleague. He was young, lean, ambitious looking. No flabby party apparatchik. Ling nodded at Barnes as he saw him and crossed the bar. They shook hands cautiously, and he gestured for them to sit. He glanced at Barnes's beer and ordered a Pepsi. He didn't order anything for the note taker.

Barnes attempted to break the ice as the drink arrived, gesturing at Ling's choice. 'The Americans aren't all bad then.'

Ling gave a half-smile. 'Their Coke is the last thing we'll sanction.' The accent was clipped East Coast America. There was a generation of Chinese students now in US and UK universities. Would they go back to change their country? Or stay and change ours? Either way, their cultural bilingualism gave them a huge slab of power.

'And the rest?'

'We'll see. We didn't pick this fight. You know that. We haven't picked any of their fights.'

'But you're in it now. And so, the rest of us are in it too.'

Ling took a long sip. 'I never believed in the Thucydides trap, that you can't get a transition from yesterday's empire to tomorrow's empire without a war. It is possible for us to overtake the Americans peacefully. That's how we want to do it. But they can't see that.'

Barnes wondered about ordering another beer. He looked at the note taker, observing everything. Not yet. 'But we all know that Elizabeth Hoon is not a normal president. Others will be less bellicose, more thoughtful. Why not wait her out? Show some of your famous patience.'

'Maybe. But she is all we have right now.'

'The election is only months away. She's going to lose. We can then all move back to something more sensible. Why give her an issue to help her popularity?'

'You Brits really think she'll go? You clearly have much more faith in the democratic experiment than we do.'

'It's still the least bad form of government.'

'Really? We've said before it's too soon to say. Did democracies respond more effectively to the last financial crash? To preparing for artificial intelligence? To the pandemics? I'm not sure your people really think that they did. You have a generation that think they'll be worse off than their parents. They might trade all this democratic churn for some strategy and delivery.'

Barnes let it go. This was part of the dance. 'We're works in progress. My question for you is whether your system can adapt to climate change. If this is a Chinese century, how can you ensure that the world you dominate is worth dominating? Do you really want to be in the smartest room in a house on fire?'

'We didn't start the fire,' Ling snapped. And then composed himself. 'Of course, the inevitable Western appeal to our pragmatism and self-interest.'

Barnes shrugged. 'You think I have a better argument?'

They sipped their drinks. Barnes watched Ling. The man was unhurried. His people clearly wanted to talk. That was something. Diplomacy was the art of giving people ladders to climb down.

'Let's work together. What do you need for a deal, Mr Ling?'

'You understand game theory, Ambassador Barnes? I studied it at Harvard. A game is cooperative if the players can make commitments that are binding, that can be enforced through law. That's how you – and most diplomats – approach climate negotiations, like a classic piece of statecraft, with trade-offs and transactions. But nothing we all agree is *remotely* enforceable. So it is pointless making these grandiose commitments and pledges. Most at the table won't ever deliver them. *Can't* ever deliver them.'

Barnes sighed. 'But without the targets we don't show people that we are serious. You know that. We lose any sense of ambition and urgency. The whole thing spins on to the next pointless summit. Conferences are forcing moments where we can see what others are prepared to do and push our own systems harder. They're as much negotiations with ourselves as with each other.'

'But these are empty words, Ambassador Barnes. It's not a zero-sum game. This is not poker, where we all have an equal amount to win or lose. Be realistic. It doesn't matter what pledges Bangladesh makes in Amman: they lose everything *whatever* we all do. Some will gain, relatively, in the short term. Look at Russia. Some, like us, will gain by watching their opponents lose. The West can't see more than a decade ahead.'

Barnes leant across the table. 'But your approach means you can't see more than a century ahead.'

The note taker raised his eyebrows. Ling smiled. 'Maybe.' He took another sip and looked out at the view. The air was cooler now, but the heat of the day was still rising from the desert. Ling gestured at the expanse. 'You know, not all of us in Beijing want our country to look like this.'

'And that's why game theory only gets us all so far, Minister. It's not a symmetric game. Human agency is at play too. And it may be the best hope we have. Someone I love told me recently that it's about being decent ancestors. Who in Beijing is playing the game on behalf of your descendants, not just your kids? Aren't you meant to be the strategic ones?'

Ling smiled. He was enjoying this. 'Careful, Ambassador Barnes. You in the West don't have a good track record in telling us what is in our interest.'

Barnes held his hands up. 'Okay, okay, fair enough. But at some point, we're going to have to take a collective leap of trust. I accept that this is not a finite game, with fixed rules and an agreed end point where we can all say we are fine. There are no fixed rules, no finish line and no start line. That's why we need to act differently. We need brave, ambitious collective targets. We need to get the top two hundred emitting companies – most of them yours or American – to get to net zero. We need to fundamentally change our behaviour, at the individual, national and global levels, make this everyone's problem. That's a generational shift of mindset. But our young people are going to demand it of us all. Yours as much as ours. And if we want to stay in power, we have to find a way to give it to them.'

'Nice speech, Ambassador. And is that what your well-meaning young prime minister will say at the conference? Or will he just blame us as usual?'

Barnes let his exasperation show. 'Maybe, Minister, but we've got to stop making this all about scoring clever debating points, pointing out the flaws in each other's arguments. We have to work together, to defy the Thucydides trap as you describe.'

Ling looked exasperated. 'But that would mean learning from history.'

'Isn't the lesson of history that we should try?'

Barnes could sense that Ling was restless, and signalled to the waiter to bring more drinks before he could get up. Ling settled back into his chair, head to one side, assessing Barnes. The file said that he had a fondness for a drink.

'And what if those in Beijing who agreed with you won the argument? *Really* won it. What would be different in how China was treated?'

'You'd get the credit for a start, be seen by the world as the key to progress rather than a domineering neighbour focused solely on its own interests. You would emerge as a genuine leader. You can't get everything you want with economic muscle and hard power alone. Ultimately a country has to be magnetic to succeed.' Barnes gestured towards the fresh can of Pepsi.

'So we get a nice consolation prize in a competition you in the West have designed and run, as always on your rules?'

Barnes shook his head. 'No. Do this deal, and you get to *design* the competition for the future. You get to genuinely build a fresh system for international cooperation. It would be a watershed moment. Recognition by the West, even by America, that we can't run the global order. That the current system has failed.'

Ling spoke more softly. 'But you broke it. *You* fix it.'

Barnes paused. 'We can't, Minister. That's the truth. That's what I've come to understand. And that's ultimately a problem for you too.'

Ling took a deep breath. 'And what about our politics? How do we make a deal stick when the US is killing our diplomats?'

Barnes shook his head. 'They're not. You don't really believe that even President Hoon would do that?'

'Why not? She's capable of worse. She has an election to win, and needs an enemy. Only escalation with us will save her presidency.'

'Then don't give her that.'

'We won't do a deal with her.'

Barnes opted to change tack. He knew they had been glancing at his case, wondering what he had to offer. He lifted it onto the table and turned it towards them, enjoying the moment of power. 'Minister Ling. I have our intelligence from Geneva. Ambassador Yang, my friend, was not killed by the Americans. Omar Ra'ad will share much of this with your ambassador there. But I trust you with the full picture.'

Ling was interested now, despite himself. 'Then who?'

43

The Thucydides Trap

Ling looked at the file for a few minutes, scanning each page thoroughly. Omar and the Swiss police had done a good job. Crawford had done a better one. The evidence, including the Wilhelm confession, was compelling. Barnes watched him closely as he read. So much hung on whether the Chinese agreed.

Ling passed the case to the note taker, who scanned it closely. 'And you are certain of this?'

Barnes nodded.

Ling held his eye. 'And how do we know that we can trust you?'

Barnes shrugged. 'Truthfully? You don't. I've learnt that. But none of us has a choice. I'm learning that too.'

Ling leant forward, but Barnes continued before he could interject. 'You can share what I've given you with the right people in Beijing and they can make their own minds up. Will you do that, Minister?'

For the first time, the minister glanced at the note taker alongside him, who gave the slightest nod of assent.

Barnes pretended not to notice. 'Do you think this means that Beijing can cool things off with Washington? You have plenty of other arguments ahead. But this is not one of them. The Russian group that killed your guy will strike again. It is your enemy now too. And maybe, at least on this, your enemy's enemy could be a friend.'

'That's above my paygrade, Ambassador Barnes. But...' Another glance at the note taker. '...I will argue for that. The problem is that no one is working to cool things off on the other side. Who will talk to President Hoon?'

'Let me work on that.'

Barnes rose from the table and messaged Hermione.

> Making progress with Ch. When do you get here?

He hoped that the Chinese would pick up that he had sent the message. The effort to get their attention, and to get a deal, relied on them seeing him as a serious player in the UK system, with the direct line in to the PM.

The message came back quickly.

> Tomorrow morning. At the airport now. Boss working on speech.

> Hoon bilat?

> Just after we land.

> OK, will send brief. Opportunity, maybe, to de-escalate with Chinese.

Having made sure that the note taker had clocked the sense of assurance with which he had tapped the message, he shook hands with Ling, who held his gaze. The next generation of Chinese diplomats: able to see a moment when they would take charge. Starting to come to terms with that responsibility. Would they do a better or worse job than the Americans and their British sidekicks?

They looked again at the dryness of the desert that surrounded them. The air was full of dust, and smelt sulphurous.

It didn't need to be repeated. Still and beautiful, but no place to live.

Barnes and Crawford didn't stop at any viewpoints on the way back to Amman, Crawford weaving in and out of lorries on the main highway. Barnes managed to doze, fitfully. He felt sharper as they reached the interminable series of roundabouts on the outskirts. They had momentum. The key was now the PM's meeting with Hoon. With Chinese flexibility, Barnes could get the mechanics of a deal in place with Omar and others. But he needed the PM to fix the politics. Back at the hotel he punched out a one-page brief to Hermione, marking it Confidential.

> CoS
>
> Saw key Chinese officials last night. Have shown them compelling evidence that US not behind Yang assassination. They are checking it out but could be reassured. Confident they won't further escalate. But they can't be seen to retreat until US also starts to back down. So PM/Hoon <u>vital</u>. Need her to see risks, make some kind of move.

On climate deal, we don't need anything more from US except that they don't block. Their officials get it, and are helping (whatever the instruction from Hoon). Can manufacture some negotiating fat to give her cosmetic wins if it helps? We have 36 hours to save deal. Massive win for PM, and for all of us. I'm convinced only way is to neutralise US and allow China credit for bringing in BRICs. PM needs to be <u>fired up</u>.

EB

He re-read it before sending, and changed 'could' to 'should'. Underlined 'confident', 'vital' and 'convinced'. He would once have resisted hyperbole, edited it out of drafts from colleagues. She would notice that he had deliberately put it in, to raise the stakes.

Barnes sought Omar out at the hotel. The UN chief had arrived the previous day. He was exhausted, wrung out, but he brightened as he saw him.

'The substance of the deal is almost in place, Ed. Everyone knows what the long-term targets need to be. But this is now all about process and politics, not the substance. We don't have enough time. The Chinese and US delegations are not playing, and the Russians are standing by to sabotage whatever we come up with. And by the way, I'm getting serious grief – from the Americans, Spanish, Somalis, Chinese – for your invitation to the Somaliland governor.'

Barnes waved away the frustration. 'I've made progress with the Chinese. Give it time to percolate through the system. What about the BRICs?' The Brazilians,

Russians, Indians, Chinese and South Africans increasingly tried to coordinate positions at summits, as a counterweight to the G7, dominated by the US and Europe.

'Hesitant. Waiting for a steer from China. But India are restless. Behind the rhetoric, I think they want to do a deal: they'll be hit harder than others if we fail.'

'So what's the package you need?'

Omar pulled a piece of paper from his pocket. Covered in crossings-out and corrections. 'We need practical changes. More of a seat at the table for China and India. Real commitments to change the top emitting companies. A new mechanism to manage global labour mobility: there is no global body overseeing the movement of people worldwide, and millions will be on the move. A UN agency with real teeth to enforce climate agreements and support those needing to change their economies. We need to amend the 1951 Refugee Convention to make it an obligation to offer asylum to climate refugees. An education passport for people on the move, so that they can contribute to their new countries, not threaten them. And we will need a strategy to create entirely new cities near the planet's cooler poles, in land that will be ice-free.'

'Doesn't sound that hard?'

Omar cocked his head. 'Maybe not in a rational world.'

'Keep at them.'

Omar slumped into a chair.

'You okay, Omar?'

He breathed deeply. 'We'll get there. But it would all be much easier without the humans.'

Barnes smiled. 'You should make that your motto.'

Omar grinned back. And then grimaced. 'You know, even with this deal, we're going to have the greatest movement of humans in history. The number of days where temperatures get over fifty degrees Celsius will mean billions head north to cooler climates. We already have 100 million refugees, half of them kids. And look what that has done to politics in the West: we quickly reached the limits of our compassion.'

'Then, my friend, we'll need to find new limits.'

'Our mistakes used to be well motivated. Can't your governments see that you need migrants? Ageing, unproductive populations will go stale. You need to move from talking about controlling migration to planning for it.'

'Then we'll need to build a new politics too. But we can't fix that today, Omar.'

Barnes wondered whether to ask his friend the question that had been haunting him, even before it was clear that Crawford, and maybe even his daughter, had found their answer. When was it right to use violence to save lives? Omar knew the rules as well as he did. But should they be changing the rules?

But Omar's mind was elsewhere. 'Migration is the human story. But this will be the end of the idea that we belong to a land, or it belongs to us. The end of borders and nation states.'

Barnes smiled again. His argument was one for another day. And maybe he did not need to know Omar's answer. Maybe he did not want to know it.

'Let's not get ahead of ourselves. We're supposed to be selling this deal to a bunch of representatives of those nation states. We need to get out there and do that.'

Omar nodded, sighed deeply, and rose. 'Leave the Indians and Brazilians to me. But you need to find a way to keep the Russians from sabotaging it.'

It was definitely best not to know what Omar felt about the ends justifying the violent means.

'We're working on that.'

44

Breakaway

Orla was doing what she loved best: trying to understand what made a person tick. But the governor of Somaliland was sending mixed signals.

Stephanie had organised for them to meet at his hotel. It was away from the other delegations. As an observer rather than head of state he didn't have a meeting room at the conference centre, and wouldn't be part of the main plenary. But he got to attend the opening and closing sessions, as well as the king's reception.

There was always a rush at summits to book a decent hotel. Many delegations would book whole floors. The US would often book an entire hotel, so as to have complete control of security. By the time the Somaliland delegation had got their invitation, there was not much accommodation left in Amman.

A man dozed behind the reception desk as Ali met them in the main lobby.

Ali was lean and wiry, with a jerkiness to his movement, like someone who was not used to staying still. Orla was still not sure why Stephanie had insisted she meet him, or why he had made it a condition for her release. But she was willing to talk to him for Stephanie, and because she knew this was how she followed the story.

She noted the genuine affection in the hug Stephanie gave him as he welcomed them. Stephanie had always been naturally affectionate, but there was genuine camaraderie there, maybe more. They took the lift to the fifteenth floor and walked along the corridor to a room.

Inside, the curtains were drawn and the room felt stuffy. When Orla asked for coffee, Ali had to take the kettle to the bathroom to fill it with water. She switched her request to tea to avoid the instant coffee. There was confusion over who should sit on which of the three chairs available.

As they sat, Stephanie nodded at Ali to start. She was in control, as ever.

Orla produced a pad and pen, and made detailed notes, mainly to reassure them both that she was taking it seriously. Once Ali started talking, he didn't need much encouragement.

He gave a detailed history, from the spice and frankincense trade through to the colonial era. The Italians took Somalia, the Brits took Somaliland. Distinct, separate. Aden as a key outpost of empire. And then when the colonists left, Somalia's draconian rule, and the decades of wars of independence. The effort to be recognised by the UN, by the big powers. 'We are the largest unrecognised state.'

Orla knew most of this. But she also knew it was a pretty hopeless cause to try and bring to public attention. Too far off the radar screen. When the West looked at the region they saw insecurity, piracy, terrorism: they wanted more state control, not less.

Ali could see that she was drifting. He leant forward. 'I know what you're thinking: it's all too complicated. But we're different to the Somalis. We govern ourselves calmly and effectively. Our education and health stats back it up. We're not like the militias and pirates over there.'

He glanced at her pad. He seemed to have an innocent confidence in her ability to tell their story to the world. She looked at Stephanie, who was nodding along with theatrical relish. Ali was a natural communicator. If he couldn't get the message across, no one could.

But to have any chance of telling the story, Orla needed an edge, an angle. 'And you're willing to use violence for independence?'

'Hasn't everyone else?' She liked his lack of finesse, the absence of prepared answers.

'And terrorism? Like in the mall in Nairobi?' Barnes would call it a shopping centre.

He inhaled deeply. She saw, for the first time, his eyes flick from side to side. 'There, we are less sure. There are those who argue we have no choice. The world will ignore us otherwise. My cousin, Hussein, who led the mall operation, was one of those.'

'And you, Ali? You're in charge. What do you think?'

Another hesitation. 'I want to show my people we can achieve what we want through negotiation. Through the UN. Through convincing the big powers that we are separate to Somalia, that we have a case that deserves to be heard.' He glanced again at her pad.

'And that's why you were so keen to be here, in Amman?'

'Yes.'

Orla was struck by the strength of the assertion. Was he trying too hard, or just nervous?

He sensed it too, and calmed his voice. 'But we have as much right to debate the climate crisis as all of them.

It is killing our people, driving new conflicts for water, bringing us more of Somalia's militia.'

'And if you fail to show progress through diplomacy?'

He seemed to withdraw, his confidence draining. 'Then the others win the argument. We do what we have been doing for fifty years, since we were denied independence. Like Hussein did. We fight and we die.'

'You fight Mogadishu? The Somalis?'

'Yes. But we also fight the world.'

Orla cocked her head. She was trying to understand the man behind the politician. There was a zeal to him, but also a gentleness, a vulnerability.

Stephanie sensed that he needed reinforcement. 'Whatever you write about all this, Orla, I want to be clear that Ali could not have been kinder to me during my time with him.'

Orla hated euphemism. 'Your time? As in when he had you taken hostage?'

Stephanie shrugged. 'He didn't know at that point who I was. They were just looking for a way to hold the West to the commitments Dad had made. But it didn't take them long to connect the dots. And for Ali to realise that they had that extra – what does Dad always call it – leverage.'

'And you don't resent him that?'

'Look, I was terrified at first. Remember that I'd just had the most frightening moment of my life.'

'The moment when Hussein threatened you with execution?'

Stephanie shook her head. Orla saw her hold herself together. 'No, the moment when he threatened Dad.'

Orla saw Ali look at her with genuine sympathy. 'I am sorry, Stephanie, you know that. And now that I have met your father, I know that he is an honest man. That he will do what he promised us.'

Orla saw again the complicity between them. Heavy footsteps outside, and the door opened. No knock.

Two strongly built men, uncomfortable in suits. They ignored Orla and Stephanie.

'Ali, it is all ready.'

Ali glanced uncomfortably at the women, and gestured at the men to stop. 'Stephanie, Orla, these are my... colleagues.'

Orla had enough experience of interviewing Northern Irish colleagues to recognise a military wing. 'Colleagues?'

The shorter of the men interjected. 'Interview over, Ali.' Orla also had enough experience of Northern Ireland to understand the complex interplay *between* the political and military wings.

Ali looked crestfallen. For a moment he looked as though he might argue, or attempt to continue their discussion. But instead, with an apologetic glance at Stephanie, he rose to indicate that they had finished. He showed them to the lift and accompanied them down to the reception.

In the hotel lobby he turned to block their departure. Orla could see the polish gone, the jerky charm of their reception. 'You see, Orla, I don't have long to show that we are making progress, that our arguments are being heard.'

Stephanie put a hand on his arm. 'You can make this invitation count, Ali. These two receptions alone – tonight and tomorrow – are surely evidence you are making progress. I'll be going with my father to the conference centre this morning. Get the photos of the reception tonight circulating. And Orla will tell your story. You have important days ahead.'

Orla saw the intensity in Ali's eyes as he shook his head. 'No, Stephanie, I only have hours. I am relying on you, and your father, to show them that this is working. Or…'

Orla sensed more. 'Or what, Ali? Is this another threat? Or are you in danger?'

He looked dejected. 'Or I lose control of it all.'

They were silent for a while in the car back to the hotel. Stephanie wanted to give Orla time to find her angle. She waited for Orla to signal that she was ready to discuss the meeting. It was only as they arrived back at the conference venue.

'That's not it, is it Steph? Your message asking me to come wasn't just about helping your dad, was it? Or even the Somalilanders, even Ali. You wanted me to decide I needed to find a way to tell the story of why Max's assassinations were necessary. You've been working with him. You played me, too?'

The smallest of nods from Stephanie. Orla narrowed her eyes. 'But when do you and Max stop? What happens when new climate change deniers, or energy investors, or airline magnates, or populist politicians emerge to replace these ones? Will you have to continue?'

Stephanie interjected. 'Not if you tell the story in the way only you can. It will make it harder for others to simply replace them.'

Orla nodded slowly. The story had brought her here. 'I can understand why you can't tell your father what you are doing, Stephanie. But you can be honest with me.'

Stephanie heard the hint of anger in her voice. 'I know how furious Dad is with me, however he hides it. I shouldn't have put him, or you, through the ringer like that. But it was the only way to make this work. And… for him too.'

Orla nodded at Stephanie, encouraging her to continue. 'What do you mean?'

She felt the ferocity before Stephanie's words came out. 'Because I want him to feel alive. He can't admit to himself that none of it matters. All that diplomacy is too… hardwired. Imagine him trying to do something else. And maybe he's regained that irritating sense of certainty?'

Orla grinned as she undid her seatbelt. 'I hope so.' She paused with her hand on the door handle. 'But I'm talking about more than all that, Steph. We never really spoke much about what happened in Paris. To Amina Joshi. You didn't want to go there. I understand that. But all this…'

Her gesture took in the room, the lies, the assassinations. 'All this is not really that different. Once you get past the idea that helping people to die can be ethical, it's really just a question of which people need to die, is that right? But that's not your call. How can it be? However much evidence you put together. However easily Max can do it. What separates him from a serial killer? What separates you?'

Stephanie was looking at her feet but when she raised her face the eyes were shining again, the zeal restored. 'The outcome.'

They walked towards the conference centre doors. Stephanie blocked Orla's path before they entered.

'Orla, tell me one thing: has Dad also worked it out about me and Max?'

Orla thought of Barnes, working the conference room, in his element. The relief when he had been reunited with his daughter.

'No.' It was her turn to bar Stephanie's way, to hold her eye. 'We must not distract him from getting this deal. And the truth is, he can't ever know.'

45

Summit or Valley?

Omar and Alice met Barnes and Stephanie as they arrived at the venue for the climate conference, a specially built complex away from the centre of Amman. The road in was lined with trees, and the 160 flags of the participating countries. Each had experts and officials who had already been there several days. Barnes passed several in the entrance, already with the ghostly new parent look of adults who had stayed up for several nights. By now, many were only still functioning through a combination of caffeine and the ticking clock of the arrival of their leader.

Omar, in a navy jacket and crumpled chinos, shook his head as they passed them. 'It's a wonder we get anything done by this stage. Everyone is utterly exhausted.'

Alice chuckled as they reached the main security desk. She was wearing an elegant trouser suit. She did not seem so tired as the others, and was clearly trying to keep Omar's spirits up. 'Each country's delegation has a head, usually their president or PM. The *grand fromage*. They won't tend to wear their gold lanyards, expecting security to recognise them. Always awkward when they don't.'

Stephanie was looking at the layout of the main entrance. 'And what about the rest of the delegation?'

Alice continued. 'The key adviser to the head is normally a chief of staff or private secretary. They'll be with them throughout. For the Brits, that will be Hermione Buckingham, I guess.' Then, with a smile, 'Your friend, eh Ed?'

Barnes nodded but refused the bait.

Alice went on. 'They get given a silver badge. The lead climate adviser joins the leader for the plenary sessions, where much of the negotiation takes place. They get a silver badge too. Other advisers and staff, four per delegation, have red lanyards. Access but not access all areas. Clear as mud, right?'

Stephanie was listening carefully. Thinking about how she might need to get Max Crawford in at some point, if the diplomacy needed to be a bit more muscular.

Barnes had been to too many of these summits. The protocol and the battle of the badges so often took over. But he was steely now: this one was different. It mattered. When the chips were down, what would they all be willing to sacrifice for a deal?

Omar chuckled in his direction. 'Veterans of the circuit like Ed will judge the hosts by their ability to keep the discipline around access for each group, even more than whether we can chair the meeting half effectively.'

Barnes grinned back. 'We also know every trick in the book to get round it. Badges and lanyards get passed around the delegation, especially when we need to get extra advisers in. We'll get as many interpreters' badges as we can, or pass officials off as security. It's a nightmare for the actual security, trying to keep bad guys out. And of course, the Americans make a point of busting through their adviser and security limits, daring the host to say no.'

He was quietly pleased to be handed a silver badge by Omar, with a mischievous wink. Omar, as the key UN convener, already had a gold one. He would be there for the endgame.

They continued through the conference centre. Every delegation had its own delegation room, and a space where leaders could hold bilateral meetings – the bilats.

Barnes was in his natural habitat now. 'These rooms are the lifeblood of summits. Most leaders loathe the plenary sessions with a passion...' He smiled at Omar, who was looking momentarily crestfallen. '...with their counterparts reading prepared statements. They do their main business through the equivalent of speed dating, their advisers setting up a different type of meeting.'

Stephanie groaned. 'Surely a meeting is just a meeting?'

Barnes raised his eyes in mock theatricality. 'No, a bilat is a formal encounter with another head of government. Less formal is a tete-a-tete, a more intimate one-to-one for trickier or more personal issues. For when we are trying to gain a genuine concession. But the real action is in the spontaneous "pull asides" from the main meeting, or "brush-bys" on the way to the plenary. Make sense?'

Alice sniggered at his earnestness. Stephanie remained serious. 'And where will any developments be announced to we mortals waiting outside, Pops?'

Omar indicated the media briefing room. Barnes pointed out the podium. 'Those will be carefully prepared, and probably only used towards the end of the conference, once the deal emerges.'

Stephanie was thinking now of Orla's ability to get to the substance of the meeting, and get the right bits of it out. 'And in advance of any deal?'

Omar indicated another part of the media centre. 'They'll do a pool spray when a leader has something to say, or just a grip and grin when they don't.'

Barnes knew what Stephanie was really asking. 'But the key for us is that media teams will be in and out of this room. It's where they interact most freely with journalists. Orla is accredited media, so she'll base here. And I'll pass her news as we want it to emerge. She'll know what to get out there and how, mainly on Twitter. She'll also hear what other delegations are saying.'

They moved through to the coffee area. The calm before the storm. Tomorrow this would be full of officials, leaders, movement, tension. For now, there were only staff, setting up spaces for the drinks and snacks, cleaning and polishing.

Alice shrugged. 'All those flags and podiums. The grandeur of what the public get to see. But it's not exactly Versailles behind the scenes.'

Omar smiled. 'Not much real diplomacy is Versailles, as you must know by now. Anyway, the key is to create space for the more informal interactions. A decent deal won't be secured in the plenary, however brilliantly...' A chuckle. '...I chair it. It will be done out here, between key officials. The more we can work that dynamic, the more ambitious we can be. Formality kills ambition.'

Barnes sipped his coffee, worrying at how tired Omar looked. How long did he really have? 'Yes, that's the key. And somehow we have to create a sense of urgency, or surprise. Most leaders won't do much actual negotiation. They'll arrive assuming that the deal is mostly done. And that deal is, but it's crap.'

A glance at Omar, who raised his hands in mock offence, but nodded agreement. 'Fair enough. Lots of hot air and platitudes. Of course, we will claim it as much more. Most climate conferences end with everyone claiming success. And yet here we all are, meeting again.'

Alice stood, looking at her watch. 'Omar, we need to keep moving. King's reception for leaders and their chiefs of staff is at seven. You can get back to all your conferencing tomorrow. And then we can all collapse tomorrow evening once they leave again.'

She gave Barnes a peck on the cheek. Omar shook his hand. Barnes held his arm for a moment. 'This can't be business as usual, my friend. Let's make this one different.'

Alice pulled at his other arm. 'See you at the reception, Ed. You don't have to worry about your frock.'

As they walked out together, Stephanie turned to Barnes. 'So *how* do we make this one different? Can you really get something serious?'

Barnes held her eye. 'We line the Chinese up to make a more ambitious set of proposals, which the Americans and Russians don't expect. We shift the undecided in their direction, and neutralise the hostile. The chair – Omar – uses the plenary to demonstrate momentum to a deal with real, concrete targets. And we rely on people's desire to do better than normal, their need to leave at five p.m. tomorrow, and a whole heap of luck.'

Stephanie chewed her lip. 'Except this time we're trying to reduce the element of luck.'

Barnes nodded. 'Yes. Because, thanks to you, we're not going to rely on diplomacy alone.'

46

The Theatre of Diplomacy

The greeting line at the reception for leaders moved fast. They had been allotted arrival times, their convoys carefully choreographed to ensure none of them had to wait too long.

The chief of protocol hovered next to the King of Jordan as he received them, partly to ensure that he remembered who they all were, partly to ensure that he didn't fall into prolonged conversation. Grip and grin: a swift handshake, the photos and into the throng. Omar and Alice were positioned nearby, to sweep the leaders and their chiefs of staff into the main reception space.

The Jordanians had gone to considerable trouble to lay on a spectacle. The palace was lit by candles, the light shimmering. Waiters glided among the guests with trays of champagne and Jordanian canapés, carefully selected so as to be easily consumed in a bite. 'No bits that get stuck in teeth,' as Alice had insisted. She was wearing a discreet diamond necklace, carefully chosen to be noticed, but not too much. A floor-length black dress: modest and unmissable.

Leaders who had done a few of these summits before liked to keep moving at the reception. Be highly visible, don't get stuck in a corner, and shake as many hands as possible. Move fast, stay low. The adviser with them would often remind them of the two to three key messages for each counterpart. *Looking forward to seeing you in September. Any progress on that trade deal? Congratulations on the football.*

There was a fair amount of insincere backslapping and laughter. Everyone wanted to be seen with those who were on the way up. Those on the way down – facing inevitable election defeat, or in terminal economic decline – could be spotted by their slightly desperate effort to be included. They would manoeuvre their way into the photos, jostling with hungrier rivals. The herd could smell weakness and decline.

Barnes stood to one side, watching the throng, checking which advisers really had the ear of their leader, watching the dynamics between different regional groups. There was a physicality to statecraft at this level. The Chinese president was working hard: a good sign. The Russian president was off to one side, with a group of minor regional allies: not playing. Not necessarily a bad sign. There was no sign of Elizabeth Hoon.

Hermione Buckingham sidled up to Barnes. The PM was in the midst of a group of Pacific Island leaders. They had most to lose from a weak outcome to the talks, but very limited leverage in the negotiations. Barnes had told them that his job was to get them to dial up their interventions, make the sense of real jeopardy much clearer.

She winked at him, mischievously. 'How did you get into this tonight, Ed? You're not on our No 10 list. I made sure of that personally.'

'So I saw. I haven't completely lost my touch, Hermione. How's it looking?' He wanted to engage her for long enough that the Chinese would notice, and carry on taking him as seriously as he needed. Hermione noticed him become more histrionic in his gestures, like a peacock attracting a mate. Not far off.

They looked across to the PM. He was unlikely to get out of the huddle for some time. He had an earnest intensity to him, but also a resigned sadness.

Hermione shrugged. 'On nights like this you get a pretty swift sense of where we are in the pecking order. Diplomacy is easy when you're a country on the rise. Other leaders answer the phone, seek you out, expand their embassies, ask for trade deals.' She sighed as she looked across at her PM. He was listening intently to a leader they didn't recognise. 'And then there's that.'

Barnes nodded. 'Hard power is back. You can see the leaders who have it behind them, who are willing to use it. Diplomacy is also easy when you've won a few battles... or can win them. We forgot that projection of force still matters. Your rivals are more inclined to see things your way, and your allies to cut you some slack. I've always been team diplomat. But the diplomats who run empires aren't the people who build them.'

Hermione was looking for a way to get the PM out of the huddle. She sensed his need to be liberated. 'Truth is we're barely Britain, let alone Global Britain. Gone from writing the list of the problems that need discussion to,' she paused to nod at the NATO Secretary General, 'appearing near the top of it.'

Barnes moved between her and the PM, to buy a few more moments. 'That's why you have to find a way to work through others tomorrow. The PM badly needs a decent deal, and everyone here knows it. But he can't be too eager, can't over-claim. Get him talking to the Chinese. Encourage them to take a few risks for once. Show them a bit of leg... sorry, that there is genuine credit for them if they do. Show them some space between us and the Americans. I think they could surprise us.'

Hermione sucked her teeth. 'The Americans have warned us off too much of that. And they're watching.'

Barnes shook his head. 'At this summit, Elizabeth Hoon is our opponent, not our ally. As they have always told us, there are no friends in statecraft, only interests.'

'Touché. You've become quite the realist in your cynical old age.'

She hadn't seen him this steely before. 'The rules have changed, Hermione. Because it matters more. Because there are players willing to turn the chessboard over.' A gesture towards the Russian corner. 'We need to work much harder than them. Maybe we've been too squeamish. Your man needs to get out there and use what power we have, not agonise about how quickly we lost it.'

Hermione rolled her eyes. 'Thanks for the pep talk, Ed. We'll try. But don't set the bar too high for him. For tomorrow. You've seen the current text. The working groups have settled around the usual lowest common denominator stuff. You can probably still remember a time when the Americans didn't have to tell people they were great, and we didn't have to say we were global. Until the Americans really engage, no one knows what flex there will be.'

Barnes blocked her path one last time. 'Foreign policy is a myth, Hermione, you know that. Leaders take decisions based on short-term pragmatism. Or make no decision at all, but simply react to a situation. It's only later, when they're done, that they try to explain it in some kind of rational way. Kissinger is only considered a great foreign policy maker because he lived long enough to explain the bits he was lucky enough to get right.' He could see he was losing her. 'Okay, I'll let you go. But can I come to the bilat tomorrow? Help the PM make the case to Hoon?'

Her eyes flashed. 'Absolutely no way. When you're in this kind of messianic mood, I can't let you anywhere near either of them. Stick to what you do, let me do what I do. Now, let me rescue the Boss.'

And she was back into the throng. Barnes spotted Ling at his president's side. Another good sign. They nodded at each other across the room.

Ali, the Somaliland governor, was suddenly in his space. Despite arriving early he had cut quite a detached, lonely figure during the evening. Most people didn't know who he was. Those that did kept a wide berth so as not to upset the rest of the African group. Those with separatist movements of their own shunned him.

But Ali looked eager, over-excited. 'High Commissioner... a pleasure.'

Barnes was looking over his shoulder, trying to spot his Indian counterpart. Normally he would have tried to hide his impatience with an unwanted interruption like this. 'I'm glad you could make it, Governor. I heard you had a good meeting with Orla. I hope we can now conclude that I've done what I promised. Everyone who matters here knows I bent the rules to get you in. My ministry are livid. The Americans are fuming with us, saying it's a reward for terrorism. They're not wrong.'

Here the power had switched. This was Barnes's world. They both knew it.

'Indeed, High Commissioner. And we are grateful. But I need you to know that it is tough for me right now. I need something to show for all this... glad-handing. I'm in a minority at home in thinking it can work. Can you introduce me to your PM? It might make a difference.'

Barnes looked at him with exasperation. 'Seriously, Ali? Do you not realise the stakes here? We have less than twenty-four hours to get the deal we need, or else the planet continues to go up in smoke. It won't matter whether you are independent of Somalia if your land can't sustain life. I've done my bit for you. Let me do what I'm here to do.' He thrust past Ali, towards the corner where the Indians had based themselves, leaving the other man a disconsolate figure again.

Alice watched Ed Barnes from across the room. As the evening gained momentum, he gave the impression of being in constant motion. In and out of the delegation rooms, moving between the groups, driving, driving, driving, even when everyone else had given up. He was working on a group of African leaders, gathered around President Obwocha of Kenya, when Alice pulled him to one side.

Barnes was not sure whether he was allowed to say how stunning she looked. 'Nice diamonds. How's Omar doing?'

She had already seen him taking her in. 'These heels are agony. Pretty demoralised. No one's saying much tonight. The Americans are sending out very negative signals.'

'Get him to focus on the Non-Aligned Movement. We need them intervening early in the plenary, to set the tone, get across the urgency. Make it harder for the Russians and Americans. I'll work on the Indian adviser. Keep his energy up.'

She smiled. 'You're loving this, aren't you? Whereas I think this is the sort of party where the invitation should have said carriages at twelve, ambulances at three, hearses at six.'

There was a clinking of glasses, and the chief of protocol came to a podium at the end of the hall. The waiters and their trays receded. 'Excellencies, the king.' The conversations ceased abruptly, and the leaders turned respectfully towards the podium.

The king looked slightly awkward, momentarily overwhelmed by the occasion. He cleared his throat.

'Dear friends, a warm welcome to Jordan. *Ahlan wa sahlan.* How do we restore society, reclaim our humanity and reimagine the future? Human society advanced one fireside discussion at a time. Much more important than decisive battles or influential individuals were the millions of unrecorded individual conversations, the millions of unrecorded moments of restraint, the millions of unrecorded simple fragments of wisdom passed on through generations. Tonight is the moment for you to have those conversations. And tomorrow is the moment to show your wisdom. This is your moment: a minute to midnight. This is our moment. To show that we can change. To make peace not just with each other, but with our planet.'

Barnes nodded at Omar and mouthed 'nicely done'.

His friend looked back grimly. He had aged several years in a few days. His skin was paler, looser on his face. The words wouldn't matter if the summit fizzled out.

–

In a small hotel on the outskirts of Amman, the militia leader attached the charges to the suicide vest, and felt the weight of it. They had lost patience with Ali's vanity exercise, and with the distracted world. Too many had died in the struggle for independence for this parade of flags and canapés. Maybe this is *our* moment.

The system did not need changing. It needed destroying.

47

Interests Not Friendships

Ed Barnes was waiting in the delegation room as the PM's breakfast with Elizabeth Hoon concluded. He watched her sweep past imperiously with Brad Curtis and her entourage. He felt an undiplomatic hatred for the president. It was vital that he had made some sort of progress in neutralising her.

Hermione emerged from the room. She looked pale. She poured herself a large coffee. At this point of the summit the caffeine was all that was keeping most of the advisers going.

'Stay hydrated.'

Her look said, *Bloody Ed Barnes.*

He needed to keep her as an ally, and so dropped the jokey attitude. 'Went badly then?'

She nodded despairingly. 'Couldn't have been worse.'

Barnes grimaced. 'She'll kill the deal?'

'She was worse than I've ever seen. Even her advisers were looking embarrassed. Ranted about lack of respect from the Chinese. Completely hostile to any deal. Focused on the threat of terrorism, the need to stop the migrants in suicide vests. Even ranted about the Brits getting the "Somaliland terrorists" along. Great work there, Ed. Planning to do her speech at the plenary and

then spend the rest of the conference in her delegation room preparing the press conference to bring it all
crashing down. All the politics work in that direction for
her.'

Barnes groaned. 'Just brinkmanship?'

Hermione looked dejected. 'No. I don't think she's
that clever. It's showmanship.'

Barnes weighed up the prospects. The Brits were not
going to be major players. But he had to keep them in
play. 'So what does the PM want now?'

'He's gone into one of his bouts of introspection.
Debating the failure of democracy and the lights going
out in the shining city on a hill.'

Barnes grimaced. 'Bit late for all that, isn't it?'

Hermione rolled her eyes in exasperation. 'I'm trying,
Ed, I really am. But he's off on one. Says democracies may
die at the hands of men with guns but they are more likely
to die at the hand of elected leaders. She was really bad in
there. I think we've all underestimated how... *evil*... she
is.' Normally they would both have flinched at the use of
the 'e' word, thinking of it as hyperbole.

Barnes held her eye. 'And so if he can't do it, then help
others lead on this deal. We don't have to be at the centre
of everything. Maybe this is how it feels to be a second
order power.'

'Maybe. But after that meeting, I'm not sure if it
is creeping irrelevance, temporary blip, or permanent
decline.'

'For the UK?'

'For democracy.'

'Then it doesn't matter which it is. We have to fight
for it. Elizabeth Hoon will be voted out in two months, a

footnote in the history of a young democracy. The checks and balances will work. Democracy is only in decline because we're not defending it.'

Hermione sighed. 'But that's the problem. The fundamental principle of democracy is that leaders leave. And Roland doesn't think she will.'

There had been media speculation that she wouldn't go if she lost, but Barnes had always dismissed it. 'Seriously? So Goebbels was right: democracy gives its enemies the means to destroy it? Surely it's unthinkable. And surely there comes a point where the UK can't accept it.'

'So what do we do?'

Barnes was pensive. 'Democracy was invented to stop people like Elizabeth Hoon. But to believe in it, ultimately you have to believe in humans.'

'I'm not sure the PM does right now. Certainly not in the US president.'

'Then she's the bug in the system. It doesn't mean the system is broken.'

'But it's not just her. Nationalists are on the move everywhere.'

'Because the fish rots from the head.'

'So, again, what do we do?'

Barnes paused. She saw his shoulders fall. And then he composed himself.

'We take the fight to her. We get this deal done. Can you allow me access to whatever intel you're getting on the other delegations?'

Hermione looked quizzical. 'Am I an interest or a friend right now?'

Barnes smiled back. 'You're both, for now.'

She shrugged. 'I guess you can see it. I never have time to read much of it anyway. Why? What do you have in mind?'

'I think we need to even it all up a bit.'

48

Plenary

Omar's pessimism appeared well placed as the leaders arrived for the first of the two plenary sessions. But Barnes, who had been at the conference centre since six a.m., was more energised, despite the failure of the UK prime minister's session with Hoon. He sought Orla out in the media zone.

'What's the mood among the press?'

Orla shrugged. 'Pretty cynical. Most of them have covered too many of these summits. They can see the chasm between the rhetoric and the substance. How is today different?'

Barnes ran through his efforts the previous night. The mood was shifting. Leaders knew that the current package wasn't ambitious enough. But the US and Russian resistance to new ideas was having a chilling effect on many.

'The key dynamic of the day is still that we need China to create the momentum shift, and then to find a way to prevent the US and Russia from wrecking it. Can you get expectations moving in that direction? Build up the hope that China sees an opportunity to provide leadership.'

'Moving the expectations is easy. Everyone in here is desperate for something to report, and it's pretty thin gruel. Can I say that the Chinese are briefing that an initiative is coming?'

Barnes hesitated. There was a risk that the Chinese delegation would react negatively. But they were too far along now. If they had decided to move, the decision was taken. If not, then any serious deal was beyond reach anyway. 'Yes. Say you got it from well-placed UN sources.' *Proceed until apprehended. Seek forgiveness later.*

Barnes went back into the main hall. It was now a mass of activity. Everyone seemed to be on the move. How much of it was actually productive? He lingered outside the Chinese delegation room. A constant stream of officials flowed in and out. Eventually he saw Ling and moved to intercept him.

Ling gave him a conspiratorial grin. '*Excellency.* I thought you would find me pretty swiftly today. Feeling optimistic still?'

'We have no choice. But it all depends on you now. Did you win the arguments you needed to win?'

Ling paused. 'You are asking a lot of us. Especially when the Americans are so belligerent. So intransigent.'

'But that means no one else can lead this shift. And it is in your interests. You know that. How can we help?'

'My president is seeing the Europeans next, and then the BRICs. The first is politics, the second is substance. If he gets enough reassurance from the Europeans that they will follow our commitments, he'll table a package with Brazil, Russia and India. We know Brazil will support it. They are major, er, beneficiaries. But all our discussions with Russia have been negative. And India are still heavily influenced by the Non-Aligned Movement.'

Barnes nodded. The message was clear. 'Thank you for your trust. Involve Omar in the BRICs meeting – he has more credibility with Brazil, Russia, India and China than us. As convener, he has more chance at shifting the Non-Aligned Movement.'

Ling looked at him carefully. 'I will consult. And we would expect him not just to be supportive but to make our leader feel that we can be in the driving seat.' He nodded briskly at Barnes and headed back into the scrum around the delegation room. Officials parted to make space as he entered.

Barnes messaged the French diplomatic adviser, Aurelie Lafont. An old friend and an old opponent from Paris.

> Vital that you ramp up the Chinese. Be as open as possible. Build their confidence that they can lead us all out of this mess.

Aurelie sent back an immediate reply.

> Any serious signs of something? The media seem to think so. Stories percolating that the Chinese are on manoeuvres. But most delegations seem in the dark. Including us.

> Yes, something's brewing. But they need to know it won't crash and burn.

She was spiky. She didn't like the sense of being manipulated, especially by Barnes.

Barnes sought Orla out again in the media suite. Stephanie was with her. 'Getting there, Pops?'

Barnes felt energised on seeing her. 'The odds are still stacked against us. But it's all still in play.'

'Max is on standby.'

Barnes winced. 'You know he can't come anywhere near this place. It's too big a risk. And we're doing this my way.'

Stephanie raised her hands in mock surrender. 'I know, I know, but just in case. In the meantime, I bring good news.' Barnes was intrigued. 'I bumped into Obwocha. The Kenyans are part of the non-aligned group. He's making progress. There is a faction who are saying that they should make much more ambitious commitments on zero carbon whether or not the big players put serious money on the table. They know this can't end with the usual fallouts where everyone has an excuse not to act: poor countries can't afford to; rich ones say they are no longer the major polluters.'

Barnes clenched a fist. 'Excellent. I'll let Omar know. Get a message into Ali to support. Say there is a fresh initiative coming. Brazil and China. Build a sense that this is going to be different.'

Orla interjected. 'I hope you're right. The media expectations are now running well ahead of where you seem to be in there. Unless this is big, they will dump all over the deal.'

341

Barnes was steely. 'We have no choice. If there is no deal, the media reaction is the least of our worries. And this is the only way to pile pressure on the US. The PM made no progress, has pretty much given up on them.'

Orla nodded. 'I told you. She's off the reservation. And what about Russia?'

'Let's leave them to the Chinese. I need to get back in there.'

Stephanie grabbed his arm. Her eyes were bright. 'Pops, you've got this.'

Barnes felt the confidence surge through him. He was where he needed to be.

–

And in the hotel room on the outskirts of Amman, Ali ignored Stephanie's call as he briefed the militia leaders on the reception the night before. He started with an effort to make the most of the brief interactions, the photos that showed that they were at least in the room.

But no one was taking that seriously. He was told firmly to stop, and his voice petered out. He received his instructions on the role he must now play in getting the world's attention.

49

BRICs

Omar ducked out of the main plenary. He had been surprised and intrigued to receive the Chinese invitation to the BRICs meeting. The four leaders were already there, and he greeted them formally and with deference, while he sought to read the room. The Chinese delegation looked anxious. The Russian president was scowling. The Chinese president motioned them to the table with a smile. This was new territory for them too.

There was no protocol on who would speak first, or even chair the session. But it was clear to all those present that the Chinese were now in charge. They put their headphones on, and the translators geared up. The Brazilian leader spoke first. 'We are all sick of these summits being driven by the West. Today risks being no different. They draft the communiqué, they set the rules, they decide who to praise and who to blame.' There were nods around the table, especially from the Indian delegation. 'But what if we change that? The Europeans want a more ambitious deal but can't deliver it. The NAM want serious financial commitments, but need us to move first. The Americans are not on the pitch.'

The Chinese president smiled benignly before he motioned for the Brazilian leader to continue. The Russian officials looked wary.

'So I propose that we agree to back whatever China is able to propose today. Change the narrative. Show that the US is not calling the shots.'

There was a pause as this settled. The Indian prime minister spoke next. His voice was quiet, thoughtful. 'But how can we back something when we haven't seen it?'

All eyes turned to the Chinese president, who glanced at Ling before taking a deep breath. 'The world is changing. The competence of our and your national strategies, combined with the decadence of the West, means that we are now in a much stronger position. And they have left us with a serious problem on climate. If this is to be a century of cooperation and partnership, to replace the colonial lectures, we need to show we can be different.'

The Chinese delegation were not taking notes: this was scripted. The note takers from the other delegations wrote everything down. Omar leant forward: the substance was coming.

Ling passed around a short document, in English. The Chinese president gestured at them to read it. It had just seven points.

1. Zero greenhouse gas emissions by 2030.
2. Every country to take action against top 20 emitting companies.
3. Fund massive reforestation programme in Amazon and Congo.
4. Ban all extraction of fossil fuels.
5. 400bn USD for renewable energy, rewilding, adaptation.
6. Ban plastic.
7. New UN body to deliver binding targets, including to limit global warming to 1%.

Omar whistled quietly through his teeth. It was almost poetic in its simplicity. But every clause was a game changer in comparison to previous agreements. Much more money and much harder commitments. It went far beyond what he had been proposing, even in his moments of wild ambition. He looked up to follow the reactions around the table.

The Brazilian nodded approvingly. He had clearly seen the document already. And he knew that China had set aside the reforestation money for the Amazon. It would secure his re-election.

The Indian leader looked intrigued, glancing at his delegation for advice. Who gets the money for renewables? What's the cost to us? Who pays? Officials looked stunned.

The Russian leader had pushed the paper away, thrown off his headphones and was shaking his head. The Chinese officials looked around the room with uncertainty. This was new territory now.

Omar had once been told at school that the key to most situations was to take twenty seconds of 'insane courage'. How many more chances would he have to do that?

He took a deep breath. 'Mr President, if I may interject here, this is an extraordinary and brave set of commitments. A moment of genuine leadership. Alongside what the negotiations have already secured it will go far beyond what any of us hoped for this meeting, and for this collective effort. It will, I suggest, also gain great public support. Globally. I cannot speak of course for the UN at this point, but I am confident that in return for this bold leadership, key players would ask China to provide the lead official for the new UN body.'

What was it Ed Barnes always said? *Proceed until appre-hended.* Maybe he should tell Ed about the cancer.

The Chinese president smiled broadly. Omar saw Ling nodding in satisfaction. But the Russian pushed his chair away from the table and stood. His delegation stood more slowly. He spoke in English now. Temporary at least, but today's alliance was with the US. 'With respect, we cannot be part of this. This proposal is unacceptable and unrealistic in every way. We will block it in the plenary, and press other friends to do so too.'

He rose and strode from the room. The Chinese pres-ident looked slightly crestfallen, and signalled that the meeting had come to an end. The air seemed to deflate from the room. Omar folded the paper into his jacket pocket, and crossed the room to where Ling was standing.

Ling raised his eyebrows. 'More than you expected?'

Omar was genuinely stunned. 'So much more. This can change everything.'

Ling looked pleased. 'And we are serious. Whatever our Russian friends say. But they must be discouraged from being too critical in the afternoon session. It will have a chilling effect on India, the NAM, and the others. We will do what we must. But we know them: they will kill it if they can.'

Omar nodded. 'And the Americans?'

Ling shrugged dismissively. 'If they are the last to join, so be it. This is not their day. And the next century is not their century.'

Omar knew that Barnes would be waiting for him outside the room. It was shaping up, as his friend had hoped. Beyond that even. But they had to find a way to block Russian and American opposition. And time was running out: the leaders would leave at five p.m. after the closing ceremony, with or without a deal.

In the media suite, Orla watched the main screen as the Russian convoy swept out of the conference venue and back towards their hotel. She screenshotted the photo and sent it to Barnes and Stephanie. 'Game over?'

And in the hotel on the outskirts of Amman, the militia leaders placed the suicide vest around Ali's shoulders. 'Too heavy a burden?'

He looked at the floor. 'No, not too heavy.'

50

Game Over?

Max Crawford smiled as the message from Barnes came through. He knew his friend had hoped that it would not be necessary. He and Stephanie had been convinced that it would.

Stephanie had messaged shortly after. 'Please be careful.'

Who was the predator here? Maybe an easier place to start was to work out who was the prey. Crawford watched as the Russian president and his delegation strode across the hotel lobby. Two burly special forces security guards held the elevator doors open, and he went up to the eighth floor. Crawford knew that they had the floors above and below also booked out.

Barnes had been adamant that there must be no violence. In any case, even Max Crawford knew that the odds of coming out on top in a direct confrontation were stacked against him. He had no desire to die again. And the mission was to save the climate deal, not to start World War Three.

Barnes had estimated that the Russians would want to return to the conference centre after roughly forty-five minutes, in order to rally support in the afternoon plenary to block the Chinese proposal. No doubt they were using the time now to start working the phones, cajoling and threatening.

Crawford made his way down the staff stairs to the basement. He was wearing the hotel's standard maintenance outfit, and so was not challenged by the first set of hotel employees to pass him in the corridor.

He pressed the security pass against the access panel to the electricity room and entered. He would need to work swiftly. The aim was to disable the power to the elevators in thirty minutes or so. The Russians would not want to risk bringing the president down the stairs, and would delay their return to the summit. But he had to be careful to make the power failure look like an accident rather than sabotage. He removed his tools from the pocket of the overalls and started to rewire the main circuit.

Crawford's back was to the door as he worked, but he heard the noise outside as someone sought access. He scooped up the screwdriver, knife and pliers, and ducked behind a large cistern. Two men entered and he slowed his breathing. They made a short circuit of the room, deep in discussion. Palestinian Arabic. Discussions of the food they missed, a girl. What sounded like a routine check. As they neared the cistern he removed the knife from his pocket, and held it at his side. But he was relieved that they continued on, their voices fading as they exited the door and moved back along the corridor.

He checked his watch. Another fifteen minutes or so until one p.m. He was behind now. But he reopened the panel, and resumed the work. He felt the phone in his pocket vibrate. Another message from Barnes.

A quick reply.

Barnes smiled and crossed the conference room to resume his efforts with the Indian delegation.

At 12:58 p.m., Crawford cut the wire connecting the power to the elevators, and disabled the backup supply. He felt the lurch as the power stopped. An alarm sounded in the maintenance room. He replaced the panel and moved swiftly back out into the corridor. He ducked into a bathroom and removed the overalls, discarding the screwdriver and pliers. But he kept the knife in the inside pocket of his jacket. As he climbed the steps to the lobby, three electricians ran past him on the stairs, not stopping to look at him. In the lobby he found a chair near the entrance and ordered a strong black coffee.

The two Russian security guards remained by the lift. But it was clear from their animated discussions that they had discovered that the power had been cut. Both were much taller than Crawford, heavily built. Shaved heads and heavy tattoos. Wagner Group mercenaries, almost certainly. Sinuous and lacklustre. He had known plenty, trained with a few, killed a few.

A duty manager approached the Russians, an obsequious half-bow. Muttered apologies, a sense of panic. They clearly did not like the news. He was pushed to one side. One of the guards went through the door to the stairs. Eight floors: Crawford calculated four minutes, max. He waited two minutes, put down his coffee and walked towards the elevators, as though heading to his room. The second Russian barred his way, a Jordanian police officer looming at his side. Crawford shrugged and turned back to his table. But he was close enough to hear the urgency in the Russian's voice as he picked the message up in his earpiece and turned to the Jordanian. 'He is coming down. The stairs.'

Crawford winced. He had hoped that they wouldn't risk it. He glanced towards the stairwell, working hard to prevent himself checking that the knife was still in his pocket. He could take out one of the Russian security guards and create enough of a scene to slow them down. It might buy them another half an hour at the venue. Would this be enough for Barnes? But they would probably kill him, slowly. He was still more useful alive.

Instead, he moved swiftly to the maintenance staircase and down to the car park. The convoy was preparing to leave. Four vehicles, all Nissan station wagons. They would not decide until the last moment which would take the Russian president. Twenty or so armed Russian security officers in position, plus the four drivers. Crawford watched as the message went round that the president was on his way. The drivers stubbed out cigarettes and started the vehicles. The rest of the security team stayed outside the vehicles, scanning the parking lot. There was no hope of getting anywhere close.

Instead, Crawford skirted the outer wall to the security barrier. Two Jordanian security guards waited to let the convoy out, nervously watching the Russian team. They did not hear him behind them, and he lowered the bodies to the floor of the booth. They would come round in half an hour. He lifted a hat from one of them and placed it on his own head, lowering the peak over his eyes. He watched from the booth as the president climbed into the second vehicle, his security team close. The convoy moved towards him, and he raised the barrier on the exit.

As the first two vehicles roared past, Crawford crouched down in the booth. The third passed, and he dived at the rear tyre of the fourth, stabbing it hard with the knife, then back to the booth. He heard the convoy screech to a halt outside the hotel. The shouts between the drivers. Would they continue with just three vehicles? He removed the Jordanian officer's hat and re-entered the stairwell, ascending fast to the lobby. From there he could see the frantic activity as the Russians examined the vehicles. And then the president was back out again, angrily cursing his security as they whisked him back towards the stairs to his room.

The sky was darkening with rain clouds. A storm was imminent. Crawford messaged Barnes.

You have another half an hour. Use it.

51

Brinkmanship

Barnes clenched a fist with satisfaction. He found Orla in the media suite amid the strange blend of bustle and lethargy. They moved to a quieter corner and he drank two bottles of water. 'News?'

Orla was edgy. 'People are pretty down. They say the body language is discouraging. They're writing up the Russian exit as a sign that any chance of a half-decent deal is dead. And the Americans are briefing that Hoon may also leave early. It feels like it is disintegrating?'

'The Russians will be back. Just not as fast as they had planned.'

Orla raised an eyebrow. Barnes nodded.

'Ed, I need more to work with. Some colour and some substance ideally. Lots of the journalists are filing their stories. We need to change the dynamic. We don't have much time.'

Barnes glanced around, reached into his pocket, and handed her the one pager that Omar had passed him. He shook his head to discourage her from opening it while he was present. 'You can use it. But hint that you got it from the Russian delegation. That they are circulating it in order to try to discredit it. Let's drive this wedge further between them and the Chinese. Raise the stakes. Heap some praise on the Chinese: responsible leadership, vision. Make them think it is all worth it. Meanwhile, Omar and the Chinese have more time to work on the NAM and the Indians. That's best coming from them rather than us.'

Orla nodded. She had never seen Barnes so determined. 'I'll get it to a couple of the less obvious broadcasters first. And the Americans?'

He grimaced. 'We can't let them block this. But they will hate this package. I have an idea. Can you get me a meeting with Brad Curtis?'

'He's not my biggest fan. But what's the carrot?'

Barnes winked. 'I don't know yet. But if anything, it's a stick. We'll think of something.'

Barnes headed back to the UK delegation room. Hermione Buckingham was in the corner with the PM. He looked fed up, deflated. She crossed the room when she saw Barnes. 'Anything to cheer him up? Cheer *us* up?'

'Maybe. The Chinese are moving hard. I can't go into details yet. But there is the potential for something extraordinary. But we have to find a way to square off the Americans. I need access to that intel.'

Hermione looked intrigued. She signalled to a colleague, who brought over a red folder. 'All yours. But Ed, be careful what you do with all this. And don't take it out of this room.'

Barnes took the folder to a table in the corner, grabbed another bottle of water, and began to leaf through it. Most was on likely negotiating positions, already long overtaken by events in the conference itself. He shook his head as he read, casting reports aside. He needed more. Something that he could use with Brad Curtis to make them calculate that they might as well swallow the deal. But there was nothing that went far beyond what they knew already.

As usual with the Americans, it was all carrots: Elizabeth Hoon wanted a state visit to the UK before the election, the gold carriage on the mall. The one thing money couldn't buy.

His phone vibrated, a message from Orla to get back to the media room. 'Brad Curtis will give you five minutes. And our friends have arrived.'

He found her in a corner of the media room with Stephanie and Max Crawford. 'What the hell are you doing here, Max? This place is crawling with security. Someone could recognise you.'

'I didn't want to miss the action.'

'Where did you get a silver badge? Oh, never mind.' Barnes shrugged. 'Well, keep your head down. And no more violence. We do this my way.'

Stephanie stood between them. 'What progress, Pops?'

Barnes sighed. 'We're three quarters of the way there. The Chinese proposal is out there.' He glanced at Orla, who held up her phone to indicate that she had made sure of it. 'And the Africans and others are coming behind it.' A glance at Stephanie, who nodded. 'The Russian resistance seems to have been stalled.' A glance at Max, who grinned.

Stephanie held her hands up. 'But?'

'But I don't have what I need to move the Americans. And I don't know yet where we get it.'

Stephanie chewed her lip. 'You've tried. And there's nothing that will shift them. Elizabeth Hoon is determined to kill any chance of this deal. She'll walk into that room and scupper it. Or simply leave the conference. It will take years to rebuild trust. We'll need to wait for the political cycle to spin round again, for leaders to go, fresh faces to arrive. The Chinese may decide to back off. Meanwhile, more catastrophes. We go past the point at which we can reverse climate change. And we will always know that we were here. That we could have done something about it.'

Barnes felt exhausted. 'We'll know we tried.'

Stephanie faced him angrily. 'That's not enough for me.'

'And it's not enough for me. But who's the antagonist here?'

Orla sighed. 'It's been Hoon all along. She is the obstacle to the deal. She is the one who is putting us all at risk.'

Crawford looked stern. 'Then use me.'

Barnes was aghast. He struggled to lower his voice. 'But seriously, Max, you're suggesting we – you – somehow take out the US president?'

Crawford nodded. 'Deadly serious. Ambassador, I've been taking on this network of people who are destroying the planet. I've dealt with many of them, permanently. Except one. That's unfinished business. Whose life is more important: Elizabeth Hoon? Or the millions who will die if there is no action on climate?'

Barnes felt disorientated. Once you had accepted that violence was justified, where did it stop? Were there moments when the majority were wrong enough that it was acceptable to go against their choice? It had always been the question of the liberal. But when did a desire to protect the people from themselves tip over into a firm of tyranny?

Stephanie sighed. 'But you always said that was the line you wouldn't cross. To kill a woman.'

Barnes held his head in his hands. Elizabeth Hoon was no Caesar. But surely no successor could allow her killers to remain free? And even if they did, would history forgive them? Would they forgive themselves?

Not for the first time, Ed Barnes envied Max Crawford his simpler code. The others were watching him closely. He avoided Stephanie's eye: he knew what she would say, and he couldn't hear it.

Barnes shook his head. This wasn't one that Max could fix. But he had no idea what his alternative was. 'What if I could show you there was another way?'

It was Orla who broke the silence, as she watched Stephanie also give a shake of the head towards Crawford. 'Maybe we're all here for a reason. Maybe we'll all have to work out what it is that matters to us. Maybe all of us are going to have to cross our line.'

She looked uncomfortable, wrestling with her conscience. 'Maybe *I* can show you there is another way.'

52

Loyalty Tests

Outside the complex, a thunderstorm. Rain hammering against the roof and walls of the conference centre. As Orla and Barnes made their way to the US delegation room, Stephanie's phone rang. Ali. She stepped away from Crawford to take it. When she rejoined him, she looked confused.

'It was odd. Even by his standards. He sounded disoriented and confused.' Crawford saw her shoulders drop. She looked crestfallen.

His antennae were up. 'What was he saying, Stephanie?'

'Not much. But before he rang off, he said he just wanted to say goodbye.'

'And?'

'There was an edge to it, a sadness. It felt sort of permanent.'

'As in *you* wouldn't see him again?'

She was trying to pick out the exact words he used. 'Sort of, I guess. But there was more of a finality to it.'

Crawford crossed his arms as he thought. 'Maybe the Somalilanders are not just here for the canapés and credibility. Maybe they want our attention. This was why they wanted the invitation. And Ed Barnes got it for them.'

Stephanie looked shocked. 'I don't think Ali is capable. But who knows about the people around him. Then we must tell Dad? Get him to warn the Jordanians? Sort the security?'

Crawford shook his head. 'No. We don't have enough to go on. It's just a hunch. And we need him to stay focused on the deal. You know him – he would feel he needed to sound the alarm. He would feel it was his fault, and he'd be right. And even a minor security alert will be enough to scupper the summit. The Americans are looking for excuses to bail out. No, time is too short. In any case, Ali isn't able to rejoin the meeting.'

Stephanie chewed a knuckle. 'But his pass does get him into the closing ceremony, when they announce the deal.' She went pale. 'And that's when most leaders are in one place.'

Crawford exhaled slowly. 'And security won't stop a head of delegation. You and I started all this. How attached are you to Ali, Steph?'

She looked vulnerable for a moment. 'We have a… connection. He's a good man. Kind. He's not a terrorist. Why do you ask?'

Crawford sighed. 'Because he clearly knew plenty about the mall attack. He's either not in control or he is more cynical than we have realised. If this hunch is right that he is part of some kind of security threat to the closing ceremony, then we – I – need to act fast.'

'As in…?'

He held her eye. 'We can't allow this risk to be out there. But we also need to avoid a great security op. It would blow your father's credibility and destroy the summit. Like Orla said, maybe we're all going to have to give something up for this deal. So, is it worth your loyalty to Ali?'

Stephanie nodded slowly. 'Would you really have tried to kill Hoon? Been exposed? Gone down in history as an assassin?'

Crawford shrugged. 'Do I have your permission to act?'

'Let me give you Ali's number. The hotel details.'

'I have all that. But we've always worked together on the targets. Do I have your permission to act?'

Stephanie sank into a chair, a tear on her cheek. 'Please don't ask me that.'

Crawford nodded grimly. He understood. He started to stride off, but turned back for a moment. 'Stephanie, this is the last one. It ends here.'

Orla and Barnes had reached the US delegation room. They waited for several minutes outside, before a flustered staffer came to collect them. Inside, Brad Curtis was alone at one of the tables, two phones in front of him. More staffers hovered nearby. There was no sign of Elizabeth Hoon. He gestured at them to sit.

'Five minutes, Orla.'

Orla introduced Barnes. Curtis eyed him suspiciously. He had read the files. Idealistic. Risk prone. A liability. 'So what do you want?'

'We want you to take the Chinese deal.'

Curtis narrowed his eyes. 'That's it? No chance. She's adamant. It stinks. And we don't believe for a second that the Chinese will see it through. It's a power play: they want to run the new UN agency. They're not serious.'

Orla interjected. 'Then you'll leave me with no choice.'

'What do you mean?' Curtis snarled. He was used to making the threats.

Orla took a deep breath. A quick glance at Barnes, who nodded at her to continue. 'Brad, I've got hours of notes and tapes from my interviews with you all. Including yours. That quote on her not thinking her voters were smart enough to carry guns. There's enough there to make her unelectable. Is she really worth your loyalty?'

Curtis laughed. 'Don't try to fuck around, Orla. Really? You think the American people haven't already priced all that in? If your material was so good, you would have got a better book deal lined up, not ended up reporting on pointless summits in Nowhereistan, hanging around with this washed-up Brit. Meeting over.'

Orla felt her cheeks reddening. 'But it's not all the usual stuff, Brad. It's also your assertion that she's a threat to national security. And more important, it's that I've joined the dots. Between your donors, and the airlines, and the fossil fuels, and the conspiracy theories in the right-wing media, and the oligarchs. You share a common interest in distracting the public from taking any serious action on climate.'

Brad curled his lip. 'Ever the conspiracy theorist. Meeting over.'

Orla persevered. 'Maybe. But the evidence is all there.'

Barnes narrowed his eyes. 'And that evidence links directly to these assassinations. Whoever is killing these individuals has picked their targets very carefully. And it is working. The public are turning against them.'

Curtis looked dismissive. 'That's a blip, not a trend. My president has a knack for moving it all on, changing the narrative.'

Barnes leant forward. 'But what if the Assassin is joined by others? What if their efforts spark the killings of those who step into these positions? It all becomes untenable.

The dam bursts. And you and your president will be swept away with it.'

Curtis sneered. 'That a threat?'

Maybe. Barnes wasn't sure any more. He was throwing everything on this last roll of the dice.

'You're wasting your time. And the Russians will block, anyway.'

Barnes shook his head. 'Not without strong cover from you. The Chinese are pushing them hard. And as this deal leaks out, your public will like it too. Especially the young. It is simple and effective. You're more isolated than you think. And there is a political cost to that.'

Curtis drummed his fingers on the table. 'Ambassador Barnes, you seem to know a lot about these assassinations. What if you were ready to do something for us?'

Curtis was enjoying the power. He had once told Orla that the only sight that still made him happy was the corpses of his political enemies in the rear-view mirror.

Barnes was intrigued. He hadn't expected to have something to offer.

Curtis continued. 'What if I were to tell you that we had almost completed our own investigation of this assassin who you seem to know so much about. Brit. Ex-Special Forces. We just need someone to testify.'

Barnes steadied himself. 'You don't have a name.'

'Not quite. But we have a pretty good lead. And it turns out that it is someone we thought we had already killed. Someone who used to work for you. Funny old world, eh Ambassador Barnes?'

Barnes flinched. And composed himself. 'I don't know who you mean.' He needed to buy time. Much of this was surely bluff. But Curtis would not have raised it unless they had a pretty good lead on Max Crawford.

Curtis smiled. 'Oh, you do, Ambassador. You do. Is he really worth your loyalty? What if you give us something to make this climate deal? Some red meat to help us distract the base from what they'll be forced to swallow? From giving up their gas-guzzling cars and plastic?'

A pause. Barnes thought of Crawford dragging him from the wreckage in Copenhagen. Standing by him even when Barnes had been convinced of his disloyalty. Coming back for him in the Nairobi mall. Out there now doing whatever he could for the right outcome. Was another moment of disloyalty the price for getting the US to acquiesce in the deal? And if so, wasn't that worth it? Given how far he had come, Crawford would think so.

Barnes held Curtis's eye for a moment and shook his head. 'No. I've got nothing to help you there. Meeting over.' He was not prepared to make the betrayal again. It was out of his hands.

Curtis rose. 'We take off in an hour, no matter what. You got closer than anyone expected, I've got to hand it to you.'

Barnes also stood. But Orla gestured at them both to sit. They could see the steeliness in her.

Orla gripped the table to steady herself. It went against all her training, and against all the integrity she had built up in the role. More painfully, it went against her instincts as a woman.

'Brad, I never thought I would use this, especially in a context like this. To be honest, I can't believe I have to.'

Curtis sat down. Intrigued, curious. This didn't feel like an idle threat. He hadn't seen her like this. He nodded at her to continue.

Orla exhaled. This deal better be worth it. Ed Barnes better be worth it.

'I know about President Hoon's abortion.'

Curtis recoiled. 'Bullshit.'

Orla shook her head.

'You would never use that. You're better than that.'

Orla looked away from him. A glance at Ed Barnes.

'We're all having to give something up. This is bigger than all of us.'

–

The governor of Somaliland adjusted his formal robes over the suicide vest. The heads of delegation line into the conference centre was moving swiftly, not going through the same security as the rest of their delegations. He felt hot and yet cold, almost dreamlike. He muttered a silent prayer to himself that Stephanie would be far from the building.

53

Endgame

Thirty minutes later, Omar and the Jordanian king stood at the podium to close the conference. The packed room was hushed as Omar produced the final communiqué and began to read it. The leaders had taken their seats. Ed Barnes was stood to one side, among the observers. He saw Ali, sweating in his traditional dress. The Chinese leader was beaming. Elizabeth Hoon fumed in her chair, shoulders hunched angrily, with Brad Curtis looking deflated in the seat behind her. The Russian president's chair had been filled by his foreign minister. The UK PM looked earnest, satisfied. Everyone would claim credit. Barnes caught Hermione's eye in the chair behind him. She winked and raised her eyebrows. *Bloody Ed Barnes.*

Omar read the introduction to the text slowly, the exhaustion on his face. He knew with certainty that this was his last summit. He paused before the final section. The room knew what was coming, and prepared to applaud. They had for once done something important, genuinely world changing. 'It has been further agreed, in the last hour, that we – the global community – will take much bolder and more audacious steps…'

The governor of Somaliland felt his heart racing. Part of him had hoped that security would stop him, prevent him from going through with this. He looked around. How many would die? And with what consequences? Would his people remember him? It was hard to go through life believing in hell. And how could he know what he now faced? He had wondered whether to say something, reveal the suicide vest before detonation. But the militia leaders had been firm. No theatre. There was too much security, someone could prevent the detonation. Get it done. Become a martyr. Change history.

He was stood in front of a curtain.

He glanced up to the balconies from where security were scanning the room.

They would issue his statement posthumously. He had expanded it to include the climate crisis, alongside Somaliland. Perhaps people – Stephanie – would be more likely to understand. *The world's leaders have shown that they are part of the problem. We, and our descendants, can wait no longer. Only by resetting the system can we deliver the change that we need.*

He watched Omar as he prepared himself to share the seven points in the agreed text. What did it matter what they said in summits like this? He looked across at Ed Barnes. He looked exhausted but elated. The room slowed. He felt lightheaded.

Ali thought of his mother, of the home he had grown up in. He heard the sounds of children playing in the tent in the refugee camp in which he had studied so hard, knowing there was a way out. In his pocket was the only memory of his younger brother – a crumpled piece of paper with stick men firing guns at other stick men – drawn a week before he was killed in a militia attack. He remembered the feel of the cool river on a hot day.

He heard the slightest of sounds in the curtain behind him. Like the first cool wind at the end of the dry season. They called it the *yaare-ha*. It brought relief, the promise of rain. He steadied his breathing, and reached inside the tunic.

Stephanie and Orla were watching on a big screen in the media room. Orla was barely able to watch, crestfallen at having used the threat against Hoon. It went against everything she believed. That she wouldn't have to see it through was no consolation. In her own eyes, she was no longer a journalist.

Stephanie paced nervously, unable to tell Orla what she and Max feared. Hoping that they were wrong about Ali. She felt again the chill that she had experienced when Hussein pointed the gun at her father's head.

Time slowed. What hubris to try to make peace with a planet. The world would carry on turning, long after the humans had gone. And yet she could see her father in the corner of the screen, excited but weary. Was that not enough?

She saw Ali by the curtain. Where the hell was Max? How long did they have?

Barnes felt his phone vibrate. The message 'Proud of you, Pops.'

He felt the tiredness overwhelm him, and he smiled, the tears rolling down his cheeks. It was over.

Behind the curtain, Max Crawford took a deep breath. And reached his hands towards Ali's neck.

Epilogue

Good Ancestors

Ed Barnes held the glass at an angle, looking at the way the slices of lemon bobbed among the ice. Always the slug of gin on the top, so that you got that first clear taste of it neat.

They were sat on the veranda of his tent, watching the night fall behind the water hole below them. While they could still taste the heat and dust of the drive they had watched the warthogs come, tails alert like antennae, snorting as they played at the edge of the water, the mother keeping a more wary eye out for crocodiles. Now a lone bull elephant scratched its hind against a tree.

The last of the sun cast a warm glow over the landscape, bathing the rolling hills and savannas in a golden light. The sky was orange, pink, and purple, as the final rays of the day faded behind the mountains. The air was crisp and cool.

Stephanie had her legs curled under her. 'They call this bush TV.'

Barnes exhaled. They were where they were meant to be. And tomorrow they would visit the community in the north that had been displaced by conflict and climate change. They would discuss how to use UK aid to help them adapt, learn new skills, get their young people into school. That was where they were meant to be, too. He felt Stephanie smiling at him.

'I remember your grandfather telling me that after the Second World War there was a moment when it felt that the world could be different.'

Stephanie cocked her head. 'And was he so wrong?' Barnes shook his head. 'I hoped not.'

She grinned. 'And you took it as a mission statement.'

A moment of silence, enveloped by nature. 'You won, Pops.'

He wondered, as so often, whether the ends had really justified the means. 'Someone once told me, it's not about winning, but the ability to keep playing. Maybe that goes for humanity too. I don't know. I just don't want to miss a minute of your life.' He paused. 'Can you forgive me all of this, Steph?'

She sighed. 'I can forgive you anything but growing old. Can you forgive me?'

'I can forgive you anything but going away.'

Stephanie caught her father's glance across to the tent where Orla was reading. She could see his mind was there, wondering whether her hair was up or down.

As so often, she thought of Ali. Max had never told her how he killed him. She had been spared that, at least. Whatever he had done with the body, his buddies in Jordanian security must have moved fast to remove it, avoiding a scene at the finale. Everything swiftly and efficiently hushed up: Ali hadn't even got his martyrdom.

'And you're now asking me to stay off-piste, Steph?'

'Dad, I don't think you were ever really on-piste.'

Alice loved to watch Omar as he read. He would furrow his brow and squeeze his beard between his fingers, concentrating intensely. Occasionally he would articulate the words out loud, rolling them around his mouth, oblivious to his surroundings. Today they were sat on a bench at the end of Lake Geneva. The season had turned towards autumn and they were wearing hats and scarves for the first time. She poured him a coffee from a small flask.

The book was a holocaust diary. Simple, profound stories of sacrifice and survival.

Sometimes it was not about winning but simply still being there, surviving. Alice watched Omar wince at the inhumanity, weep at the loss, and smile at the moments when humans occasionally hit back. *Look for the helpers*. Every generation faced its own battles, its own choices about what it would give to defend freedom.

Barnes had once told Omar a story about peace-making. 'In Northern Ireland it was, in the end, not the politicians, churchmen or men of violence who really made the peace, but ordinary men and women. At one reconciliation event in Lebanon, I was introduced to two people promoting direct links between individuals across the divide in places that had been cut deep by conflict, like Rwanda, the Balkans and South Africa. The room was full of trauma, grief and pain. Assuming they were a couple, I asked why they had come. "My father was killed in a terrorist attack," the woman told me. I sympathised, feebly, one of those moments where you feel the inadequacy of words. "And you, sir?" "I was the bomber." That's why all this matters.'

Omar put the book aside for a moment. 'We must never underestimate our potential for violence. Humans are works in progress. So we have to heal the wounds of history. We have to forgive each other. We have to forgive ourselves.'

Alice smiled. 'You did what you needed to do, Omar.'

The air was clear and bright. Every conversation felt like it might be the last. She took out her phone and sent her daughter a photo of the view.

–

In her tent, the breeze in the green canvass, Orla opened her laptop and started to write. The behind-the-scenes manuscript on Elizabeth Hoon lay to one side. She wouldn't need to share the intimacy of those encounters. It felt somehow prurient. The characters were too preposterous. It was all too farcical. It was still too painful to reflect on whether she would have been ready to see through her threat on revealing Hoon's abortion. Of course it was about hypocrisy, not the abortion itself. But part of her integrity had died in using it to get Brad Curtis to acquiesce in the climate deal.

Early evening was the best and the hardest time to write. But you had to keep showing up. Getting words, any words, on the page.

She thought of how many politicians had disappointed her. And how many men. Lives eaten up with failure, envy, disappointment. She thought of Brad Curtis.

What does the man of destiny do when destiny is eluding him? He frets and manoeuvres. He makes joyless money and dubious friends. He seethes at his enemies and resents his allies. He settles scores. He writes books that don't get read, bar the index. He gets more obsequious with those in power, and more obnoxious with everyone else. He invents new ways of describing old ideas. He watches friends die or peter out, and celebrates or mourns their lack of impact on history. He becomes a bull with no china shop. Pity the ambitious man who does not attain his ambitions. And pity the man who does.

Ed Barnes felt different. But didn't they all at first? It would be worth finding out.

The cursor flicked on the screen. Only when she started writing a book did she realise that it had already taken her a lifetime. But where to go next? How to tell the story of the lengths that humans might have to go if they were to stop climate change? The sacrifices they would have to take and the risks they would have to run? Would it take the upending of moral and ethical codes, the transformation of ingrained ways of being in the world? The science and the numbers were obvious and yet impenetrable. Humans struggled to go there. And so ultimately the subject had to be humanised to be understood.

Imagine a world in which we failed to do that, and fail to unleash great waves of creativity, innovation, discovery and opportunity.

Imagine a world in which we succeeded.

Orla relished lining up the shoeboxes, and starting to fill them. *Write what excites you.*

She said the words out loud. To no one. And to everyone. 'Very well then, a novel.' Follow the story. Stephanie had led her to it. She would tell the story of an assassin, bring it to life, try to change the world, not simply describe it.

The sunset was blood red behind Mount Kenya. The heat of the day receded as the dead man drove towards the trophy hunter.

That was enough for now. It was time to see if Ed Barnes still made a great gin and tonic.

–

Max Crawford took his father's arm briefly as they descended the rough track up the old man's favourite mountain.

They had wanted to do it together one last time. So many climbs it had been Max, stumbling as a child, who had needed to be coaxed and carried, shown where the rocks were less slippery, kept fortified by biscuits, and kept distracted by stories and songs.

Now it was his turn to point out the peak in the distance, to try to discern the sheep tracks that would take less scrambling, to pretend that they were closer to the summit than they were. For periods Max would go ahead, clearing bracken to make the route easier to see. On more straightforward stretches he would walk behind, placing his boots as closely as possible in the prints left by his father.

Fifty years ago, his father had told him the stories of the early mountaineers. He had always been struck by the image of Mallory on Everest, a speck on the ridge as the clouds rolled in. He had heard from his father the mountaineer's prayer: *O Lord, spare me from death in valleys.*

The old man was stubborn, refusing to let on how much it was already hurting, silent for periods. But Max could hear the quiet groans as knee and ankle and hip were pushed through the pain. The man who had carried him up this mountain so many times was now leaning more and more heavily on his stick.

Max had noticed himself getting more sentimental as he got older. He had made sure he had brought the custard powder.

Our ancestors had a much stronger sense of the circle of life, the passing of the seasons and years. It was hardwired into the social calendar, the rituals and the rites of passage, and was often the glue that held together communities. The stories were preserved, embellished, cherished, shared. His father had once said to him that one of the hardest things about losing parents is the realisation that you are now the story bearer.

At moments he had wondered whether to insist they turn back, leave it for another day, take in the view from lower altitude. But he had known better than to try.

His father would not take this path again. He was seeing these views for the last time. But Max *would* take this route again. Alone on days of remembrance and gratitude. And with his own boys, probably when his own joints were too old to heave up. He would keep the climbing stick.

Max wondered whether to articulate any of this. What did it mean to be a good ancestor? What were the patterns of habit and DNA that we had to strive hardest to pass on? Or to filter out? What made life worth staying alive for? What's your song? And is it unsung?

He wondered whether he should ask his father what he should say in his eulogy, tried to articulate the question in his head.

They walked on in silence for a while, and then Max Crawford gestured across the valley at the fine mists rolling towards them. So familiar and yet always so different. Max felt time slow for a moment.

'We should be getting down.'

Acknowledgements

As ever, I seek forgiveness from former colleagues and (hopefully not former) friends for dialling it all up so shamelessly. My characters are based on no-one I've met, and on everyone I know. Thank you to Kim Stanley Robinson for the idea of killing for the planet, and to Professor Anette Mikes for insisting I read Stan's life-changing *Ministry of the Future*. Alexandra Asseily made me want to think and write about being a good ancestor. General Sir Graeme Lamb gave me some great lines, though he thinks that Max Crawford needs some work on 'ways and means'. Thank you to Sony TV and Elizabeth Kesses for their faith in Ed Barnes, and for helping me think more cinematically. Russel McLean has been heroic in helping me understand character agency and jeopardy – there is an actual ticking clock in the book for him. Thank you to Michael Bhaskar, Hannah Taylor, Miranda Ward and the rest of the excellent Canelo team for giving me the chance to do this, and for helping to conceal the flaws. Charlie Brotherstone and Sheila David are brilliant agents, always a few steps ahead of me. I'm grateful to Andy McNabb, Frederick Forsyth, Alastair Campbell and Matthew d'Ancona for their encouragement of this strange zag away from my normal zig. Guy Winter, Sarah Zeid, David Cameron, Cathy Ashton, Sarah Brown, Antonia Romeo and Colin Firth helped with advice on specific characters. Plus many serving colleagues who can't be mentioned, including two former High Commissioners to Kenya. And a cast of bad guys who I've met along the way. Thanks to friends who have bumped around Jordan and Kenya in Land Rovers with me. Rebecca Cox and Dannie Godrey help me to manage a complicated life in a way that allows time to write. The Fellows of Hertford College remain a tolerant if sometimes perplexed bunch. Thanks to Mum and Dad for many climbs up Cnicht, and to Granny for Ed's generous approach to gin and tonic. Louise, Charlie and Theo make it all possible with their encouragement, support and patience for those very early writing mornings at Casa Antares when we are meant to be on holiday. Every book I write is a flawed love letter.

This isn't a drill. We have tough choices ahead of us if we are to be good ancestors. We all have to ask ourselves what we are prepared to sacrifice to protect the things we must not sacrifice.